CANADIAN CASES IN FINANCIAL ACCOUNTING

Second Edition

Carol E. Dilworth

Joan E. D. Conrod

IRWIN

Homewood, IL 60430
Boston, MA 02116

This symbol indicates that the paper in this book is made of recycled paper. Its fiber content exceeds the recommended minimum of 50% waste paper fibers as specified by the EPA.

The first edition of this text was published under the authorship of Conrod and Dilworth.

Vice president: Sarah Iles
Senior sponsoring editor: Roderick T. Banister
Marketing manager: David J. Collinge
Project editor: Waivah Clement
Production manager: Mary Jo Parke
Cover designer: Amy Osborne
Designer: Larry J. Cope
Compositor: Better Graphics, Inc.
Typeface: 10/12 Times Roman
Printer: R. R. Donnelley & Sons Company

ISBN 0-256-11140-5
Library of Congress Catalog Card No. 92-73934
Printed in the United States of America
1 2 3 4 5 6 7 8 9 0 DOC 0 9 8 7 6 5 4 3

CANADIAN CASES IN FINANCIAL ACCOUNTING

This book is dedicated to our fathers with love,

H. L. (Roy) Dilworth
J. Ivan Davison

Preface

We are delighted to present the second edition of *Canadian Cases in Financial Accounting*. We would like to thank the numerous students, instructors and course authors who encouraged us after the first edition.

The cases in this book cover a wide variety of financial accounting issues at various levels of depth and complexity. There are over 100 cases in the book, forty-six of which are brand new. All cases retained from the first edition have been updated for changes in accounting standards and circumstances, where appropriate. We think you'll enjoy exploring issues such as environmental accounting, complex financial instruments, and many other current topics.

The Introduction to this casebook gets case analysis started. This is done by examining a multisubject natural resource company and then providing a solution followed by a sample student response.

In response to comments, we have increased the number of intermediate single-subject cases. Please let us know how these are working for you. Long and more complex cases are included for use in advanced undergraduate, graduate, or executive courses. *Canadian Cases in Financial Accounting* has been used in courses in intermediate accounting, accounting theory, corporate reporting, and various "capstone" and professional programs.

We're pleased that it is so adaptable! As with the first edition, the book can be used on its own or in conjunction with another text.

We have not reproduced sections of the *CICA Handbook* or relevant background materials to any great extent. Instructors may wish to place selected items on reserve in their campus library or leave the library research to the student.

We are aware of the variances in course content and coverage across Canada. We also realize that courses have different prerequisites. Some students are distance education learners and do not have the corporate or library facilities or personal contact that other students may benefit from. However, we believe that you can adapt cases for specific purposes and situations. We provide guidance for this in the instructor's manual, which is available to the instructor or course author.

Our thanks for permission to adapt material go to the copyright holders: the Canadian Institute of Chartered Accountants, the Society of Management Accountants of Canada, the Institute of Chartered Accountants of Ontario, and the Atlantic School of Chartered Accountancy. Canadian corporations continued to provide outstanding disclosure that led to so many of our cases.

We have had constant support from our colleagues at the University of Waterloo School of Accountancy and the Schools of Business at Dalhousie University and at Wilfrid Laurier University.

In particular, we thank Len Eckel, Morley Lemon, John R. E. Parker, and Howard Teall.

Our reviewers provided insight and good advice. For this assistance we thank Maureen Fizzell, University of Saskatchewan, Pamela Ritchie, University of New Brunswick, Wendy Roscoe, Concordia University, and Terry Litovitz, Scarborough College, University of Toronto.

The quality of the finished product is due to detailed work of the people in Toronto and Homewood. They have done another wonderful job. Sarah Iles, vice president of Irwin Dorsey, was always cheerful, encouraging, and there for us. Waivah Clement, project editor, was patient and serene. We also thank Mary Jo Parke, production manager, and the designer, Larry J. Cope.

Things have not been dull personally or professionally over the past four years. Joan is now a tenured associate professor at Dalhousie University, has a computer (!) and *another* baby. While there are "new editions" in Joan's current five-year plan, they are all books—no more babies! Carol is now an independent author and educator, with a clientele in industry and education. We are both actively involved in professional accounting education and have a total of 27 years of full-time teaching behind us—and many more in front of us!

We hope our experiences keep our case material fresh and interesting for you.

February, 1993

Carol E. Dilworth, Toronto
Joan E. D. Conrod, Halifax

Contents

Introduction to Case Analysis

Why do cases? Because they're fun? Interesting? Challenging? Because they relate cut-and-dried techniques to the more complex real world? Yes, all of that, and more! Case analysis should make you think. It should help develop your judgment, which is an integral part of financial accounting. Strange as it may seem, the numbers themselves are often not the most important part of financial accounting. Choice and application of accounting policy is the real root of professional accounting practice.

Professional judgment is required in case scenarios to identify unique and compelling elements in the environment, to identify and rank problems, and to solve those problems in a practical, integrated fashion. Technical knowledge is still necessary to solve the accounting problems. After all, an accounting professional must have mastery of the body of knowledge that is defined as "financial accounting." Judgment is necessary, though, to define the tools, techniques, and rules that are appropriate in a given set of circumstances.

This introduction to case analysis will:

1. Provide an outline of an approach to case analysis.
2. Allow practice, for a case with a suggested solution.
3. Review feedback, as you look at a sample student submission.

BACKGROUND

A financial report can be viewed as a method for one group (e.g., a business owner) to communicate with another (e.g., a chartered bank). The person who receives this communication will use it to make decisions (e.g., lend money, change interest rates). If financial accounting is seen as having the power to affect behavior, it is only natural to expect the preparer to wish to present it in a way that might increase the likelihood of getting the desired behavior. This is neither good nor bad, it is merely a factual observation. Professional accountants have to understand the potential biases in a situation in order to be effective.

In financial accounting, generally accepted accounting principles (GAAP) exist to establish the basic ground rules. In some instances, they are specific, rule-oriented pronouncements that leave little room for the exercise of professional judgment. For example, the *CICA Handbook* sections on earnings per share and leases are very specific. In other areas, the standards require that the environment be carefully considered, and judgment used, when establishing an accounting policy. For example, the accounting policy chosen to translate the statements of a foreign subsidiary into Canadian dollars depends on *Handbook*-specified individual circumstances. In other areas, a variety of accounting policies are acceptable under GAAP, with few indications of the factors that should dictate choice. For example, inventory costing methods (FIFO, LIFO, weighted average, and the like) and depreciation methods (straight line, declining balance, and so on) are not narrowed in any directive manner.

How does a professional make decisions when there is choice? If application of certain policies produces statements that are more suitable for the purpose for which they are intended, then the choice seems obvious. But "suitability" is subjective. The professional accountant must guard against biasing the statements to attempt to ensure a given outcome. Fair presentation is an overriding concern.

The value of accounting information is partly a function of reliability, of which a major component is neutrality.[1] Accounting information would soon lose its credibility if it were biased or expected to be biased.

Think of the role of the professional accountant like this: First, to understand the environment, circumstances, and motivations of the providers (and users) of accounting information who produce (or use) an accounting policy or a desired policy. Second, to judge the acceptability of a policy in relation to established standards, a combination of technical knowledge and judgment. Usually, the standards are GAAP and fair presentation, but in some cases all parties are better served by tailor-made policies. Third, the accountant must have the ability to implement the policy—the application of technical knowledge.

There are few black-and-white areas in the practice of accounting. Case analysis will make you appreciate the various shades of grey.

---

[1] "Financial Statement Concepts." *CICA Handbook,* Section 1000, par. 1000.21.

APPROACH TO CASE ANALYSIS

The following steps are offered to help in case preparation:

1. **Skim**
   a. Read all material quickly.
   b. Determine your role.
   c. Read the required.
   d. See what information is available.
2. **Read**
   a. Read all material carefully.
   b. Understand all information.
   c. Work through numeric exhibits.
   d. Gather information for steps 3 and 4.
3. **Identify problem areas and issues**
4. **Recognize situational variables, as applicable**
   a. Environment analysis—identify the industry, state of the economy, the competitive factors that help this organization succeed, and so forth.
   b. Organization analysis—Identify planning and control systems including incentive schemes, reporting structure, and so on.
   c. Financial statement analysis—Identify financial strengths and weaknesses.
   d. Statement uses analysis—Identify users, types of decisions to be made, and the motivation of the key players.
5. **Analysis**
   For each problem:
   a. Identify alternatives.
   b. Analyze each alternative:
      (1) Qualitative, both sides of the argument.
      (2) Quantitative (if possible).
      (3) Analysis of situational variables.
6. **Recommendations**
   Consistent with analysis.

SAMPLE CASE

Take an hour and write a solution to the NSTR case that follows. You'll learn more from the exercise if you resist temptation and ignore the suggested solution until *after* you finish!

NSTR[2]

Nova Scotia Timber Resources Ltd. (NSTR) is a privately held company incorporated under the companies legislation of Nova Scotia. It is owned by a family syndicate based in Bonn, Germany. The syndicate has been actively involved in acquiring timberland in the province of Nova Scotia for the past five years. Early in 1993, the decision was made to roll the assets into a corporation and harvest timber for the first time. Previously, land acquired had been left idle.

While a primary purpose of the land acquisition was to gain profit from the timber resource, the syndicate's long-term goals included profit on the land itself. Germany has high-density population, and recreational land is scarce. Nova Scotia waterfront properties represent attractive acquisition targets.

The syndicate members have retained finance contracts on the properties in their personal names—the land, not the debt, has been transferred to NSTR, although the land is often collateral for the debt. In addition, though, the syndicate members provided personal guarantees on an operating line of credit for NSTR of up to $4 million with the Chartered Bank of Canada. This loan is also secured by a floating charge on inventory and receivables.

NSTR, in its first year of production, leased a building (for 10 years) which housed sawmill operations, administrative offices, and a warehouse. It also acquired about $400,000 of processing equipment, trucks, tools, and other necessary assets.

As trees are harvested, the decision must be made whether to sell the logs to other sawmills or users of timber, or to process the logs in NSTR's own facilities. The quality of logs varies. A five-year contract was signed with a plant in Nova Scotia that used low-quality logs to produce chipboard and paneling. The price agreed on was ''fair market value,'' determined monthly, and minimum delivery quantities were established for each month.

Higher-quality logs, processed internally, become lumber of various dimensions, sold to both building supply companies and independent contractors in the Maritimes and in the Quebec and Ontario markets. Transportation costs make it difficult to compete strongly in the Quebec and Ontario markets. Terms are usually cash payment within 60 days of delivery.

Prices of these finished products are a function of supply and demand at the date of sale. Inventory is stored in NSTR's warehouses, incurring interest and storage costs, if the current market price is deemed unacceptably low by management. They have refused to accept prices below cost,

---

[2] Adapted with permission from the Atlantic School of Chartered Accountancy.

and lumber prices were quite volatile in 1993. For example, one of the by-products associated with the sawmill process, wood chips, can be sold in retail stores (bagged), sold to industrial concerns for fuel, or sold as an input to chipboard plants. Management has decided that the prices offered for the last two uses do not cover costs and are carrying wood chips in inventory.

Management has the responsibility for making these decisions; they also make decisions concerning how much lumber to harvest in any one year, based on their market predictions.

The syndicate has set a policy of reforestation of harvested land, consistent with their long-term goals of land appreciation. The costs to fulfill this policy, while not large in 1993, are expected to be material in future years.

The company's first year-end has just passed. The syndicate has not indicated how net income is to be computed, nor has the Canadian management spent much time considering financial accounting policies. There has been some indication that the syndicate wishes to be able to draw funds, in the form of dividends, to meet debt service charges and principal repayment. In addition, some consideration had been given to awarding senior management a bonus on net income, although details have yet to be worked out.

Required

Assume the role of an accounting adviser to the company and explain the financial accounting policies and principles the company should adopt.

NSTR—Suggested Solution

Size Up. Users of the financial statements are as follows:

1. Syndicate members: Two goals: —Profit on timber harvest.
   —Long-term land appreciation.
   Also —Want enough cash from operations to pay debt costs.
   —Need to evaluate management.
2. Tax—File corporate tax returns.
3. Bank—Evaluate $4 million line of credit.
   —Bankers reasonably sophisticated; commercial credit.
   —Need cash flow information to be able to evaluate operation.
   —Inventory and receivables are pledged; must assess collateral.

A reasonable conclusion is that the syndicate members, at a distance from the operation, will be the primary users, but the banker is a close second.

(Since accounting policies are chosen with an eye to GAAP and to satisfy the users of the financial statements, the case analysis begins by identifying those users and their motivations.)

Issues.
Financial accounting policies:

1. Initial investment valuation.
2. Asset valuation.
3. Revenue recognition.
4. Inventory valuation.
5. Depletion of timber resources.
6. Reforestation costs.
7. Depreciation of fixed assets.
8. Lease classification.
9. Loan disclosure.

(The case did not list these issues. Professional judgment must be used to define the areas for which NSTR must set accounting policies. You have to think about it!)

Analysis and Recommendations

1. *Valuation of initial investment.*

   How should the land transferred from the syndicate to NSTR be valued on the initial NSTR balance sheet?

   - One alternative is the original cost to the syndicate.
   - Could also be recorded at fair market value (FMV) per appraisal on day of rollover. This would help in the assessment of management stewardship, economic performance, and return on investment.

   Recommendation: Record at fair market value on day of rollover.

2. *Asset valuation.*

   - Since a long run goal of the syndicate is to earn profits on the land itself, appraisal values could be used to measure land value. NSTR could separate land value from the timber rights on the land. Timber values would be subject to depletion, while land values could appreciate. Appraisals could be done every two to three years, to be cost effective.
   - Use of FMV on land would lead to a qualified audit opinion, but would the syndicate mind? There would be a trade-off between relevance and reliability.
   - No one—except maybe the banker, who is relatively sophisticated—needs an unqualified report.

- On the other hand, historical cost (or FMV on date of rollover) is more reliable, understandable, and comparable to other companies. Separation of land versus timber values could be very subjective.
- Users may not need appraisal value in statements if they are well aware of the value of the assets (less likely—problem of distance!).

Recommendation: Record land values at historical cost, disclose FMV in notes. This should meet everyone's needs!

3. *Revenue recognition.*
   Process internally/sell outside.

   - If tax minimization is a major concern, NSTR should consider deferral to point of cash collection. (possibly justified, since NSTR is a new company with no collection history?)
   - This method does not serve the needs of bankers or shareholders, evaluating performance.
   - Normal revenue recognition point is the point of delivery: Set up revenue, receivable, allowance for doubtful accounts. This allows for adequate performance evaluation. Note that the bank requires receivables as security.
   - Early recognition is not justifiable (e.g., when timber cut) because there are uncertainties prior to delivery. The market price of this commodity is also quite volatile.
   - If the risk of noncollection cannot be established (lack of history, etc.) then revenue recognition must be delayed until payment. There is no evidence to suggest this is a problem.

   Recommendation: Recognize revenue when product is delivered; an allowance for doubtful accounts must be established.

   Long-term contract.

   - NSTR has a long-term contract for delivery of low-grade timber for chipboard—what is the appropriate point for revenue recognition? Alternatives include signing the contract, production, delivery, or payment.
   - NSTR should not want early revenue recognition even if it could be justified, as it would incur tax prior to cash collection.
   - Performance evaluation needs are critical here—needs well served by using delivery as the critical event.
   - If the risk of noncollection cannot be established (lack of history, etc.) then revenue recognition must be delayed until payment. There is no evidence to suggest this is a problem.

Recommendation: Recognize revenue when product is delivered. An allowance for doubtful accounts must be established.

4. *Inventory valuation.*

NSTR must consider the following four areas in inventory valuation:

a. Cost flow assumption.
Alternatives are LIFO, FIFO, and weighted average.
- LIFO is not acceptable for tax. NSTR would have to use a different method for accounting versus tax, and establish deferred taxes. LIFO will match the most current costs on the income statement, but undervalue inventory on the balance sheet. It is poor for the banker, if trying to assess security, but may be better for performance evaluation, since matching is well served.
- FIFO is better for collateral evaluation, but may not be as good for other uses.
- Weighted average tends to be in the middle of the two alternatives.

Recommendation: Use weighted average as a compromise position, as it will work towards most user needs.

b. Direct versus absorption costing.

- Direct —avoids income manipulation caused by deferral of fixed costs
  —shows only variable costs in inventory
  —low valuation of inventory on balance sheet
- Absorption —better for collateral evaluation
  —more likely to be industry practice
  —but, involves allocations

Recommendation: Absorption costing should be adopted to serve the banker. The owners can request additional information on volume of production versus sales to check for deferrals that may impact on their assessment of performance evaluation.

c. Valuation at lower of cost or market.

Market is often defined as net realizable value. In the face of volatile prices, there is a potential problem, as net realizable value will fluctuate as market prices fluctuate.
- Such write-downs reflect poorly on management, who made the decision to harvest when cost exceeded market value, and should be highlighted on statements used for performance appraisal.
- Write-downs also reduce collateral pledged to secure the operating line and are important to the bank.
- Wood chip inventory may require a write-down to NRV. Note

that a decision to sell this inventory should be based on *relevant* costs.

Recommendation: NSTR should value inventories at the lower of cost or net realizable value. They should adopt a definition of net realizable value based on a short-term average at year-end.

d. Interest and storage costs.

Lumber doesn't get more valuable as it sits around. Expense interest and storage costs immediately. This will portray cash flow, and aid in performance evaluation.

5. and 6. *Depletion of timber resources and reforestation costs.*

Two alternatives exist:

1. Record no depletion, and expense reforestation costs as a cost of doing business and preserving future land value. Matching is questionable, as timber has been cut and new trees are far from maturity. NSTR cannot realistically avoid reforestation without seriously hurting land values.
2. Deplete existing timber resource costs and capitalize reforestation costs, to be expensed as timber costs when the stand of trees matures, and is eventually cut. This clearly reflects that reforestation is done for future benefit.

This is an allocation problem, and allocations are incorrigible. The efficient market hypothesis says that since cash flow is the same under both methods, users should not make different decisions because of the accounting policy chosen.

The timber rights should be amortized (depleted) over their useful life. Since harvest fluctuates from year to year based on volatile market prices, units of production seems to be the method that will provide the best matching. This method introduces subjectivity to the depreciation calculation, since total timber reserves must be estimated.

Original cost (or fair market value at time of establishing the corporation) will have to be allocated between land cost and timber rights.

Recommendation: NSTR should deplete timber costs on a units-of-production basis. The reforestation costs should be capitalized to be consistent with the depletion policy and demonstrate the future value created. The level of expenditures made for reforestation should be disclosed in a note to the financial statements.

7. *Depreciation of fixed assets.*

Methods to be considered:
Straight-line.

Declining-balance.
Units of production.
Same depreciation as CCA claim.

The decision will not affect tax or cash flows. This is another incorrigible allocation. Units of production may seem the most logical, but may be hard to assess. Declining balance methods produce depreciation that is very high in early years and depress income. Straight-line is simple and easy to understand. Claiming the same depreciation as CCA is not GAAP and would result in a qualified audit report. It's one thing to consider a qualification over something important, like asset values. It's another thing to consider a qualification over something this trivial.

Recommendation: Any depreciation method except CCA is acceptable. Units of production would provide the best information for performance appraisal and is recommended.

8. *Lease classification.*

The lease must be classified as an operating lease (expense the payments, disclose five years' minimum lease payments) or capital lease (capitalize asset and obligation, recognize interest and depreciation on the income statement, disclose five years' minimum lease payments). As the area is covered by Section 3065 of the *CICA Handbook,* there is no leeway to choose a policy.

Recommendation: Ascertain the terms of the lease, and classify and account for it as appropriate. If a capital lease, the amortization method chosen for the asset should be consistent with other assets (#7).

9. *Loan disclosure.*

NSTR's assets are collateral for another entity's loans. This should be disclosed in financial statements. Users, especially creditors, should not be fooled into thinking this corporation is in better shape than it really is.

Recommendation: Disclose the fact that NSTR's land is pledged as collateral for syndicate members' personal loans.

The fact that NSTR's operating line of credit is secured by the personal guarantee of syndicate members should also be disclosed.

(Notice that this analysis ties the alternatives to the users and uses of the financial statements. If disclosures (or techniques) are appropriate for those users, then the disclosures should be made even if not required *under GAAP. This makes the statements more useful to users!)*

SAMPLE STUDENT RESPONSE

Overview

NSTR is a newly formed corporation that needs guidance on policies for accounting. No constraint on accounting policy choice is based on consistency. GAAP is not necessarily a constraint, because the company is not public. Also, note that the owners may not understand Canadian GAAP, because they are German-based. They may prefer German GAAP.

There are conflicting objectives in the user groups. Syndicate members want dividends to meet debts (high net income to support dividend declaration?) (or maximize cash flow and minimize tax, so report low net income?). Their objectives are likely the latter, because tax minimization is important to cash flow. Management would like to see high net income to maximize their bonus. Banks are mostly interested in cash flow but also in respectable earnings figures.

Conclusion. Syndicate members are the most important users, tax minimization is the most important use.

(This section is reasonably well done, but, *since NSTR is a Canadian company, has a major Canadian creditor and must use its statements to pay Canadian income tax, it is likely they will use Canadian GAAP. Also, the apparent conflict with management re: use of net income number for a bonus—remember that the bonus plan has yet to be established—could easily be resolved by careful formulation of the bonus plan.)*

1. Revenue Recognition

When should revenue be recognized? NSTR could recognize revenue as trees grow, or when sales occur.

A ready market exists for the product in raw form (i.e., NSTR can sell directly to saw mills). A market exists even for low-quality logs; therefore, NSTR can estimate revenue for at least a minimum amount. They have a five-year contract, so there is a reasonable expectation of profit. Furthermore, markets for this commodity do exist and are a function of supply and demand—that is, are reliable. Collectibility of revenues should be reasonably assured.

On the other hand, the quality of logs can only be determined when trees are processed. It would be very costly to figure out how much revenue to accrue each year—it would require experience to figure out how much trees had grown, and it would be very subjective.

Since syndicate members are concerned with cash retention, they should minimize taxes by recognizing revenue at a later point in time.

(This section is poorly done. Would NSTR really recognize revenue as trees grow? Alternatives should be sensible! Analysis of sales should be organized according to the two major types of sales, and criteria for revenue recognition have to be examined in a substantive fashion. Saying something like "collectibility of revenues should be reasonably assured" with no reason is unacceptable.)

2. Building

NSTR will need to disclose the lease commitment over the next five years.

(Missed the issue of whether the lease is an operating or capital lease.)

3. Depreciable Assets

NSTR must establish appropriate amortization policies. Canadian GAAP requires amortization over the expected useful life of the asset. Amortization periods may not exceed 40 years, unless it can be demonstrated that life clearly exceeds 40 years.

(Where are the alternatives? The analysis tied to user needs? Where is the recommendation?)

4. Land and Timber Resources

Since NSTR has a land resource that is partially "used up" as timber is harvested, depletion may be necessary. However, since NSTR is spending money on reforestation, there may, in fact, be no depletion of the resource. It seems as though they plan to sell the land in the future (they're interested in future capital gains). Will it be sold for just the land value? Or land, plus timber? This should be clarified with the owners.

Costs spent on restoring the condition of the timberlands can either be capitalized or expensed as incurred. Capitalization would require that the expenditure has caused an increase in the value of the asset. It's unlikely that *restoration* caused an increase in asset value! It's far more likely that an increase in value is caused by simple appreciation of land values in general. Costs are not large this year, but NSTR should pick a policy they can maintain for consistency. Tax minimization is not a factor here, since the costs may be written off for tax purposes regardless of accounting treatment.

It is doubtful that future economic value could be justified to the extent needed to establish the asset value. Therefore, the costs should be written off.

(What criteria were used to establish the policy in the absence of tax minimization as a deciding factor? Shouldn't user needs—the syndicate members or the bank—be mentioned? Do you agree that the future economic benefit of reforestation is so uncertain as to preclude capitalization?)

Inventory Cost Flow

Options open to NSTR include FIFO, LIFO, and weighted average. FIFO would likely increase income and increase inventory levels. This would allow for higher dividends and bonuses. LIFO would do the opposite. Weighted average would be between the two. Specific identification is not possible due to the nature of the process.

(No recommendation?)

Value of Inventory

NSTR would need to evaluate "obsolesence" or the need for a lower of cost or market write-down. In Canada, companies use the lower of cost and market (net realizable value). In the United States, they use the lower of cost and market value, but market value cannot be lower than net realizable value less a normal profit margin. NSTR has to establish a market value policy. Once written down, inventory cannot be written back up.

(Why are U.S. rules quoted? What kind of a policy should NSTR establish? How will it affect collateral levels with the bank? Performance evaluation of managers?)

Case 1

Acme Construction Ltd.

Bob Bothwell had started Acme Construction Ltd. early in 1992 after working for several years as a supervisor for a local construction company. An inheritance from his parents had provided the start-up capital. Bob's wife, Susan, did all of the bookkeeping on weekends without pay to help conserve cash.

For the 1992 and 1993 year-ends, the firm where you are employed as a student-in-accounts had performed a review of the financial statements and prepared the tax returns for the company. In late December 1994, Bob Bothwell phoned the partner in charge of the engagement to arrange

EXHIBIT 1

ACME CONSTRUCTION LTD.
Statement of Income (draft)
For the Year Ended December 31

	1994	*1993*
Net revenue from completed contracts	$365,000	$136,000
General and administrative expenses	172,000	100,000
Income before taxes	193,000	36,000
Income taxes	48,250	9,000
Net income for the year	$144,750	$ 27,000

Significant Accounting Policies

Revenue recognition: the company follows the completed contract method of recognizing revenue from construction projects.

Institute of Chartered Accountants of Ontario, adapted.

a meeting in Bob's office on December 30, 1994. The partner asked George Cathcart, chartered accountant, the senior on the engagement in 1992 and 1993, to represent him at the meeting and asked that you accompany George.

EXHIBIT 2 Summary of Contracts Undertaken

Started in 1992

Mainline Apartments

The contract price was $600,000, and costs were estimated at $450,000. The project was one-half complete at the end of 1994, and costs were on target at $225,000. In 1993, the project was completed but costs were $14,000 higher than estimated. The customer was billed $600,000 and all but $90,000 was received in 1987. The balance was collected in 1994.

Started in 1993

Harbour View Apartments

The contract price was $940,000 and costs were originally estimated at $800,000. At the end of 1993, the project was 80 percent completed, but price declines on materials resulted in costs of only $600,000. Progress billings were sent out for $470,000, of which $310,000 had been received at the year-end.

In 1994, the project was completed with additional costs of $150,000. The customer paid the full contract price by November 1994.

Sunnyside Curling Rink

The contract was awarded at $1,425,000 and costs were estimated at $1,250,000. At the end of 1993, the project was 20 percent completed, and costs were on target at $250,000. Progress billings had been sent for $200,000 and one half had been received by December 31, 1993.

The contract was completed in 1988. Costs were higher than estimated because of a subcontractor that delayed the project. Completed contract income of $148,000 is included in income, and all of the contract price was received from the customer before December 31, 1994.

Started in 1994

Victoria Mall

This contract for a three-unit mall was completed in 1994. The contract price of $450,000 has been billed, but $70,000 has not been received. Total costs of $423,000 were incurred.

DaVinci Apartments

The contract price was $1,825,000 and costs were estimated at $1,500,000. At the end of 1994, the project was 15 percent completed and actual costs included in construction in progress were $225,000. Although progress billings were sent out for $150,000, nothing had been received by December 31, 1994.

Discount Don's Department Store

The contract was awarded in November of 1994, but no construction has started. The cost of preparing the bid was $9,000 and this has been included in general and administrative expenses.

At the meeting, Bob explained that business was booming, and that he was considered privately raising additional equity capital to undertake some very large projects. He wanted to retain control of the company but was willing to relinquish sole ownership instead of increasing his bank loan. However, the preliminary draft statements for 1994 did not look as impressive as he had expected.

He handed George and you a copy of the income statement (Exhibit 1), along with a summary of contracts undertaken (Exhibit 2). He shook his head and said, "I didn't bring the balance sheet because I don't think it is correct. The materials in inventory are worth $200,000 now, not the $150,000 I paid for them. The same thing applies to the temporary investments. My broker assures me that they are worth twice what I paid. I also don't see anything reflected in the financial statements about the lawsuit that I'm involved in. My lawyer says that, when we go to court next week, I'll be sure to win $27,000 from the subcontractor that delayed the curling rink project."

"My biggest problem is with the income figure," he continued. "I don't seem to get credit for the projects that are in progress, even though my costs are usually in line, and I know I'm making money. Is there any way to improve my net income without paying any additional income tax?"

Required

Prepare a memo to George Cathcart. The memo is to include a revised net income figure for both 1992 and 1993 assuming that the company changes its revenue recognition policy from completed contract to percentage-of-completion, but continues to calculate taxes on the completed contract basis. You should also include your thoughts on the best way to deal with the problems Bob raised. Cathcart will be using your work as a basis for his report to the partner.

Case 2

Aggregate Corporation Limited

Aggregate Corporation Limited is a medium-sized processor and marketer of canned and frozen vegetables and fruit and frozen fruit-flavoured beverage concentrates for retail, food service, and industrial markets. The corporation also manufactures, mostly on a custom basis, freeze-dried foods for industrial customers. The corporation markets products across Canada under a variety of well-known brand names. Sales are also made under generic and private labels for major retail chains and food service distributors which service hotels, restaurants, and institutions. The corporation also exports products to Europe and the United States.

The corporation is in poor financial condition, following years of losses from operations in price-competitive markets. In the early 1990s, in the face of severe operating losses, the company sold a variety of divisions and property to rationalize the core operations and reduce debt. In the current year their major shareholder, who is financially strong, forgave $3.5 million in debt to improve Aggregate's financial position and partially appease external lenders.

Financial statements for the current year (Exhibit 1) and information from the *CICA Handbook* relating to the assessment of the going concern assumption (Exhibit 2) follow.

Required

Evaluate the accounting and reporting policies of Aggregate Corporation. Your response should include a revised 1992 Statement of Changes in Financial Position and any other analysis deemed appropriate.

EXHIBIT 1 Aggregate Corporation Limited Financial Statements

AGGREGATE CORPORATION LIMITED
Consolidated Balance Sheets
As at April 30

	1992 ($000)	*1991 ($000)*
Assets (note 2)		
Current assets		
Cash	$ 100	$ 100
Accounts receivable	5,076	6,004
Inventories	24,783	37,867
Prepaid expenses	347	542
Deferred closure costs	1,172	1,172
	31,478	45,685
Capital assets (note 3)	20,599	24,100
Other assets	664	707
	$ 52,741	$ 70,492
Liabilities		
Current liabilities		
Bank indebtedness (note 2)	$ 16,128	$ 26,436
Demand debenture payable to an affiliated company, non-interest bearing (note 2)	1,500	6,000
Accounts payable and accrued liabilities	8,317	11,735
Current portion of long-term debt (note 4)	2,751	2,838
	28,696	47,009
Long-term debt (notes 2 and 4)	38,081	38,035
	$ 66,777	$ 85,044
Shareholders' Equity		
Capital stock (note 5)	$ 35,429	$ 35,429
Deficit	(49,465)	(49,981)
	(14,036)	(14,552)
	$ 52,741	$ 70,492

AGGREGATE CORPORATION LIMITED
Consolidated Statements of Operations and Deficit
For the Years Ended April 30

	1992 ($000)	*1991 ($000)*
Gross Sales	$ 91,460	$112,704
Trade discounts and freight	15,321	19,061
Net sales	76,139	93,643

EXHIBIT 1 *(continued)*

AGGREGATE CORPORATION LIMITED
Consolidated Statements of Operations and Deficit
For the Years Ended April 30

	1992 ($000)	*1991 ($000)*
Costs and Expenses		
Cost of sales, selling, and administrative	$ 73,526	$ 89,954
Depreciation and amortization	2,381	3,399
Interest		
Short-term debt	1,653	3,487
Long-term debt	2,039	1,729
	79,599	98,569
Loss before the following	(3,460)	(4,926)
Gain on sale of beverage business and farmlands	976	—
Gain on reduction of debenture principal (note 6)	3,500	—
Plant closures and reorganization costs (note 7)	(500)	(10,740)
Net income (loss) for the year	516	(15,666)
Deficit—Beginning of Year	(49,981)	(34,315)
Deficit—End of Year	(49,465)	(49,981)
Net income (loss) per share	$ 02	$ (60)

AGGREGATE CORPORATION LIMITED
Consolidated Statements of Changes in Financial Position
For the Years Ended April 30

	1992 ($000)	*1991 ($000)*
Operating activities		
Net income (loss) for the year	$ 516	$(15,666)
Charges (credits) to income not involving cash -		
Depreciation and amortization	2,381	3,399
Accrued debenture interest	570	—
Gain on sales of assets	(1,866)	—
Gain on reduction of debenture principal	(3,500)	—
Write down of capital assets	—	7,922
Other	(52)	(120)
	(1,951)	(4,465)
Net change in non-cash working capital balances related to operations	10,789	10,678
	8,838	6,213

EXHIBIT 1 *(continued)*

AGGREGATE CORPORATION LIMITED
Consolidated Statements of Changes in Financial Position
For the Years Ended April 30

	1992 ($000)	*1991 ($000)*
Financing activities		
Reduction of bank debt	**(10,308)**	(5,972)
Short-term borrowings from an affiliated company	—	1,500
Repayment of long-term debt	**(1,611)**	(1,330)
	(11,919)	(5,802)
Investing activities		
Proceeds on sale of assets	**5,087**	907
Purchase of capital assets	**(2,006)**	(1,318)
	3,081	(411)
Change in cash during the year	**0**	0
Cash—Beginning of Year	**100**	100
Cash—End of Year	**$ 100**	$ 100

AGGREGATE CORPORATION LIMITED
Notes to Consolidated Financial Statements
For the Years Ended April 30, 1992 and 1991

1. **Summary of significant accounting policies**

Basis of consolidation

These consolidated financial statements include the accounts of the company and all subsidiary companies. The purchase method has been used to account for all acquisitions.

Inventories

Inventories are valued at the lower of cost and net realizable value, with cost determined on a first-in, first-out basis.

Prepaid expenses

Prepaid expenses include advances to growers and cost of growing crops which are deferred until the crops are harvested.

Deferred closure costs

Deferred closure costs will be charged against the anticipated gain to be realized on the sale of the property.

Depreciation

Depreciation of capital assets is calculated using the straight-line basis over their estimated useful lives. The estimated useful lives for buildings and improvements range from 20 to 40 years and for machinery and equipment range from 4 to 12 years.

EXHIBIT 1 *(continued)*

2. Security for debt

All of the company's assets have been pledged as security, either directly or through floating charge debentures, for the bank indebtedness, the demand debenture and the long-term debt.

AGGREGATE CORPORATION LIMITED
Notes to Consolidated Financial Statements
For the Years Ended April 30, 1992 and 1991

3. Capital Assets

	1992			*1991*
	Cost ($000)	*Accumulated depreciation ($000)*	***Net ($000)***	*Net ($000)*
Land	$ 711	—	$ 711	$ 1,187
Buildings and improvements	17,495	$ 6,027	11,468	11,873
Machinery and equipment	23,580	15,160	8,420	11,040
	41,786	21,187	20,599	24,100

4. Long-term debt

	1992 ($000)	*1991 ($000)*
Loans, mortgages and debentures, bearing interest at rates ranging from 0.0% to 12.4%, due at various dates through 1997	$ 6,060	$ 7,128
Amounts payable to affiliated companies -		
Debentures, bearing interest at bank prime plus 1/4% and repayable within 366 days upon receiving written notice demanding repayment and which have been subordinated to the banks' position	17,070	20,000
Advances, bearing interest at rates ranging from prime plus ¼% to 12.55% and a noninterest bearing advance, all with no fixed terms of repayment and of which $6,770,000 has been subordinated to the banks' position	7,370	7,370
Noninterest bearing debenture due April, 1994 and a noninterest bearing demand debenture repayable in annual principal payments of $500,000	9,975	5,475
Other—noninterest bearing, due at various dates through 2002	357	900
	40,832	40,873
Less: Current portion	2,751	2,838
	38,081	38,035

EXHIBIT 1 *(continued)*

AGGREGATE CORPORATION LIMITED
Notes to Consolidated Financial Statements
For the Years Ended April 30, 1992 and 1991

The company is renegotiating the repayment terms of a debenture payable to the Provincial Business Capital Corporation with a balance owing of $4,975,124 at April 30, 1992. A principal payment of $750,000, which was due on April 30, 1992 has not been paid.

The aggregate amount of payments required in each of the next five years to meet retirement provisions (assuming no repayment of the debentures payable to affiliated companies is required) is as follows:

		($000)
Year ending April 30,	1993	2,751
	1994	9,346
	1995	596
	1996	594
	1997	605

5. Capital stock

(a) Authorized—

An unlimited number of common shares without nominal or par value
An unlimited number of nonvoting equity shares without nominal or par value which rank equally with the common shares
An unlimited number of preference shares which shall be issued in series by the directors, each such series carrying such rights and conditions as the directors may determine.

(b) Issued and fully paid —	*Shares*	*($000)*
Common shares	26,125,255	$35,429

(unchanged during each of the years)

6. Related party transactions

(a) Debt reduction—

During the year, the principal balance owing on debentures payable to affiliated companies was reduced by $3,500,000 by the debt holders.

(b) Transactions—

During the year, the company was charged approximately $4,300,000 (1991 - $4,400,000) by related companies for supplies, services, and interest.

7. Plant closures and reorganization costs

As a result of the company's plans to reorganize and rationalize its investment in plant and warehouse facilities in Ontario and Atlantic Canada, a provision of $500,000 (1991—$10,740,000) has been made in the accounts to record the

EXHIBIT 1 *(concluded)*

AGGREGATE CORPORATION LIMITED
Notes to Consolidated Financial Statements
For the Years Ended April 30, 1992 and 1991

anticipated costs related to this reorganization. The provision includes the following:

	1992 ($000)	*1991* *($000)*
Write-down of capital assets to net realizable values . . .	—	$ 7,922
Other costs	$500	3,990
	500	11,912
Less: Deferred closure costs	—	(1,172)
	$500	$10,740

8. Pension plans

The company sponsors a defined-benefit pension plan covering substantially all hourly employees and a money-purchase plan covering all of the executive employees. The pension plan for salaried employees was converted from a defined benefit plan to a money-purchase plan effective January 1, 1992. An actuarial valuation of all plans was made on December 31, 1990, and was then extrapolated to April 30, 1992. The company's actuarial obligations for pension benefits arising from service prior to April 30, 1992 are estimated to be $3,132,000 (1991 - $3,354,000). The actuarial estimate of the market value of the assets available to meet these obligations at April 30, 1992, is $3,387,000 (1991—$3,387,000).

9. Future income taxes

The company and its subsidiaries have accumulated losses for tax purposes of approximately $23,700,000 which may be carried forward and used to reduce taxable income in future years. These losses may be claimed no later than:

		($000)
Year ending April 30,	1993	$3,800
	1994	500
	1995	3,300
	1996	8,600
	1997	2,700
	1998	2,300
	1999	2,500

In addition, the undepreciated capital cost of capital assets as at April 30, 1992, exceeded their net book value by approximately $23,000,000.

The potential income tax benefits associated with the above items have not been recorded in the accounts.

EXHIBIT 2 Evaluation of the Going Concern Assumption

Extracts from "Reservations in the Auditor's Report," Section 5510 of the CICA Handbook: par. 51–53.

An assumption underlying the preparation of financial statements in accordance with generally accepted accounting principles is that the enterprise will be able to realize assets and discharge liabilities in the normal course of business for the foreseeable future. This is commonly referred to as the "going concern" assumption.

During the examination, however, the auditor may become aware of conditions that cast doubt on the ability of the enterprise to continue as a going concern. Some of the conditions which, individually or collectively, may indicate a potential problem or could jeopardize the continuance of the enterprise as a going concern are:

(a) recurring operating losses;
(b) serious deficiencies in working capital;
(c) an inability to obtain financing sufficient for continued operations;
(d) an inability to comply with terms of existing loan agreements;
(e) the possibility of an adverse outcome of one or more contingencies;
(f) insufficient funds to meet liabilities;
(g) a plan to significantly curtail or liquidate operations; and
(h) external factors which could force an otherwise solvent enterprise to cease operations.

In some cases the enterprise may be experiencing many of the problems outlined above, but it is, nevertheless, reasonable to anticipate its continued operation. On the other hand, the problems may be such that the enterprise has, in fact, been placed in receivership or bankruptcy. Between these two extremes, there is a range of possible circumstances. Accordingly, the auditor must assess the circumstances in each particular case to determine to what extent the existence of the conditions would affect the enterprise's ability to realize the carrying value of its assets and continue as a going concern. In light of this assessment, the auditor's responsibility is to review and evaluate the accounting treatment, disclosure and presentation by the enterprise so that (s)he can report whether the financial statements are presented fairly in accordance with generally accepted accounting principles. . . . In assessing the adequacy of the financial statement diclosure, however, the auditor must consider whether the information explicitly draws the reader's attention to the possibility that the enterprise may be unable to continue realizing its assets and discharging its liabilities in the normal course of business.

Case 3

Air Canada

Air Canada is an international air carrier providing scheduled and charter flights for passengers and for cargo. The airline's passenger route network travels to 24 cities in North America and to 24 cities in Europe and the Caribbean. The cargo division serves 60 national and international destinations.

The government of Canada created Air Canada's predecessor, Trans-Canada Air Lines, in 1938. The airline was renamed Air Canada in 1965. By 1989, Air Canada was the free world's 18th-largest passenger airline.

Until August 1988, the airline was a Crown corporation, operating under the Air Canada Act, 1977. A Crown corporation is one that is wholly or majority owned by the federal or a provincial government, or one where the majority of members of the board of directors are appointed by the government. The government of Canada owned all the shares of Air Canada. Lenders throughout the world held the debt.

In September 1988, there was an initial public offering of 31 million common shares. In July 1989, there was a secondary offering of 41 million common shares. The government no longer holds shares in the airline.

In 1989, Air Canada changed its accounting policy for frequent flyer points. The airline's annual report described that change as follows (amounts are in millions):

> In the third quarter of 1989, the Corporation changed its policy with respect to its frequent flyer program "Aeroplan," whereby the estimated incremental cost of providing travel awards is charged to expense when entitlements to such awards are earned. Previously, the Corporation recorded such costs as they were incurred.
>
> As a result of this change in accounting policy, which has been applied retroactively, net income for 1989 and 1988 has been reduced by $3 and $7, respectively. The cumulative effect to January 1, 1988, of $9 has been reflected as a decrease in retained earnings at that date. The estimated liability as at December 31, 1989, was $34 (1988, $24).

The 1988 audited financial statements reported the following items:

Net income	$ 96
Opening retained earnings	$270
Closing retained earnings	$366

The 1989 audited net income was $149. The cumulative effect of the new policy at January 1, 1989, was an increase in expenses of $16.

The new policy is the same as the Canadian Airlines International and PWA policy.

Required

Present the 1989 Consolidated Statement of Retained Earnings for Air Canada. Discuss why the airline changed its accounting policy for frequent flyer points.

Case 4

Allingham Ltd.

Allingham Ltd. is a private company incorporated in Ontario. The company is located near Windsor and manufactures components that are used in the automotive industry. Ten years ago, Allingham's president decided that the company should become more involved in the local community. A wholly owned subsidiary was formed to purchase a small piece of land and a building. The building is used for fall fairs, hockey games, and summer craft programs. The land, the building, and an ice-making machine are the subsidiary's only assets. The subsidiary has no debt; however, Allingham Ltd. has long-term bank financing and a line of credit.

The subsidiary was very profitable until several years ago when difficulties in the auto industry reduced disposable income. In November 1992, an additional problem arose. Parents watching their children's hockey games noticed cracks in the walls and ceiling and demanded that Allingham Ltd. hire an inspector to determine if there was an asbestos risk. The report indicated that no asbestos was being released. However, rentals have almost ceased, and people have said that even if repairs were made they would not use the building. As yet there are no reports of illness, but the parents have hired a lawyer in case a lawsuit develops.

Allingham's board of directors is considering either selling the assets and winding up the subsidiary or tearing down the old building and constructing a new one. No decision has been made on the alternatives.

Required

For the year ended December 31, 1992, determine the impact that the subsidiary's loss and the asbestos problem will have on the financial statements of the parent company, Allingham Ltd.

Institute of Chartered Accountants of Ontario, adapted.

Case 5

Atlantic Trust Company

Atlantic Trust Company (ATC) was incorporated in 1964. Until 1980, ATC was a relatively passive and conservative financial institution in the Nova Scotia marketplace. Revenues were derived primarily through mortgage lending and investment income, and only a small portion of revenue was generated from commercial business and from brokerage fees on real estate transactions.

For many years, ATC was run by a part-time president, with the board of directors exercising considerable control over the operation. In 1980, an investor group headed by Joseph Potter acquired 80 percent of ATC's outstanding common shares, and Potter was installed as president and CEO. Potter was determined to follow a more aggressive course with the company, both through its trust company operation and through other activities, including real estate joint ventures and stock market investments.

From 1980 to 1982, ATC grew quite rapidly (see Exhibit 1). Unfortunately, however, there was a significant mismatch in maturities between assets and liabilities. The vast majority of the company's asset loan portfolio was in fixed-rate mortgages, while funding was provided by demand loans and short-term certificates. The rapid rise in interest rates during 1980 and 1981 caused a deterioration in interest rate spreads, which was largely responsible for ATC's poor profitability.

In 1982, ATC was found to be in violation of certain provisions of the Trust Act, which required minimum levels of cash reserves to be maintained and also specified the nature of asset composition. Consequently, the Nova Scotia superintendent of insurance assumed temporary control of the assets of the company, pending resolution of these issues.

A portion of ATC's investments were real estate joint ventures, which could not be liquidated readily. The company's stock market portfolio, however, was sold, resulting in the recognition of a loss of $767,761, after provision for $240,216 of income tax. (See Exhibit 3). Consistent with the

EXHIBIT 1 Atlantic Trust Company Operating Statistics

Year	*Assets*	*Revenue*	*Net Income*	*Equity*
1979	$ 38,506,448	$ 5,581,870	$ 36,996	$1,952,192
1980	44,981,435	6,566,895	122,029	2,427,030
1981	56,888,717	8,790,976	36,181	2,931,485
1982	60,097,890	10,451,572	(141,425)	4,636,817
1983	68,283,600	10,790,739	(408,356)	4,228,461
1984	73,305,277	11,432,047	8,097	4,179,484
1985	86,390,813	12,273,870	16,705	4,471,189
1986	93,240,798	11,228,130	73,497	5,703,757
1987	109,048,740	11,755,597	204,294	8,086,446
1988	141,567,463	15,504,140	61,488	8,147,286

EXHIBIT 2 Atlantic Trust Company Share Issue Data

	Per Share Figures	
Year	*Issue Price*	*Book Value*
1980*	$2.99	$2.99
1981*	3.87	3.13
1982*	5.00	3.13
1983*	—	2.78
1984*	2.13†	2.56
1985	—	2.58
1986	2.70	2.63
1987	2.70	2.73
1988	2.67‡	2.68

* Restated for 5-for-1 stock split in 1985.
† Conversion of subordinated debt issued in 1982.
‡ A $2.70 issue price, less costs.

classification rules in force in 1982, this loss was properly disclosed as "extraordinary."

This loss exacerbated the problems of ATC, since the size of the deposit base that the company was allowed to accept from customers was regulated, under the Trust Act, to a specific multiple of the capital base. Net losses that reduced this capital base would mean the company's deposit base had to shrink as well.

There were two ways to increase the capital base in the circumstances: obtain more investment or "manage" a gain into income. Both courses were followed. Additional capital investment of $900,000 was forthcom-

EXHIBIT 3

ATLANTIC TRUST COMPANY
1982 Financial Statement Exerpts

Notes to the Financial Statements:

12. Extraordinary Items:

Gain on sale of head office premises (net of income tax of $134,517)	$839,159
Loss on liquidation of stock portfolio (net of income tax benefit of $240,216)	767,761
Total	$ 71,398

During the year the company, as a first step in a redevelopment plan, sold its head office premises for cash consideration of $1,800,000, resulting in an after-tax gain of $839,159. The premises were leased back from the purchaser for a 10-year term. In the opinion of management the gain on disposal of this property was income earned in 1982 as:

(a) The sale was at fair market price to a party dealing at arm's length.
(b) The cash consideration was received in 1982.
(c) The leaseback of the premises is a cost equivalent to fair market rentals.
(d) The lease is subject to termination prior to the expiry of its term upon the happening of specified events.

Accordingly, the gain is reported as extraordinary income for the year as noted above.

Generally accepted accounting principles as set out by the Canadian Institute of Chartered Accountants recommend that such a gain be deferred and amortized over the [10-year] lease term. If this recommendation had been followed, the extraordinary items would have been decreased by $839,159.

From the Auditor's Report:

The company has recorded as extraordinary income a gain arising from the sale of a property. This property was leased back by the company, and generally accepted accounting principles require this gain to be deferred and amortized over the [10-year] lease term. The effect of this departure from generally accepted accounting principles is explained in Note 12 to the financial statements. In our opinion, except that the gain from the sale of property has not been deferred as explained in the preceding paragraph, these consolidated financial statements present fairly the financial position of the company as at December 31, 1982, and the results of its operations and the changes in its financial position for the year then ended. . . .

(signed) Doane Raymond
Chartered Accountants

ing from the existing shareholders, and a gain was recognized on the "sale" of ATC's head office building.

In fact, ATC arranged for the sale and lease-back of their premises with a finance company. ATC recorded the entire gain on this transaction in the 1982 fiscal year, contrary to the rules in Section 3065 of the *CICA Handbook,* which requires the gain to be amortized to income over the lease term—in this case 10 years. Accordingly, the auditors qualified their report for a departure from GAAP (see Exhibit 3). However, the gain was included in capital by the superintendant for insurance in Trust Act calculations, and the income and capital base as recorded were widely reported in the financial press (Note that, under 1982 rules, the classification of this gain as "extraordinary" was entirely appropriate.)

By the end of 1982, control of assets was returned to the company. Mr. Potter resigned and rebuilding commenced. ATC reported large losses in 1983, but subsequent operating performance showed gradual improvement.

During the period, new capital was invested in ATC, often to support the deposit base. Generally, capital investment was made at approximate book value per share (see Exhibit 2). A notable exception to this was 1982, when shares were issued to existing shareholders for a price 60 percent higher than their book value, and convertible debt issued (as part of the same transaction) with a conversion price 32 percent lower than book value. This debt was converted to common shares in 1984.

Required

1. Discuss the likely rationale for the *CICA Handbook* requirement to defer gains arising on a sale-leaseback.
2. Recalculate income and equity for ATC from 1982 to 1988, using GAAP for the sale-leaseback transaction.
3. Comment on the impact these figures might have had on the financial statement users, including current and potential investors, depositors, and regulators.

Case 6

Azzip Limited

Azzip Limited is a medium-sized, successful public Canadian company incorporated in 1963. Azzip is engaged in the exploration for, and production of, natural resources in several Canadian provinces. The officers, directors, and one "friendly" financial group control 35 percent of the company. The remainder of the outstanding shares are widely held in Canada, the United States, and the United Kingdom. Azzip's shares are not listed in the United States, nor does the company plan to obtain any financing there in the future.

The company purchases exploration rights and carries out exploration and development activities. On approximately 10 percent of its successful properties, it undertakes production and sale of the minerals and hydrocarbons that have been discovered. Production rights associated with the remainder of the successful properties are sold.

You have recently been retained as a consultant to the audit committee of the board of directors to help resolve a dispute that has arisen. The president, the vice president of finance, and the vice president of exploration and development, as well as two of the directors on the audit committee, disagree strongly among themselves about the most appropriate approach for reporting the firm's asset values. Through discussion with these officers and directors, you realize that a major concern is that they believe Azzip may be a potential target for a takeover bid within the next two years. In fact, they see signs that some anonymous small share accumulation may be getting under way right now. This, in their view, is not in the best interests of the company or of its other shareholders.

Adapted, with permission, from the *Uniform Final Examination Handbook,* 1979. © The Canadian Institute of Chartered Accountants, Toronto. Changes to the original question and/or suggested approach to answering are the sole responsibility of the authors and have not been reviewed or endorsed by the Canadian Institute of Chartered Accountants.

Two of the officers and one director, while understanding the basics of certain technical accounting requirements, believe that the company may be unwittingly contributing to the possibility of its own takeover by refusing to recognize as assets the discovery (exit) values of the firm's undoubtedly successful activities. This is of major concern, they suggest, because other shareholders may not be fully aware of the firm's success and might easily be convinced to sell their shares at low prices to individuals or groups seeking control.

Another officer shares the concern about a potential takeover but believes that the firm's assets should be valued on a replacement cost basis, rather than on either the present historical cost or on the suggested discovery-value basis.

The remaining director also readily acknowledges the possibility of a takeover. He believes, however, that conservative accounting policies and historical cost valuation are in the best interests of the firm and its shareholders. He argues that the management group should be able to explain the real situation to the shareholders, solicit their proxies, and obtain support for present policies. At an appropriate time in the future the entire firm would be sold at prices representing real economic value substantially in excess of the market and what may be offered in a takeover.

Upon returning to your office, you received a telephone call from the president. The president asked you to prepare a position paper, which would be discussed at the next audit committee meeting. In the position paper, you are to analyze the subject of the disagreement among the officers and directors, explain the financial impact that may be expected from possible approaches, and recommend a preferred approach for Azzip Limited.

Required

Prepare the requested position paper.

Case 7

Bender Capital Limited

Bender Capital Limited is a well-established leather goods company, manufacturing and distributing various items through retail chains. It has been a public company for nearly 25 years. Income and return figures generally have been respectable but not spectacular. In 1993, management became concerned that the company might become the target of a takeover bid, especially since sizeable cash balances had accumulated in the corporation.

At a meeting of the board of directors, several measures were approved to help reduce the attractiveness of the company as a takeover target. Among these was to increase the dividend payout, in order to help reduce cash balances on hand.

You, an assistant to the VP finance, have been asked to evaluate the advisability of each of the following policies for dividend payout:

1. Distribute a constant percentage of historical cost net income (see Exhibit 1).
2. Distribute a constant percentage of "operating income, replacement cost," that is, revenues less expenses stated at their replacement cost at the time of sale. (see Exhibit 1).
3. Distribute a constant percentage of "total wealth increase, replacement cost," that is, operating income using replacement costs, plus real holding gains (losses) and a purchasing power gain (loss) (see Exhibit 1).
4. Distribute a constant percentage of "cash from operations" (see Exhibit 2).

You note that the VP finance has asked a finance consultant to investigate the likely impact of dividend payouts on market price and takeover

---

Adapted, with permission, from the Atlantic School of Chartered Accountancy.

EXHIBIT 1

BENDER CAPITAL LIMITED
Income Information, 1993
(in thousands)

	(1)	*(2)*		*(3)*
Sales	$5,244	$5,244		$5,244
Cost of goods sold	3,737	4,018		4,018
Depreciation	221	412		412
Selling, general, and administrative expenses	399	399		399
Interest	199	199		199
Income tax	121	121		121
Total	4,677	5,149		5,149
Net income, historical cost	$ 567			
Operating income, replacement cost		$ 95		95
Holding gains, realized			$472	
Less inflation component			450	22
Holding gains, unrealized			616	
Less inflation component			209	407
Purchasing power gain				131
Total wealth increase, replacement cost				$ 655

(*1*) Historical cost, nominal dollars.
(*2*) Replacement cost, nominal dollars.
(*3*) Replacement cost, constant dollars, average dollars.

EXHIBIT 2

BENDER CAPITAL LIMITED
Cash Flow from Operations,
1993
(in thousands)

Net income	$567
Adjustment for:	
1. Noncash items: depreciation, etc.	221
2. Changes in noncash working capital	(265)
3. Changes in long-term items related to operations:	
Increase in deferred product development costs	(110)
Cash from operations	$413

potential; your evaluation should avoid these issues and discuss the alternatives using the other areas of your expertise.

The VP finance is particularly concerned that dividend payouts not be too aggressive, since the board would likely adopt the policy on a permanent, ongoing basis. He has pointed out that cash will be needed internally to fund development of new products, to support new products through their early growth cycles, and to maintain operations. This latter concern is especially important because increased general and specific prices are expected to hit Bender hard in the next year. Capital maintenance is important. Replacement costs have already escalated by 10 percent, on average, and are expected to continue to climb in the first two quarters of 1994.

Required

Respond to the requests of the VP finance.

Case 8

Black Corporation I

Black Corporation is a widely held public company. The company has suffered a recent decline in earnings due to general economic conditions. In an effort to improve performance, the company introduced an executive compensation plan last year. The plan provides that bonuses to management be paid out of a bonus pool. The excess, if any, of audited net income before extraordinary items over 20 percent of average total assets employed during the year goes to the bonus pool.

The company has a $52 million, 8 percent debenture issue outstanding that has 15 years to maturity. Five years ago, the debentures were issued at par. They are not publicly traded and are neither convertible nor callable. There is no provision in the debt agreement for either the early extinguishment of debt or the maintenance of a sinking fund, but there are various covenants on working capital ratios, debt/equity ratios, and dividend payments.

Interest rates are significantly higher now than at the time of the original issue of the debentures. The company's management is contemplating an early extinguishment of the debt.

Their plan is referred to as "in-substance extinguishment" or "defeasance." The company would need to invest $32 million in Government of Canada bonds with a coupon rate substantially higher than the rate on its issued debentures. The annual interest revenue and principal at maturity of the government bonds would be sufficient to fund both the annual interest expense and principal at maturity of the debentures. The bonds would be placed in an irrevocable trust solely for use in satisfying the debenture liability and interest payments. The company would finance

---

this Government of Canada bond investment with the proceeds of a new equity issue.

Management proposes the following journal entries to record the contemplated transaction:

Cash	31,900,000	
Share issue costs (legal expense and commissions)	100,000	
Common shares		32,000,000
To record new common share issue.		
Investment in Government of Canada bonds	32,000,000	
Legal expenses and commissions	100,000	
Cash		32,100,000
To record purchase of Government of Canada bonds.		
Debentures payable	52,000,000	
Investment in Government of Canada bonds		32,000,000
Gain on in-substance extinguishment of debt		20,000,000
To record the in-substance extinguishment of corporate debenture liability.		

Management believes that the proposed accounting treatment properly reflects the substance of the transaction and is justified by the facts. They argue that the debenture liability is extinguished in substance, even though there is no legal discharge. In addition, they argue that, since the company is currently in a strong financial position, it is unlikely there will be a breach of debt covenants or corporate bankruptcy. Therefore, the face value of any corporate debt would not become due prior to maturity. They point out that accountants are supposed to attach more importance to the economic substance of a transaction than to the legal form.

The gain would dramatically reduce the drop in earnings per share. Management proposes that the gain be included in "miscellaneous income" accompanied by a note explaining the transaction and the accounting treatment. They assert that an efficient market is indifferent between separate line-item disclosure of the gain (as an unusual item) on the income statement and complete note disclosure.

To support its views, management points out that reflecting debentures at current replacement value would allow recognition, as unrealized holding gains, of the gains which would be recorded in the contemplated transaction. They contend this would be more realistic than recording the debentures under historical cost accounting.

The partner in charge of the Black Corporation audit engagement has expressed concern about management's proposed treatment of the gain for the transaction. He points out that the company's liability for the face amount of the debt still exists after the transaction. He also points out that, if the stock market is efficient as management suggests, the market will not be fooled by management's efforts to bolster earnings. Finally, he has reminded management of its stewardship responsibilities to shareholders, since the advance refunding of corporate debt normally takes place in order to secure lower interest rates.

Required

Prepare a memo to the board of directors of Black Corporation that discusses the accounting and business issues of the proposed transaction. The memo should also address whether any economic effects would result for the company.

Case 9

Black Corporation II

Black Corporation is a widely held public company. The company has suffered a recent decline in earnings due to general economic conditions. In an effort to improve performance, the company introduced an executive compensation plan last year. The plan provides that bonuses to management be paid out of a bonus pool. The excess, if any, of audited net income before extraordinary items over 20 percent of average total assets employed during the year goes to the bonus pool.

The company has a $52 million, 8 percent debenture issue outstanding that has 15 years to maturity. Five years ago, the debentures were issued at par. They are not publicly traded, and are neither convertible nor callable. There is no provision in the debt agreement for either the early extinguishment of debt or the maintenance of a sinking fund, but there are various covenants on working capital ratios, debt/equity ratios, and dividend payments.

Interest rates are significantly higher now than at the time of the original issue of the debentures. The company's management is contemplating an early extinguishment of the debt.

This would be achieved through a debt-equity swap arrangement. Common shares of Black Corporation would be issued to the debenture holders in exchange for cancellation of the debt. Using discounted cash flow analysis, management appraised the fair value of the debt at $30 million. Management has proposed the following journal entry to record the contemplated transaction:

Legal expenses and commissions	200,000	
Debentures payable	52,000,000	
Common shares (management's appraised debt value)		30,000,000
Gain on extinguishment of debt		22,000,000
Cash		200,000
To record the debt-equity swap and related extinguishment of corporate debenture liability.		

Management believes that this treatment simply recognizes a realized holding gain, which is analogous to the gain resulting from the routine disposal of land or a capital asset.

The gain resulting from this transaction would dramatically reduce the drop in earnings per share. Management proposes that the gain be included in "miscellaneous income" accompanied by a note explaining the transaction and the accounting treatment. They assert that an efficient market is indifferent between separate line-item disclosure of the gain (as an unusual item) on the income statement and complete note disclosure.

To support its view, management points out that reflecting debentures at current replacement value would allow recognition, as unrealized holding gains, of the gains which would be recorded in the contemplated transaction. They contend this would be more realistic than recording the debentures under historical cost accounting.

The partner in charge of the Black Corporation audit engagement has expressed concern about management's proposed treatment of the gain for the transaction. One of his concerns is whether the discount rate used to determine the fair value of the debt is appropriate. He also points out that, if the stock market is efficient as management suggests, the market will not be fooled by management's efforts to bolster earnings. Finally, he has reminded management of its stewardship responsibilities to shareholders, since the replacement of corporate debt normally takes place to secure lower financing costs.

Required

Prepare a memo to the board of directors of Black Corporation that discusses the accounting and business issues of the proposed transaction. The memo should also address whether any economic effects would result for the company.

Case 10

Black Corporation III

Black Corporation is a widely held public company. The company has suffered a recent decline in earnings due to general economic conditions. In an effort to improve performance, the company introduced an executive compensation plan last year. The plan provides that bonuses to management be paid out of a bonus pool. The excess, if any, of audited net income before extraordinary items over 20 percent of average total assets employed during the year goes to the bonus pool.

The company has a $100 million, 14 percent debenture outstanding that has 18 years to maturity. Two years ago, the debenture was issued at par. At the same time, an interest-rate swap was arranged.

The swap agreement is with another Canadian public company that has $100 million in floating-rate debt outstanding, at a rate of prime plus 2 percent. Black had access to fixed-rate financing but, believing interest rates were due to fall, wanted a floating-rate instrument. The other company preferred the security of fixed-rate financing. Accordingly, Black agreed to pay the other company prime plus 2 percent each year; the other company pays Black $14 million each year. This, in essence, turns Black's fixed-rate financing into variable-rate financing.

The interest-rate swap was arranged through a financial intermediary, who guaranteed all payments in exchange for an up-front fee. The two companies signed an agreement, which outlined their respective responsibilities, and agreed to continue the swap for the entire 20-year life of Black's debenture.

Black has, in accordance with industry practice, continued to show their legal liability (14 percent long-term, fixed-rate debt) on the balance sheet. The existence of the swap is clearly described in the notes to the financial statements.

As the management of Black had predicted, prime rates fell subsequent to the issuance of the debenture, from 12 percent to 8 percent. As a result, throughout this year, Black has had a 10 percent (prime plus 2) cost of debt financing.

The other company in the swap, burdened with 14 percent financing, has approached the management of Black with a view to ending the swap arrangement. They are willing to pay Black a $5 million fee to end the contract.

Black's management team has examined the interest-rate market, and believes that interest rates will climb back to their previous level, or higher. They are willing to accept the deal.

Management has proposed that the $5 million fee be included as an "unusual item" on the current year's income statement. They argue that, because there are no remaining cash flows or risks associated with the agreement, any gains or losses should be recognized immediately in income. This treatment also parallels the cash flow to Black.

The auditors, on the other hand, have suggested that the $5 million payment should be deferred and amortized as an interest adjustment over the remaining life of the debenture. They argue that the $5 million represents a payment in advance for future interest-rate reductions and is properly accounted for as such.

FASB, in Statement No. 80, *Accounting for Futures Contracts,* has concluded that deferred exchange gains and losses on hedges should become part of the carrying value of the hedged asset or liability. On early termination of the hedge, the cost or carrying value of the hedged asset or liability is not to be adjusted by writing off the deferrals; they are to be linked continuously to the hedged item, and the accounting for them should be consistent with the accounting for the hedged item.

The auditors argue that the "defer and amortize" treatment of the payment is consistent with this rationale, while the "immediate recognition" alternative violates the logic.

Management is not pleased with the view the auditors have taken. They point out that a deferred item adds "clutter" to the balance sheet, and the credit is not a liability because it does not require any "future sacrifice of economic benefits" by the corporation.

The auditors have collected a variety of opinions on the interest-rate market and have concluded that interest rates are expected to stay low for the next few years, subject to various fluctuations.

Required

Evaluate the position taken by management and the auditors. Conclude with a recommendation on the proper accounting treatment for the transaction.

Case 11

CCB

"You can't have a system where you pay more for deposits, and you have higher operating costs, and you charge less on loans and take less security in order to grow faster than other institutions. Life isn't that way."

Richard Thompson, *chairman and CEO of the Toronto Dominion Bank,* commenting on the CCB in May 1985.

The Canadian Commercial Bank (CCB) was created in the mid-1970s as an Alberta-based operation, lending to small- and medium-sized businesses that needed loans in the $1 million to $10 million range. It was strictly commercial and had no retail outlets. Most deposits were short-term, from institutions and corporations, attracted by higher interest rates. Under CEO Howard Eaton, the bank loaned aggressively. Profits, $13,000 in 1978, reached $8.5 million in 1982. Assets, mostly loans, totaled $1.9 billion by 1982. Since the bank's loan clients were centered in western Canada, the CCB ended up with many real estate and oil industry related loans—in effect, an undiversified loan portfolio.

Eaton's goal had been growth: when Alberta had failed to deliver the targeted $5 billion asset base, he began oil industry lending in the United States as well. He also masterminded the CCB's purchase of 39 percent of the Westland Bank in 1981. Eaton was fired on January 24, 1983, partially due to his links with Leonard Rosenburg, of Crown Trust fame. Rosenburg had been attempting to accumulate, illegally, a 27 percent interest in the CCB. Gerald McLaughlan was installed as the new CEO.

The National Energy Policy and the recession in the western provinces had disastrous effects on the CCB. Land prices in Alberta and British Columbia fell as much as 50 percent. Oil properties and drilling equipment plunged in value. More than 40 percent of the CCB's loan base was in real estate and construction, or in energy and drilling rigs.

Between 1982 and 1983, net income slumped 88 percent, and there was a before-tax loss of $7 million in 1984 (see financial statements, Exhibit 1).

Return on assets declined from 0.88 percent in 1981 to 0.03 percent in 1984. On average, Canadian chartered banks earn 0.50 percent to 0.55 percent on assets.

Throughout 1984, the CCB continued aggressive lending practices, trying to diversify the loan portfolio away from real estate and energy. Assets grew almost 30 percent. The audit report for the 1984 fiscal year was unqualified, with loan losses of approximately $70 million on a $3 billion asset base. This, despite the fact that most of the loans which eventually were determined uncollectible were already on the books. Indeed, McLaughlan claimed that less than 2 percent of the bad loans were booked after Eaton left.

EXHIBIT 1

CANADIAN COMMERCIAL BANK
Consolidated Statement of Assets and Liabilities
As at October 31
(in thousands)

	1984	*1983*
Assets		
Cash resources:		
Cash and deposits with Bank of Canada	$ 55,406	$ 36,132
Deposits with other banks	196,004	18,726
Cheques and other items in transit, net	—	25,292
	251,410	80,150
Securities:		
Issued or guaranteed by Canada	66,197	107,447
Other securities	205,885	88,801
	272,082	196,248
Loans:		
Day, call and short loans to investment dealers and brokers, secured	71,000	170,000
Mortgage loans	70,471	25,691
Other loans	2,274,456	1,810,540
	2,415,927	2,006,231
Other:		
Customers' liability under acceptances	20,600	43,900
Land, buildings, and equipment	22,819	12,206
Other assets	103,778	58,538
	147,197	114,644
	$3,086,616	$2,397,273

EXHIBIT 1 Financial Statements (*continued*)

CANADIAN COMMERCIAL BANK
Consolidated Statement of Assets and Liabilities
As at October 31
(in thousands)

	1984	*1983*
Liabilities		
Deposits:		
Payable on demand	$ 137,324	$ 8,897
Payable after notice	7,802	—
Payable on a fixed date	2,693,297	2,165,061
	2,838,423	2,173,958
Other:		
Cheques and other items in transit, net	735	—
Acceptances	20,600	43,900
Liabilities of subsidiaries, other than deposits	1,303	815
Other liabilities	55,019	39,422
	77,657	84,137
Subordinated debt:		
Bank debentures	49,000	33,800
Capital and Reserves		
Appropriations for contingencies	16,596	23,947
Shareholders' equity:		
Capital stock:		
Class A preferred shares	30,000	—
Common shares	49,148	48,725
Contributed surplus	25,680	25,334
Retained earnings	112	7,372
	121,536	105,378
	$3,086,616	$2,397,273

EXHIBIT 1 (*continued*)

CANADIAN COMMERCIAL BANK
Consolidated Statement of Income
For the Year Ended October 31
(in thousands, except per share amounts)

	1984	*1983*
Interest income:		
Income from loans, excluding leases	$252,335	$208,841
Income from lease financing	2,071	2,606
Income from securities	18,176	7,638
Income from deposits with banks	11,546	2,502
Total interest income, including dividends	284,128	221,587
Interest expense:		
Interest on deposits	251,253	188,402
Interest on bank debentures	5,016	2,867
Interest on liabilities other than deposits	614	150
Total interest expense	256,883	191,419
Net interest income	27,245	30,168
Provision for loan losses	14,832	9,024
Net interest income after provision for loan losses	12,413	21,144
Other income	21,698	24,040
Net interest and other income	34,111	45,184
Noninterest expenses:		
Salaries	18,209	17,252
Pension contributions and other staff benefits	1,785	1,781
Premises and equipment expenses, including depreciation	9,739	8,220
Other expenses	11,306	9,706
Total noninterest expenses	41,039	36,959
Net income (loss) before provision for income taxes	(6,928)	8,225
Provision for (recoverable) income taxes	(7,732)	1,720
Net income for the year	$ 804	$ 6,505
Net income (loss) per common share	$ (0.22)	$ 1.57
Net income (loss) per common share fully diluted	$ (0.22)	$ 1.55

EXHIBIT 1 *(continued)*

CANADIAN COMMERCIAL BANK
Consolidated Statement of Appropriations for Contingencies
For the Year Ended October 31
(in thousands)

	1984	*1983*
Balance at beginning of year:		
Tax allowable	$22,849	$20,992
Tax paid	1,098	1,438
Total	23,947	22,430
Changes during the year:		
Loss experience on loans	(25,183)	(14,507)
Provision for loan losses included in consolidated statement of income	14,832	9,024
Transfer from retained earnings	3,000	7,000
Net change during the year	(7,351)	1,517
Balance at end of year:		
Tax allowable	13,555	22,849
Tax paid	3,041	1,098
Total	$16,596	$23,947

CANADIAN COMMERCIAL BANK
Consolidated Statement of Changes in Shareholders' Equity
For the Year Ended October 31
(in thousands)

	1984	*1983*
Capital stock:		
Balance at beginning of year	$48,725	$38,560
Issued during the year:		
Class A preferred shares	30,000	—
Common shares	423	10,165
Total	30,423	10,165
Balance at end of year	$79,148	$48,725
Contributed surplus:		
Balance at beginning of year	$25,334	$15,225
Addition from common share issues	346	10,109
Balance at end of year	$25,680	$25,334

EXHIBIT 1 *(continued)*

CANADIAN COMMERCIAL BANK
Consolidated Statement of Changes in Shareholders' Equity
For the Year Ended October 31
(in thousands)

	1984	*1983*
Retained earnings:		
Balance at beginning of year	$ 7,372	$ 7,395
Net income for the year	804	6,505
Dividends paid	(4,065)	(2,894)
Transfer to appropriations for contingencies	(3,000)	(7,000)
Income taxes related to the above transfer	—	3,444
Expenses of capital stock issues, net of deferred income taxes of $924 (1983—$76)	(999)	(78)
Balance at end of year	$ 112	$ 7,372

Notes to Consolidated Financial Statements
October 31, 1984

1. Prescribed Accounting Principles

The consolidated financial statements of banks in Canada follow accounting principles prescribed by the Bank Act, 1980, and the related rules issued by the Inspector General of Banks under the authority of the Minister of Finance. The significant accounting policies are as follows:

a. Basis of Consolidation

The consolidated financial statements include the accounts of all subsidiaries after eliminating intercompany transactions and balances. The Bank accounts for the acquisition of subsidiaries using the purchase method; any difference between the cost of the investment and the proportionate share of the fair value of assets acquired is amortized on a straight-line basis over 40 years. See the Schedule of Subsidiaries for a listing of subsidiary companies.

Investments in corporations of which the Bank owns between 20 percent and 50 percent of the voting shares are accounted for using the equity method and are included in "Other securities" in the Consolidated Statement of Assets and Liabilities. The Bank's share of earnings of such corporations is included in "Income from securities" in the Consolidated Statement of Income for the period of such percentage ownership.

EXHIBIT 1 *(continued)*

Notes to Consolidated Financial Statements
October 31, 1984

b. Securities

Securities include both investment account and trading account securities.

Debt securities held in the investment account are carried at amortized cost. Realized gains and losses relating thereto are amortized on a straight-line basis in the Consolidated Statement of Income over five years. Unamortized balances of realized gains and losses are carried in "Other liabilities" and "Other assets" on the Bank's Consolidated Statement of Assets and Liabilities.

Other securities held for investment purposes are carried at cost, with due provisions for losses in value which are other than temporary. Gains and losses are reported in the Consolidated Statement of Income in the year in which they occur.

All securities held in the trading account are carried at market value. Gains and losses are reported in the Consolidated Statement of Income in the year in which they occur.

Realized gains and losses on Government of Canada Treasury bills are reported in the Consolidated Statement of Income in the year in which they occur.

c. Translation of Foreign Currencies

Assets and liabilities denominated in foreign currencies are translated into Canadian dollars at rates prevailing at the balance sheet date. Revenue and expenses in foreign currencies are translated into Canadian dollars at the average of the prevailing month-end exchange rates. Realized and unrealized gains and losses from foreign currency translation are included in "Other income," with the exception of unrealized gains and losses in respect of net investment positions in foreign operations, which are included in retained earnings, net of applicable income taxes, in the Consolidated Statement of Changes in Shareholders' Equity together with any gains and losses arising from economic hedges of these net investment positions.

Prior to November 1, 1983, unrealized gains and losses in respect of net investment positions in foreign operations and related economic hedges of these net investment positions were reported in "Other income" in the Consolidated Statement of Income. In accordance with instructions issued under the authority of the Minister of Finance, this change in accounting policy has been applied prospectively and the prior year's financial statements have not been adjusted. The effect of this change is not material in relation to the prior year's financial statements.

d. Loans

Loans are carried at their principal amount less any specific provisions for anticipated losses. The actual net loss experience on loans for the year comprises the amount of loans written off, recoveries on loans previously written off, and net

EXHIBIT 1 *(continued)*

Notes to Consolidated Financial Statements
October 31, 1984

changes in provisions. This amount is charged to the Consolidated Statement of Appropriations for Contingencies.

The provision for loan losses is based on a formula designed to average the loss experience on loans over a five-year period as prescribed by the Minister of Finance. This provision is included in the Consolidated Statement of Income and that amount is carried to the Consolidated Statement of Appropriations for Contingencies.

Loan income is recorded on the accrual basis. Accrued but uncollected loan income is generally reversed whenever loans are placed on a nonaccrual basis. The accrual of loan interest income is discontinued where interest or principal is contractually past due 90 days unless senior credit management determines that there is no reasonable doubt as to the ultimate collectibility of principal and interest. Interest payments received in respect of nonaccrual loans are first applied to the recovery of specific provisions, if any, and secondly, to income.

e. Appropriations for Contingencies

In addition to provisions against specific loans, the Bank maintains appropriations for contingencies to provide for unforeseen future losses in respect of loans.

The appropriations for contingencies consists of two portions: tax-allowable and tax-paid. The tax-allowable portion includes the net loss experience on loans and the provision for loan losses charged to the Consolidated Statement of Income in respect of the Bank itself, together with tax-allowable transfers from retained earnings, which are subject to a cumulative limit prescribed by the Minister of Finance.

The tax-paid portion includes the net loss experience on loans net of related income taxes, if any, and the provision for loan losses charged to the Consolidated Statement of Income in respect of subsidiaries of the Bank, together with transfers from retained earnings in excess of the prescribed limit.

f. Land, Buildings, and Equipment

Land, buildings, and equipment are recorded at original cost and depreciated over their estimated useful lives, using primarily the straight-line method of depreciation. Gains and losses on disposals are included in "Other income."

h. Provision for Income Taxes

The Bank follows the tax allocation method of providing for income taxes. The cumulative difference between tax calculated on such basis and that currently payable is essentially a timing difference and results in deferred income taxes included in "Other assets" or "Other liabilities."

EXHIBIT 1 *(concluded)*

Auditors' Report

To the Shareholders of Canadian Commercial Bank:

We have examined the Consolidated Statement of Assets and Liabilities of Canadian Commercial Bank as at October 31, 1984, and the Consolidated Statements of Income, Appropriations for Contingencies and Changes in Shareholders' Equity for the year then ended. Our examination was made in accordance with generally accepted auditing standards, and accordingly included such tests and other procedures as we considered necessary in the circumstances.

In our opinion, these consolidated financial statements present fairly the financial position of the Bank as at October 31, 1984, and the results of its operations for the year then ended, in accordance with prescribed accounting principles applied on a basis consistent with that of the preceding year.

Edmonton, Alberta	Clarkson Gordon	Peat, Marwick, Mitchell & Co.
December 4, 1984	Chartered Accountants	Chartered Accountants

In early 1985, a decline in OPEC oil prices placed the CCB's oil drilling loan portfolio, both in Canada and the United States, in grave jeopardy and prompted a call from the U.S. Federal Reserve Board to the Canadian Inspector of Banks concerning the CCB's U.S. loan portfolio. Although the Canadian Inspector of Banks had been closely monitoring the CCB since Eaton's firing in 1983, neither they, nor the auditors, nor the investment community sounded any alarms during the 1983–84 period. The CCB even sold shares in a subsidiary, CCB Realty Trust, in February of 1985.

On March 14, 1985, McLaughlan notified the inspector's office that approximately $544 million of the CCB's loans were bad, and that the bank would require assistance or have to fold. On March 22, a private bailout proposal, to be financed by six major Canadian chartered banks, was rejected by those banks as an inappropriate use of their shareholders' investments. On March 24, a package involving the federal government ($165 million), the Alberta and B.C. governments ($18 million each) was announced that would provide additional capital to the CCB.

Despite public assurances of the bank's stability, 30 percent of the bank's $2.8 billion of deposits were withdrawn over the next six weeks. By July, $1.6 billion had been removed, and the CCB was little more than a shell. Bad loan estimates, $70 million in the 1984 audited financial statements and $544 million in March of 1985, were estimated to be in the $800 million to $1 billion range by August. During this period, the CCB was permitted to draw on the Bank of Canada to cover its cash requirements. By the end of August, they were overdrawn by more than $1.3 billion.

A final bailout or merger package found no takers at the end of August, and, on September 1, 1985, a formal announcement was made. Canada had its first bank failure since 1923. The cost to the Canadian taxpayer has been estimated at $1 billion.

The Fallout on the Accounting Profession

Many reasons have been suggested for the bank's failure:

> the recession, the vulnerability of the western economy, the mischievous over-expansion of the chartered banking system in the name of more regionalism and variety, the willingness of politicians to spend taxpayers' money on a cynical vote-buying adventure; or else a board of directors that had failed in its clear duty, auditors who didn't signal irregular practices, an inspector general who could have moved sooner and with more force, the chartered bankers who said one thing and did another (*Canadian Business,* December 1985).

Whatever the actual reason or combination of reasons, the federal enquiry into the bank collapse, chaired by Mr. Justice Willard Estey, served to focus attention on the role of the auditors, Peat Marwick Mitchell & Co. and Clarkson Gordon (now Peat, Marwick, Thorne and Ernst and Young). One can suggest that one purpose of the enquiry was to deflect criticism from the federal government and focus on the other players.

A series of headlines in the financial press illustrates the tone of Estey's (and others') open criticism:

"Estey shows impatience at methods of auditors" (*Globe and Mail,* November 23, 1985).

"'Bank management, the auditors and the Government's bank inspection system must share the blame for the collapse,' Bouey says" (*Globe and Mail,* December 14, 1985).

"Bank failures put auditors under fire" (*Financial Post,* November 23, 1985).

"Glare of spotlight reveals warts in auditing system" (*Globe and Mail,* December 7, 1985).

"Auditors didn't blink at bank's poor loans" (*Toronto Star,* September 25, 1985).

Accounting Policies

In the early 1980s, banks did not have to comply with the *CICA Handbook*. Instead, they followed the requirements of the federal Bank Act (see the auditors' report in Exhibit 1). The following accounting policies of the CCB were examined and criticized at the hearings:

1. When a loan initially went into arrears, overdue interest would be added to the amount owed (i.e., capitalized) and brought into income regardless of the fact it had not been paid. In addition to that, however, the bank would charge a flat fee to the client, which was also capitalized and brought into income. Income from such loan fees alone totaled $16.8 million in 1984. This was not disclosed in the notes. The now higher loan balance, of course, would be subject to loan loss review.

2. Part of the bank's compensation for a loan deal would often include an up-front fee. Common with industry practice of the time, this fee would be included in income when the loan was booked. Since many of the loans that involved up-front fees went sour, and may not have even paid the fee, the revenue recognition policy appears, in retrospect, questionable.

3. The loan loss was based, not on the amount deemed appropriate for the current year but, rather, on a five-year average. (See **note 1d** to the financial statements.)

4. Loans in arrears on principal and interest payments were often "sold" to a third party who was willing to speculate on recovery of collateral. The CCB would replace the "loan" asset with a "note receivable" asset, making no write-down. If the third party made a profit, the note was repaid. If not, the bank's only recourse was against the original security. Obviously, the notes receivable are quite risky.

The $350 million of such notes were not separately disclosed in the 1984 financials.

5. In the loan loss review, loans in arrears were evaluated against the security lodged against them. In many cases, the current value of real estate or oil properties was nowhere near the loan value. However, CCB management apparently valued much of the real estate security at theoretical prices that might be fetched years in the future. Presumably, these were values following recovery of the western economy. The bank was also getting into novel oil exploration agreements to create work for the rigs on which it had lent money. The auditors commented that the bank's credit officers continued to demonstrate "creative and imaginative" workout capabilities.

6. "The 1984 [loan reserve, on the audited financial statements] was only 0.68 percent of total loans, which suggested a reasonably healthy position. . . . The Bank Act did not permit the CCB to take a larger reserve, since that would have given it negative retained earnings. Management and the auditors suggested to the Inspector General of Banks that a larger reserve be taken . . . this was rejected." (*Financial Post,* November 23, 1985). In their annual report, the CCB claimed that the 0.68 percent "continues to compare favorably with industry averages." Even though bound by the Bank Act, the additional reserve requested could have been disclosed in the notes.

Required

1. Evaluate the accounting policies outlined, including an evaluation of the adequacy of disclosure in the 1984 financial statements. Which of CCB's policies are *not* according to GAAP, as outlined in the *CICA Handbook?*
2. Evaluate the content of the 1984 auditors' report (Exhibit 1), which states that the CCB's financial statements *present fairly the financial position of the bank* . . . in accordance with prescribed accounting principles (the Bank Act).

Case 12

CNR

Canadian National Railway Company (CNR) is the largest railway in North America. Included in its assets are 45,000 kilometres of track and 1,845 diesel electric locomotives. The railway is one of the 40 companies controlled by the Canadian National Railway System. In addition to the railway, "System" controls firms in the hotel, telecommunications, steamship, delivery, and technology marketing industries and has joint venture arrangements with numerous American companies involved in land and sea transportation. In 1986, System employed approximately 57,000 people (a drop of 10,000 from the level five years earlier). That same year Railway provided 74.8 percent of System's revenues.

History

Until the early 1800s, transportation in Canada was via her waterways. Ships could sail up the St. Lawrence River to Montreal, where they reached the Lachine Rapids. Passengers and cargo would have to continue past the rapids by boats through the Great Lakes and by canoe on rivers farther west. For up to six months of the year, these routes were frozen and transportation stopped. In 1836, the first Canadian railway opened; its 23 kilometres connected towns on the St. Lawrence and Richelieu rivers. By 1850, six companies had laid track, three of them bypassing obstructions in water routes; and, by 1860, there were 3,200 kilometres of track in Canada, heavily financed by the government. Many of the provinces that joined Confederation in 1867 and later did so on the understanding that they would receive railway connections to the rest of the country.

The most important railway company established in the 1850s was the Grand Trunk Railway Company of Canada. It was designed to have one main line, with smaller branch lines joined to it. The first component ran from east of Quebec City to Sarnia, Ontario. In the first decade of the

1900s, Grand Trunk built a line from Winnipeg to British Columbia, and created a new seaport called Prince Rupert. Across the prairies, railway stations were built every 24 kilometres, to encourage the development of new farming communities. In addition, a holding company called Grand Trunk Corporation ultimately purchased or constructed lines in the United States.

On June 6, 1919, the Canadian National Railway Company was incorporated by a special act of parliament. The company's mandate was "to consolidate the railways, works, and undertakings compiled in Canadian Northern System and operate them, together with the Canadian Government Railways, as a national railways system to provide transportation and communications facilities and to develop and utilize the resources of its undertaking."[1] The new company was composed of two predecessors, the Canadian Northern Railway and the Canadian Government Railways, 90 percent of whose financing had been by government loans. Ownership of Grand Trunk Pacific was acquired the following year.

One of the later acquisitions occurred in 1949, when Newfoundland became the 10th and last province to join Confederation. The publicly owned Newfoundland Railway and Steamship Services became the TerraTransport division of CNR at that time. Newfoundland has 705 miles of narrow-gauge track on which a special fleet of freight cars must be used. The line runs from the provincial capital, St. John's, to Port aux Basques, where passengers and cargo are transferred to ferries for the 90-mile crossing to North Sydney, Nova Scotia.

Current Operations

CNR is a Crown corporation. A Crown corporation is one that is wholly or majority owned by the federal or by a provincial government, or one where the majority of members of the board of directors are appointed by the government. By 1987, there were approximately 400 federal and 500 provincial Crown corporations in Canada.

CNR is wholly owned by the government of Canada, which appoints the company's chairman, president, and directors. Under the requirements of the Financial Administration Act, CNR must provide an annual report, including audited financial statements, and a capital and operating budget to the Minister of Transport. The Minister of Transport then presents the annual report and the capital budget to parliament. The government must approve the location and construction of any additional lines of railway, and, if these lines exceed 20 miles, it must also approve the expenditure. Any purchase, sale, or lease of any part of the railway

---

[1] *Crown Corporations and Other Canadian Government Corporate Interests,* Treasury Board of Canada, Ottawa, 1984.

and the granting of any trackage rights also must be approved by the government.

The railway operates coast to coast, although 70 percent of the work load is located in western Canada. The major items transported by the railway include lumber, grain, and fuel from the west, potatoes from Prince Edward Island, potash from Saskatchewan, and newsprint, steel, and automobiles from central Canada. In 1986 responsibility for passenger services was transferred by legislation to Via Rail.

Among the competitive pressures the railway faces are:

Lower world demand for Canadian resource products.

Increased competition in international markets.

Protectionist moves affecting lumber exports to the United States.

Alternative modes of transportation.

Protective measures ensuring that rates are fair and nondiscriminatory.

In addition, other components of System are contending with lower world oil prices and new products in the telex market.

The following article appeared in the *Globe and Mail* on May 2, 1987:

CN Loses $86.3 Million after Taking Write-Downs

Canadian National Railway Co. of Montreal took write-downs of $110 million in 1986 to be rid of a money-losing trucking division and to whittle down its work force.

An operating profit of $281 million on revenue of $4.7 billion was turned into a loss of $86.3 million after the write-downs and losses for services provided for the federal government. The corporation paid $382 million in interest on long-term debt of $3.5 billion.

This compares with an operating profit of $440 million in 1985 on revenue of $5 billion. Final profit was $117.6 million in 1985. The Crown corporation also lost $41.3 million on TerraTransport in Newfoundland, the passenger and freight service that it runs for the federal government.

CN sold its trucking company last year for $23 million to a group of Toronto business people. In recent years, the division consistently lost about $50 million annually.

To get rid of the trucking company, CN took a write-down of $71 million, including a shut-down cost of $26.9 million. It also took a loss of $9.4 million for a Newfoundland dockyard that was spun off by the company. In addition, CN wrote off $41 million in severence pay to employees last year.

Chief executive Ronald Lawless said the overall loss reflected one-time expenses and that 1987 results should be better. For one thing, Ottawa is expected to pay a bigger share of the cost for TerraTransport.

One of the worst turnarounds last year was in the rail division, which accounts for the bulk of the company's revenue. It had a loss of $11.2 million, compared with a profit of $105.5 million a year earlier.

This resulted from receiving lower payments from Via Rail Inc. of Montreal for the use of its facilities and from carrying reduced volumes for companies in the automotive and natural resources sectors.

Grand Trunk Corp., the U.S. rail division, and the CN Hotels chain, which has been put up for sale, also posted losses. Grand Trunk had a loss of $14.2 million, compared with a profit of $13.6 million. CN Hotels reduced its loss to $659,000 from $3.4 million.

The communications group had a profit of $36.2 million, compared with $43 million in 1985. Profit at the exploration division dropped to $4.5 million from $30.6 million, and the real estate arm increased profit to $18.8 million from $14.7 million.

The write-downs were disclosed after operating results but before extraordinary items. Regarding TerraTransport, the annual report said:

TerraTransport, which manages CN's rail, highway freight and intercity bus services in Newfoundland, experienced a 5 percent drop in freight tonnage in 1986, mainly because of a Canadian Transport Commission decision requiring increases in CN's freight rates for containerized traffic, increases which served to favor competing carriers.

The future of rail services in Newfoundland has been under consideration for some years and, in June of 1986, the federal government decided that services will be continued at least until 1990 and that government will provide some funding during this four-year period.

The government's decision did not provide for compensation to CN Rail for an inevitable operating deficit, with the result that the company has been obliged to carry out this imposed public duty without adequate financial compensation. CN will pursue resolution of this matter with the government.

Extracts from the 1986 financial statements of Canadian National Railway System follow in the exhibits.

EXHIBIT 1

CANADIAN NATIONAL RAILWAY SYSTEM
Consolidated Statement of Income
Year Ended December 31
(in millions)

	1986	*1985*
CN Rail:		
Revenues	$3,652,655	$3,753,190
Expenses	3,663,826	3,647,658
Income (loss)	(11,171)	105,532
Grand Trunk Corporation:		
Revenues	531,399	551,782
Expenses	545,556	538,200
Income (loss)	(14,157)	13,582

EXHIBIT 1 (*continued*)

CANADIAN NATIONAL RAILWAY SYSTEM
Consolidated Statement of Income
Year Ended December 31
(in millions)

	1986	*1985*
Enterprises Group:		
CN Communications:		
Revenues	303,384	303,930
Expenses	267,145	260,882
Income (loss)	36,239	43,048
CN Hotels:		
Revenues	146,911	129,846
Expenses	147,570	133,289
(Loss)	(659)	(3,443)
CN Exploration:		
Revenues	33,869	56,730
Expenses	29,368	26,123
Income	4,501	30,607
CN Real Estate:		
Revenues	35,157	29,582
Expenses	16,330	14,885
Income	18,827	14,697
Other:		
Income (loss)	1,822	(489)
Total Enterprises	60,730	84,420
Total CN Rail, Grand Trunk, Enterprises	35,402	203,534
Imposed public duty:		
TerraTransport:		
(Loss)	(41,291)	(39,908)
Total continuing operations	(5,889)	163,626
Discounted operations:		
CN Route		
(Loss)	(70,961)	(42,590)
Dockyard		
(Loss)	(9,430)	(2,933)
Total discontinued operations	(80,391)	(45,523)

EXHIBIT 1 (*concluded*)

CANADIAN NATIONAL RAILWAY SYSTEM
Consolidated Statement of Income
Year Ended December 31
(in millions)

	1986	*1985*
Income (loss) before income taxes and extraordinary item	(86,280)	118,103
Income taxes	—	57,823
Income (loss) before extraordinary item	(86,280)	60,280
Reduction in income taxes on application of prior years' losses		57,359
Net income (loss)	(86,280)	117,639

EXHIBIT 2

CANADIAN NATIONAL RAILWAY SYSTEM
Consolidated Balance Sheet
December 31
(in millions)

	1986	*1985*
Assets		
Current assets:		
Accounts receivable	$ 494,597	$ 486,922
Material and supplies	377,132	406,184
Other	252,915	234,849
Total current assets	1,124,644	1,127,955
Insurance fund	8,905	9,176
Investments	75,270	380,011
Properties	6,248,505	6,193,468
Other assets and deferred charges	385,290	428,171
Total assets	$7,842,614	$8,138,781

EXHIBIT 2 *(concluded)*

CANADIAN NATIONAL RAILWAY SYSTEM
Consolidated Balance Sheet
December 31
(in millions)

	1986	*1985*
Liabilities		
Current liabilities:		
Bank indebtedness	106,894	152,719
Accounts payable and accrued charges	899,189	954,235
Current portion of long-term debt	305,812	223,885
Other	186,273	155,732
Total current liabilities	1,498,168	1,486,571
Provision for insurance	8,905	9,176
Other liabilities and deferred credits	274,097	271,891
Long-term debt	3,052,486	2,948,347
Minority interest in subsidiary companies	4,345	4,345
Shareholders' Equity		
Capital stock	2,278,867	2,606,425
Retained earnings	725,746	812,026
Total liabilities and shareholders' equity	$7,842,614	$8,138,781

EXHIBIT 3 Extracts from the Notes to the Consolidated Financial Statements, December 31, 1986

Note 1: Summary of Significant Accounting Policies

Introduction

All references in these Notes to the "Company" refer to Canadian National Railway Company, which is wholly owned by the Government of Canada and, unless the context otherwise requires, its consolidated subsidiaries, and all references to the "System" mean Canadian National Railway Company and its consolidated subsidiaries together with the lines of railway, telecommunications, and other property entrusted by the Government of Canada to the Company for management and operation. A division designated in the Consolidated Statement of Income as an "Imposed public duty," as is TerraTransport, is one whose operations are continued by the Company in accordance with directions from the Government of Canada despite the fact that such continued operations are contrary to the economic interests of the Company.

EXHIBIT 3 *(continued)*

a. Principles of Consolidation

With the exception of Coastal Transport Limited, the consolidated financial statements include the accounts of all subsidiaries and the Company's share of the assets, liabilities, revenues, and expenses of CNCP Telecommunications, which is accounted for by the proportionate consolidation method; CN's share in the activities of CNCP Telecommunications represents slightly less than 60 percent of the activities of CN Communications. Also, consistent with the legislation governing the System, the accounts of the Canadian Government Railways entrusted to the Company by the Government of Canada are included in the consolidated financial statements. Coastal Transport Limited and the net assets of the Company's dockyard operation in Newfoundland, which formerly formed part of the consolidation, have been included in investments in anticipation of their forthcoming divestiture.

Investments in entities in which the Company has less than a majority interest are accounted for by the equity method, where appropriate.

* * *

d. Properties

Accounting for railway and telecommunications properties is carried out in accordance with rules issued by the Canadian Transport Commission and the Canadian Radio-television and Telecommunications Commission, respectively (Canadian properties), and the Interstate Commerce Commission (U.S. properties). Generally, major additions and replacements are capitalized and interest costs are charged to expense.

The cost of depreciable railway and telecommunications assets retired or disposed of, less salvage, is charged to accumulated depreciation in accordance with the group plan of depreciation. Other depreciable assets retired or disposed of are accounted for in accordance with the unit plan whereby gains or losses are taken into income as they occur.

The Company follows the successful efforts method of accounting for its oil and gas operations whereby the acquisition costs of oil and gas properties, the costs of successful exploratory wells, and the costs of drilling and equipping development wells are capitalized.

e. Depreciation

Depreciation is calculated at rates sufficient to write off properties over their estimated useful lives, generally on a straight-line basis. For railway and telecommunications properties, rates are authorized by the Canadian Transport Commission, the Canadian Radio-television and Telecommunica-

EXHIBIT 3 *(continued)*

Note 1: Summary of Significant Accounting Policies

tions Commission, and the Interstate Commerce Commission. The rates for significant classes of assets are as follows:

	Annual Rate (percent)
Ties	2.89%
Rails	1.87
Other track material	2.23–2.83
Ballast	2.76
Road locomotives	5.23
Freight cars	1.73–3.18
Commercial communication systems	6.40
Hotel properties	1.00–10.0

Acquisition costs of oil and gas properties are amortized on a straight-line basis over the term of the lease until such time as they are determined to be productive or judged to be impaired. Acquisition costs of productive properties and costs of successful exploratory drilling and of drilling and equipping development wells are charged against income on the unit-of-production method based upon proven reserves of oil and gas. Exploratory dry hole and acquisition costs judged to be impaired are charged against income in the current period. Other exploratory expenditures are charged against income as incurred.

f. Transportation Revenues

Transportation revenues are generally recognized on completion of movements, with interline movements being treated as complete when the shipment is turned over to the connecting carrier. Costs associated with uncompleted movements are generally deferred.

Note 2: Special Charge and Discontinued Operations

a. Special Charge

CN Rail expenses include a special charge of $60.2 million (1985—$40.4 million) relating to a provision for rationalization costs in connection with an ongoing program to reduce the size of the CN Rail work force.

EXHIBIT 3 (*continued*)

b. Discontinued Operations

During 1986 the Company disposed of its former division CN Route and its investment in CN Marine Inc. (see Note 6*a*) and entered into negotiations for the disposition of its dockyard operations in Newfoundland. Details of the charges (income) incurred on these operations are as follows:

Year Ended December 31 (000s)

	1986	*1985*
CN: Route:		
Operating loss	$25,641	$42,590
Loss arising from disposal	45,320	—
Total CN	70,961	42,590
Dockyard:		
Operating loss	4,530	2,933
Provision for loss arising from disposal	4,900	—
Total Dockyard	9,430	2,933
Total discontinued operations	$80,391	$45,523

Note 4: Properties

December 31, 1986 (000s)

	Cost	*Accumulated Depreciation*	*Net*
CN Rail	$7,978,729	$2,869,139	$5,109,590
Grand Trunk Corporation	557,864	153,150	404,714
Enterprises Group:			
CN Communications	742,175	312,045	430,130
CN Hotels	236,247	75,551	160,696
CN Exploration	85,728	25,261	60,467
CN Real Estate	63,279	13,861	49,418
TerraTransport	89,919	56,429	33,490
	$9,753,941	$3,505,436	$6,248,505

EXHIBIT 3 *(continued)*

Note 4: Properties

	December 31, 1985 (000s)		
CN Rail	$7,755,679	$2,766,643	$4,989,036
Grand Trunk Corporation	561,570	153,718	407,852
Enterprises group:			
CN Communications	708,538	288,916	419,622
CN Hotels	217,059	72,351	144,708
CN Exploration	74,947	12,211	62,736
CN Real Estate	72,750	18,221	54,529
Other	17	4	13
TerraTransport	95,484	52,430	43,054
Discontinued operations:			
CN Route	95,284	55,257	40,027
Dockyard	34,555	2,664	31,891
	$9,615,883	$3,422,415	$6,193,468

Amounts included above with respect to Canadian Government Railways entrusted to the Company by the Government of Canada:

1986	$1,060,097	$ 569,633	$ 490,464
1985	$1,037,108	$ 556,142	$ 480,966

At December 31, 1986, the gross value of assets under capital leases included above was $119.4 million (1985—$108.4 million) and related accumulated amortization thereon amounted to $9.3 million (1985—$5.5 million).

Note 6: Shareholders' Equity

a. Capital Stock

The capital stock of Canadian National Railway is as follows:

Common shares of no par value authorized, issued and outstanding, December 31, 1985	6,523,902	$2,606,425
Less: Shares canceled in December 1986 in consideration of transfer of all the common shares of CN Marine Inc. and certain assets held by the Company to the Government of Canada pursuant to the enactment of June 27, 1986, of the Marine Atlantic Inc. Acquisition Authorization Act, which act also changed the name CN Marine Inc. to Marine Atlantic Inc.	655,116	327,558
	5,868,786	$2,278,867

EXHIBIT 3 *(continued)*

b. Retained Earnings

Under its governing legislation, the Company is required to pay to the Receiver General for Canada a dividend equal to 20 percent of net income for the year or such greater percentage as the Governor in Council may direct.

* * *

Note 8: Subsidies

Revenues include the following subsidies:

	December 31 (000s)	
	1986	*1985*
Payments under the Railway Act paid under authority of that act and the related Appropriation Act in respect of certain uneconomic operations, services, and prescribed rates which railways are required by the Railway Act to maintain	$39,641	$37,151
Maritime Freight Rates Act and Atlantic Region Freight Assistance Act subsidies	18,735	20,460
Sundry	2,502	6,074
Other assistance	163	167
	$61,041	$63,852

* * *

Note 13: Other Matters

a. The Company carries on ordinary business transactions with various entities controlled by the Government of Canada on the same terms and conditions as current transactions with unrelated parties.

In addition, the Company provides, under contractual arrangements, rail transportation and maintenance services to the Government of Canada and to entities controlled by the latter. The revenue derived from such services rendered in 1986 aggregated $203.0 million (1985—$320.0 million).

b. Following enactment of the Western Grain Transportation Act, which became effective on January 1, 1984, the Government of Canada, in order to minimize the cost to grain shippers, pays a portion of the cost of shipping grain. Amounts received from the Government of Canada under the Western Grain Transportation Act amounted to $378.0 million in 1986 (1985—$278.9 million), a reflection of the volume of grain handled.

c. Commencing in 1977, the Government of Canada has agreed to pay to the Company, by way of capital grants not exceeding $557.9 million, certain amounts with respect to expenditures incurred in carrying out rehabilitation programs for branch lines in Western Canada. Total payments received up to December 31, 1986, amounted to $431.4 million of which $34.5 million was received in 1986 (1985—$43.7 million).

EXHIBIT 3 (*concluded*)

Note 13: Other Matters

d. As part of the program commenced in 1981 for the testing and evaluation of railway operations in Newfoundland, the Government of Canada reimbursed CN for certain costs. Total billings under this program amounted to $5.3 million in 1986 (1985—$7.6 million).

Required

Discuss the importance of accounting policy selection and disclosure alternatives for Canadian National Railway System.

Case 13

Campeau Corporation I

In 1986, Campeau Corporation purchased Allied Stores Corporation (Allied). The cost was $3.6 billion (U.S.). Debt covered 82 percent of the purchase price (20 percent short-term, 62 percent long-term), and 36 percent of the assets acquired were designated for sale.

In 1987, Allied issued junk bonds and sold assets totalling $1.1 billion. The bond issue and the asset sale proceeds reduced debt.

In 1988, Campeau Corporation purchased Federated Department Stores (Federated) for $6.6 billion (U.S.). Financing was 100 percent debt. Robert Campeau paid $73.50 per share for Federated despite advice to offer $70.00. Also in 1988, Campeau sold eight Federated divisions and two Allied divisions. One of the Allied divisions sold at a loss. The sale of the divisions reduced investors' confidence in the group's bond issues. In 1988, Federated attempted to sell $1.15 billion of junk bonds and raised $750 million.

During 1989, attempts to restructure the group's debt failed. In January 1990, Allied and Federated filed for protection under Chapter 11 of the United States Bankruptcy Code. Two creditors sued Robert Campeau for defaulting on personal loans, and a Canadian bank wrote down a loan from Campeau Corporation. Shares in Campeau were the collateral for this loan.

Required

Calculate the following ratios for 1986 to 1989 inclusive:

Current ratio

Working capital/Total assets

Net cash flow from operations/Current liabilities

Total liabilities/Owners' equity

Total liabilities/Total assets

Income before taxes and interest/Interest

Using the information presented in the attached exhibits, evaluate the financial position of Campeau Corporation.

EXHIBIT 1

CAMPEAU CORPORATION
Balance Sheet
January 31
(in millions of U.S. dollars)

	1989	*1988*	*1987**	*1986*
Assets				
Current assets	$ 3,999	$ 4,212	$1,336	$1,541
Properties & equipment	3,410	3,419	940	996
Rental properties	892	1,052	1,171	858
Development properties	422	473	336	556
Notes receivable	1,276	1,298	45	0
Other assets and deferred charges	318	524	245	261
Goodwill	1,854	2,862	1,227	977
Discontinued real estate assets	203	411	435	527
Assets for sale	0	44	46	1,320
Total assets	$12,374	$14,295	$5,781	$7,036
Liabilities and Shareholder's Equity				
Current liabilities	$ 2,834	$ 4,550	$1,686	$2,944
Long-term debt	2,874	7,858	3,447	3,780
Convertible subordinated debentures	155	416	144	0
Other liabilities	122	184	16	0
Deferred income taxes	754	787	70	64
Minority interest	3	412	280	0
Chapter 11 liabilities	7,299	0	0	0
Total liabilities	$14,041	$14,207	$5,643	$6,788
Shareholders' Equity				
Preference shares	101	101	101	107
Ordinary shares	165	165	165	59
Retained earnings (deficit)	(1,954)	(195)	(132)	93
Foreign currency adjustments	21	17	4	(11)
Total shareholders' equity	(1,667)	88	138	248
Total liabilities and shareholders' equity	$12,374	$14,295	$5,781	$7,036

* As reported in the 1988 annual report; 1987 reports on 13 months.

EXHIBIT 2

CAMPEAU CORPORATION
Income Statement
For the Year Ended January 31
(in millions of U.S. dollars, except per share amounts)

	1989	*1988*	*1987*	*1986*
Revenues:				
Department & specialty stores	$ 7,574	$6,546	$3,263	$786
Supermarkets	2,556	1,842	0	0
Real estate	309	280	267	191
Total operating revenues	10,439	8,668	3,530	977
Expenses:				
Cost of goods sold:				
Department & specialty stores	5,314	4,486	2,110	481
Supermarkets	2,140	1,545	0	0
Real estate	161	138	148	81
Selling, general, and administrative	1,927	1,618	821	155
Total operating expenses	9,542	7,787	3,079	717
Net income	$ 897	$ 881	$ 451	$260
Financing	1,185	877	485	92
Depreciation and amortization	371	308	134	27
Corporate expenses	80	57	40	11
Gain on sale of assets	(208)	(491)	(8)	(9)
Write down of goodwill	958	0	0	0
Reorganization costs	259	0	0	0
Income taxes	7	130	(34)	78
Minority interest	(119)	34	30	0
Net loss—continuing operations	(1,636)	(34)	(196)	61
Net loss from discontinued real estate assets	104	0	0	65
Net loss	(1,740)	(34)	(196)	(4)
Dividends on preference shares	15	12	10	6
Net loss attributable to ordinary shareholders	($1,755)	($46)	($206)	($10)
Net loss per ordinary share	(39.59)	(1.04)	(5.06)	(0.26)

EXHIBIT 3

CAMPEAU CORPORATION
Statement of Changes in Financial Position
For the Year Ended January 31
(in millions of U.S. dollars)

	1989	*1988*	*1987*	*1986*
Operating activities:				
Loss, continuing operations	$(1,636)	$ (34)	$ (196)	$ 61
Items not requiring a current outlay of cash:				
Deferred income taxes	7	122	(45)	11
Depreciation and amortization	296	238	98	23
Amortization of financing costs	161	84	112	9
Amortization of goodwill	75	70	36	4
Minority interest	(119)	34	30	0
Write-off of financing costs	252	0	0	0
Write-down of goodwill	958	0	0	0
Gain on sale of division	(101)	(350)	0	0
Total items	(107)	164	35	108
Net change in noncash, working capital balances				
Accounts receivable	(61)	(51)	(2)	(130)
Merchandise inventory	28	(105)	(76)	79
Accounts payable and accrued expenses	(74)	138	156	(116)
Income taxes payable	(6)	0	(15)	67
Cash provided by operating activities	(220)	146	98	8
Financing activities:				
Issue of capital stock, net	0	0	100	81
Debt issued	2,265	6,395	2,975	3,384
Debt issue cost	(202)	(355)	(112)	(177)
Debt repaid	(1,695)	(7,795)	(4,610)	(3,005)
Debt issued on acquisition	0	6,207	0	3,477
Minority interest	67	99	250	0
Cash provided by financing activities	435	4,551	(1,397)	3,760

EXHIBIT 3 *(concluded)*

CAMPEAU CORPORATION
Statement of Changes in Financial Position
For the Year Ended January 31
(in millions of U.S. dollars)

	1989	*1988*	*1987*	*1986*
Investment activities:				
Properties and equipment	(289)	(305)	(78)	(28)
Rental properties	(22)	(26)	(309)	(45)
Development properties	(190)	(189)	81	(158)
Costs recovered from sale of properties	471	285	242	46
Proceeds from sale of division	430	740	0	0
Notes receivable	15	(1,236)	(22)	1
Acquisition of subsidiaries	0	(6,591)	0	(3,583)
Other	71	51	(3)	38
Assets for sale	33	3,108	1,055	(7)
Discontinued real estate assets	67	41	109	6
Cash applied to investment activities	586	(4,122)	1,075	(3,730)
Dividends	(13)	(28)	(13)	(9)
Increase (decrease) in cash	$ 788	$ 547	$ (237)	$ 29

Case 14

Campeau Corporation II

In 1986, Campeau Corporation purchased Allied Stores Corporation (Allied). The cost was $3.6 billion (U.S.). Debt covered 82 percent of the purchase price (20 percent short-term, 62 percent long-term), and 36 percent of the assets acquired were designated for sale.

In 1987, Allied issued junk bonds and sold assets totalling $1.1 billion. The bond issue and the asset sale proceeds reduced debt.

In 1988, Campeau Corporation purchased Federated Department Stores (Federated) for $6.6 billion (U.S.). Financing was 100 percent debt. Robert Campeau paid $73.50 per share for Federated despite advice to offer $70.00. Also in 1988, Campeau was able to sell eight Federated divisions and two Allied divisions. One of the Allied divisions sold at a loss. The sale of the divisions reduced investors' confidence in the group's bond issues. In 1988, Federated attempted to sell $1.15 billion of junk bonds and raised $750 million.

Campeau Corporation's January 31, 1988, annual report showed an increase in goodwill. A note explained the increase as being "attributable to the disposition of divisions held for sale in amounts less than the estimated fair value at the time of the business combination, estimated costs of certain assets to be disposed of and additional costs associated with the merger, net of amortization." Campeau amortizes goodwill on a straight-line basis over 40 years.

During 1989, attempts to restructure the group's debt failed. In January 1990, Allied and Federated filed for protection under Chapter 11 of the United States Bankruptcy Code. Two creditors sued Robert Campeau for defaulting on personal loans, and a Canadian bank wrote down a loan from Campeau Corporation. Shares in Campeau were the collateral for this loan.

During the year ended January 31, 1989, Campeau wrote down its goodwill value for the first time. The annual report disclosed that "the original value attributed to Federated's goodwill has been impaired and accordingly has been written down by $958 million after considering a range of valuations. Due to the uncertainties described (in an earlier section of the annual report), further adjustments to goodwill may be required in the future."

Required

Discuss Campeau Corporation's goodwill valuation. Use the financial statement extracts presented in Exhibit 1 or the full set of financial statements in "Campeau Corporation I."

EXHIBIT 1 Extracts from the Financial Statements, January 31 (in millions of U.S. dollars)

	1989	*1988*	*1987**	*1986*
From the balance sheet:				
Goodwill	$ 1,854	$ 2,862	$1,227	$ 977
Total assets	12,374	14,295	5,781	7,036
Chapter 11 liabilities	7,299	0	0	0
Total liabilities	14,041	14,207	5,643	6,788
Retained earnings (deficit)	(1,954)	(195)	(132)	93
From the income statement:				
Net loss—				
continuing operations	(1,636)	(34)	(196)	61
From the statement of changes in financial position:				
Operating activities:				
Items not requiring a current outlay of cash:				
Depreciation and amortization	296	238	98	23
Amortization of goodwill	75	70	36	4
Write-down of goodwill	958	0	0	0
Gain on sale of division	(101)	(350)	0	0
Investment activities:				
Proceeds from sale of division	430	740	0	0
Acquisition of subsidiaries	0	(6,591)	0	(3,583)

* As reported in the 1988 annual report; 1987 reports on 13 months.

Case 15

Canadair Limited

In 1984, Canadair Limited was a Crown corporation, acquired from General Dynamics Corporation of St. Louis in 1976 for $46.6 million. The company had been formed to serve the needs of the Canadian military; but when military spending began to deteriorate in the 1960s, Canadair began to evolve into something closer to a maintenance center than a development company. Acquisition by the Canada Development Investment Company was meant to reverse this.

Work on the Challenger jet program began in the mid-1970s. The jet was plagued with problems from the very beginning. Canadair had little expertise in jet design. Their engineering staff was at an all-time low of 150 at the inception of the project. They selected an unproven engine. They committed to a design and certification schedule they could not meet. Their prototype had a shorter range and needed a longer runway than called for in the original design.

These design problems cost the company significant amounts for development costs, and their rising cash needs were met entirely by borrowing at a time when interest rates were high. The debt issued was all government guaranteed.

As costs escalated, the viability of the jet program was continually reevaluated. In March 1980, the company predicted that it would break even with sales of 255 planes by mid-1984. In December 1982, the numbers had become 389 planes by the end of 1992. As the number of planes required for break-even increased, so did the optimism of management, who were confidently predicting required sales targets would be met.

In 1983, the aircraft was in commercial production. However, most aircraft delivered to that date had been sold at a loss. The company was so anxious to keep orders and compensate for shortfalls in performance that it was willing to sell at low prices. This encouraged buyers to turn around and resell at a profit, competing with Canadair's own marketing efforts.

By the spring of 1983, however, the bubble burst. Management finally acknowledged that the Challenger program would never break even. They were requesting a $240 million injection of capital from the government in order to stay afloat until the end of the year. Senator Jack Austin was appointed to investigate.

Concurrently, the financial statements for fiscal year 1982 were released with an audit report dated May 18, 1983. These showed a $1 billion write-off of deferred development expenses relating to the Challenger program. The write-off left the company with assets of $267,024, and a shareholder's deficit of $1,160,787. (See Exhibit 1.) The loss made headlines in the financial press.

Canadair had followed a policy of deferring costs associated with new aircraft development. The costs would be amortized to net income when the aircraft started commercial production. This would match the costs to the revenues generated by the project. This method of accounting recognizes the unique nature of an industry that makes huge investments at the

EXHIBIT 1

CANADAIR LIMITED
(Incorporated under the laws of Canada)
Consolidated Balance Sheet
As at December 31, 1982 and 1981
(in thousands)

	1982	*1981*
Assets		
Current assets:		
Cash	$ 5,497	$ 3,012
Accounts receivable	43,045	65,516
Contracts in process and inventories, less advances and progress billings (Notes 3 and 4)	127,651	1,031,619
Prepaid expenses	5,040	3,322
	181,233	1,103,469
Property, plant, and equipment	118,353	110,401
Less accumulated depreciation	60,174	54,600
	58,179	55,801
Other assets:		
Note receivable, net of current portion	5,129	—
Deferred charges, net	22,483	(1,443)
	27,612	(1,443)
Total assets	$ 267,024	$1,157,827

EXHIBIT 1 *(continued)*

CANADAIR LIMITED
(Incorporated under the laws of Canada)
Consolidated Balance Sheet
As at December 31, 1982 and 1981
(in thousands)

	1982	*1981*
Liabilities		
Current liabilities:		
Bank loans	$ 10,575	$ 322,087
Accounts payable and accrued liabilities	352,949	117,019
Customer deposits	2,620	13,186
Principal due within one year on long-term debt	86,062	50,212
	452,206	502,504
Long-term debt	975,605	601,160
Shareholders' Equity (Deficit)		
Capital stock:		
251,700 Preferred shares, Class B	25,170	25,170
3,102,206 Common shares, Class A	17,244	17,244
	42,414	42,414
Contributed surplus (Note 2)	200,000	—
Excess of appraised value of land over cost	10,760	10,788
Retained earnings (deficit)	(1,413,961)	961
	(1,160,787)	54,163
Total liabilities and shareholders' equity	$ 267,024	$1,157,827

EXHIBIT 1 (*continued*)

CANADAIR LIMITED
Consolidated Statement of Income
and Retained Earnings (Deficit)
Years Ended December 31, 1982 and 1981
(in thousands)

	1982	*1981*
Sales	$ 429,379	$285,662
Expenses (Note 3):		
Cost of sales	500,971	273,991
Selling, general, and administrative	57,311	3,363
Research and development	16,189	1,800
Interest and other financing (Note 12)	215,477	3,430
	789,948	282,584
Income (loss) before unusual items and income taxes	(360,569)	3,078
Unusual items relating to Challenger program (Note 3)	(1,054,327)	—
Income (loss) before income taxes	(1,414,896)	3,078
Income taxes (Note 11)	26	43
Net income (loss) for the year	(1,414,922)	3,035
Retained earnings (deficit) at beginning of year	961	(2,074)
Retained earnings (deficit) at end of year	$(1,413,961)	$ 961

Notes to Consolidated Financial Statements
Years Ended December 31, 1982 and 1981

1. Summary of Significant Accounting Policies

b. Accounting for long-term contracts and programs

Under long-term contracts and programs, the company does not recognize earnings until such time as sufficient production has been accomplished to minimize the risk in estimating total contract earnings. At such time, earnings are recorded as they have been earned to date. Estimated losses are recorded in full as soon as they are identified. Earnings and losses recorded in the current year may include the cumulative effect of adjustments to prior years' estimates.

Estimated earnings or losses on contracts and programs are determined from projected revenues and manufacturing costs, taking into account factors such as expected sales, price levels, production costs, and other variables which are beyond the company's control. Because these factors cannot be measured with precision, the estimates are subject to periodic

EXHIBIT 1 (*continued*)

Notes to Consolidated Financial Statements
Years Ended December 31, 1982 and 1981

revisions. If future assessments indicate that any unamortized costs are not recoverable, the excess will be charged to earnings immediately.

Development costs which qualify for deferral are inventoried and amortized over the number of units to be produced. When the recovery of amounts deferred to future periods becomes uncertain, such costs are written off as a charge to earnings in the year.

Title to work performed under certain contracts in process and to related inventories is vested in the customer in accordance with contract provisions.

Costs relating to claims by Canadair arising out of contractual disputes are included in contracts in process when management is of the opinion that the amount of such costs does not exceed the net realizable value of the claims. Losses on claims are recorded in full as soon as they are identified.

2. **Government Guarantees and Financing Requirements**
The government of Canada has the authority to guarantee certain financial arrangements of the company with financial institutions to a maximum of $1.350 million. On December 30, 1982, the government of Canada contributed $200 million to the company's equity account.

The company's forecast cash requirements indicate that, without additional financing arrangements, the total debt for which the company expects to need government guarantees will exceed the authorized limit of $1.350 million in 1983. Additional capital subscriptions or an increase in the guarantee limit, or both, will be necessary to provide the company with the working capital required to ensure that the company will continue as a going concern, the basis on which these financial statements have been prepared.

The government of Canada, through an item in supplementary estimates introduced in the Parliament of Canada on May 18, 1983, has requested parliamentary authority for additional government equity financing of $240 million for the company.

3. **Challenger Program—Commercial Production and Unusual Items**
The Challenger 600 program commenced in late 1976 with first flight in November 1978 and type certification in November 1980. Modifications developed through the certification process were incorporated in the aircraft in production during 1981. As a result of continual review and monitoring of production throughout 1982, management has determined that the program development process was completed by December 31, 1981, and the commercial production commenced in 1982. Type certification of the *Challenger 601*

EXHIBIT 1 *(continued)*

Notes to Consolidated Financial Statements
Years Ended December 31, 1982 and 1981

was received in March 1983. At December 31, 1982, 67 aircraft had been delivered under the program.

Prior to 1982, costs such as development, finance, marketing, product support, and general and administrative expenses had been included as part of contracts in process inventory as the management of the company believed at the time that all such inventoried costs would be recovered in the future. Concurrently with the commencement of commercial production, the company ceased charging these costs to contracts in process inventory, and such costs incurred since January 1, 1982, have been expensed in the year. Before the commencement of commercial production, the cost of each aircraft delivered was removed from contracts in process and charged to cost of sales in an amount which equaled the selling price of the aircraft delivered.

Management no longer believes that there is reasonable assurance that the inventoried costs discussed in the preceding paragraph will be recovered from future sales. Thus, these costs have been written off to 1982 earnings as unusual items. Unusual items written off in the amount of $1,054.3 million also include estimated excess early production cost, development costs incurred in 1982 for the Challenger 601, provisions for claims, surplus and obsolete materials, and other related estimated losses, aggregating $361.2 million.

4. Contracts in Process and Inventories

	1982	*1981*
	(in thousands)	
Finished goods including aircraft, less advances and progress billings of $19.1 million (1981—nil)	$ 68,553	$ 5,820
Government contracts in process	1,749	5,461
Commercial programs and contracts in process, less advances and progress billings of $180.9 million (1981—$201.4 million)	$ 44,446	$1,008,766
Inventories of commercial products, materials and spare parts	12,903	11,572
Total	$127,651	$1,031,619

EXHIBIT 1 *(concluded)*

Auditor's Report

To the Shareholders of
Canadair Limited:

We have examined the consolidated balance sheet of Canadair Limited as at December 31, 1982 and 1981, and the consolidated statements of income and retained earnings (deficit) and changes in financial position for the years then ended. Our examination was made in accordance with generally accepted auditing standards, and accordingly included such tests and other procedures as we considered necessary in the circumstances.

In our opinion, these consolidated financial statements present fairly the financial position of the company as at December 31, 1982 and 1981, and the results of its operations and the changes in its financial position for the years then ended in accordance with generally accepted accounting principles applied on a consistent basis.

Montreal, Canada
May 18, 1983

Thorne Riddell
Chartered Accountants

beginning of an aircraft program and realizes a profit only after many years.

According to the description of their deferral policy contained in the notes to the financial statements, Canadair treated all costs which were in any way related to the Challenger program as costs of the program and eligible for deferral. These included materials, labour, factory overhead, development, tooling, interest, marketing, after-sales support, and general administration. The cumulative interest charges alone on the Challenger program were $440 million by the end of 1982.

In 1982, the company had made a chain of decisions that resulted in the write-offs. First, they designated January 1, 1982, as the date for accounting purposes on which the Challenger came into commercial production. Second, they came to the realization that the company "could never reasonably hope" to break even; that is, they became more realistic in their sales estimates. Finally, and most importantly, they decided to more closely follow the accounting policies of the other North American aviation companies. Interest, marketing, after-sales support, administrative overhead and ongoing development, and tooling costs were no longer considered appropriate for deferral as aircraft development.

Questions for Discussion

1. At the inception of the program, management faced three basic alternatives for the accounting treatment of the Challenger program costs:
   a. Defer all costs.
   b. Defer only those costs directly related to the program (as other aviation companies chose to do).
   c. Expense all costs.
   Canadair chose alternative (1). Were they in error? Your answer should include a complete analysis of all alternatives.
2. Do you think that the write-down was properly treated in the 1982 financial statements? Your answer should include a review of the alternative treatments. Why do you think they chose the alternative they did?

Case 16

Canadian Conglomerate

Canadian Conglomerate (CC) is one of Canada's largest and oldest public companies, with controlling interests in the tobacco industry, drugstores, and financial services. At the end of 1992, CC's total assets amounted to $3 billion; the 1992 revenue was $4.3 billion and net income was $242 million.

In November 1993, the vice president of accounting met with the company's audit partner to discuss the procedures for the year-end audit and the presentation to be adopted in this year's statements. There were two items in particular that the vice president, Jacques Anthony, wanted to review with the auditors. One concerned the $17.5 million gain on the sale of the company's interest in an oil and gas exploration company. This investment had been in preferred shares only (there had been no vote attached to the shares), and the holding represented an insignificant portion of the outstanding preferreds. The other issue to be discussed was a provision made in August relating to an early retirement program that had been announced by CC in 1992. By coincidence the provision had also amounted to $17.5 million. The provision included estimated company pension contributions for the employees electing early retirement, as well as an extra months' salary, vacation pay, and career counseling. It was CC's hope that by the end of 1996 almost 500 employees would retire so layoffs during the forecast downturn in the next 18 months would not be necessary.

Anthony had several ideas concerning the treatment of the two items. Regarding the gain on the sale of the investment, he would be delighted to show it in this year's income statement included with the other sources of revenue; operating revenues were down from the previous year and the gain would help offset this drop. Anthony suggested that the related tax of $4.75 million could be netted against the gain (although this was not his preference, as he wanted to maximize revenue) or be included in the tax expense.

Regarding the provision for the early retirement program, Anthony felt there were a number of possible alternatives. Because the program had been announced the previous year, Anthony suggested that the majority of the provision could be charged retroactively to 1992. Another possibility would be to spread out the charge over the succeeding four years, with a minimal charge to 1993 as the program had just started and the smallest number of retirements was forecast to have occurred during this past year. The third alternative arose due to the fortunate coincidence of the two items being identical amounts: the gain on the sale of the investments and the provision for early retirements could be offset so no reference to either would be necessary as the total was zero. Expensing the entire $17.5 million provision in 1993 would have the worst effect on net income of all the alternatives. However, there would be a benefit to the company's employee relations if the provision was expensed and netted against the gain from the sale of the investment, in that the employees and the public would not see the extent of the downsizing forecast by the company.

Required

Assume the role of the auditor and respond to Anthony's ideas.

Case 17

Canadian News Ltd.

Lunch at the Courtyard Cafe, one of Nashville's most expensive restaurants, is more for gathering information than for eating. Today was no exception. Alison Edwards ran into a friend, Michael Maguire, whom she had not seen for several months.

Maguire is president and CEO of U.S. Conglomerate Inc.(USCI). USCI recently sold its interest in a company that did not fit well into the overall direction of the firm and now has some cash to invest. Maguire is considering a USCI investment of up to 25 percent in Canadian News Ltd. (CNL), a medium-size Canadian public company. CNL has had steady growth since its founding 90 years ago, and Maguire thinks it would be a good match with USCI's operations and long-run investment strategy. He has analyzed the 1991 audited financial statements of CNL, as published, but wants to ensure that he doesn't have to worry about differences between Canadian and U.S. GAAP.

Michael was delighted to see Alison, because he remembered that she had worked for a public accounting firm in Canada for several years. During their conversation, Alison agreed to take a look at CNL's most recent statements.

Company Background

James Barnett founded Canadian News Ltd. in Toronto in 1898. Although only in his early 20s, Barnett was already the assistant editor of the city's daily newspaper. There was so much news on agricultural prices and developments that Barnett decided to start a specialized publication, *The National Field,* for people involved in all aspects of growing and selling produce. The new magazine was an immediate success.

From the one English-language magazine, CNL expanded over the decades to bilingual periodicals aimed at the Quebec market and to the publication of a weekly business paper in Great Britain. By 1960, the year of the founder's death, CNL published 13 items and had established a small Canadian subsidiary, Plato Ltd., to print limited-edition handbound books. Over the years the firm invested in other printing and publishing businesses. In 1960, ownership of the firm passed to James's son, Robert, who did not have to go to the public capital markets for funds until 1973. The shares are all common shares and are now widely held.

Current Operations

By 1991, CNL was publishing three consumer magazines: *Haute Couture, Le Gourmet,* and *Designer Homes*. The company also publishes seven daily newspapers and a number of community weekly papers in Canada and in the northeastern United States. The well-known Canadian business newspaper *Bay Street Week* is a Barnett publication. The firm also has expanded into specialty printing, catalogues, and business forms and keeps its presses running six days a week, three shifts a day. Plato Ltd. continues to publish limited-edition books.

The firm has remained in the publishing business despite the tendency of competing companies to diversify into broadcasting and cable television. Robert Barnett remains committed to his father's view of engaging in only one activity and doing it well.

Required

Analyze the audited financial statements and accompanying notes of Canadian News Ltd. as presented below. Include in your analysis an explanation of the differences between Canadian and U.S. GAAP and, where possible, the impact of the difference on the statements.

EXHIBIT 1

CANADIAN NEWS LTD.
Consolidated Balance Sheet
December 31, 1991
(in thousands of dollars)

	1991	*1990*
Current assets:		
Cash and short-term investments	$ 7,440	$ 0
Accounts and loans receivable (Note 3)	24,506	22,369
Inventories (Note 4)	12,380	10,859
Total	$44,326	$33,228
Current liabilities:		
Bank indebtedness	0	4,086
Accounts payable and accrued liabilities	16,929	16,773
Income taxes	5,913	1,318
Long-term debt due within one year (Note 6)	1,164	2,538
Total	$24,006	$24,715
Working capital	$20,320	$ 8,513
Add:		
Capital assets, less accumulated amortization (Note 5)	41,388	39,379
Investment in Lawrason Paper Limited (Note 11)	0	6,191
Deduct:		
Deferred revenue	2,709	2,372
Long-term debt (Note 6)	26,151	31,739
Deferred income taxes	5,348	5,265
Total	$27,500	$14,707
Owners' equity:		
Capital stock (Note 7)	$15,350	$15,350
Retained earnings (deficit)	11,650	(1,643)
Excess of appraised value of capital assets over amortized cost (Note 8) [Also, see **1** in Exhibit 5]	500	$ 1,000
Total	$27,500	$14,707

EXHIBIT 2

CANADIAN NEWS LTD.
Consolidated Statement of Income
and Retained Earnings (Deficit)
Year Ended December 31, 1991
(in thousands of dollars except per share amounts)

	1991	*1990*
Revenue from operations:		
Newspapers and magazines	$ 75,289	$ 69,572
Printing	62,216	51,126
Books	14,280	14,504
Business information	13,580	9,995
Total	$165,365	$145,197
Cost of operations:		
Operating expenses	$147,033	$127,466
Amortization	5,672	4,744
Interest (Note 6)	4,416	3,295
Earnings of subsidiary (Note 2)	(215)	0
Gain on sale of investment (Note 11)	(11,263)	0
Total	$145,643	$135,505
Income before income taxes	$ 19,722	$ 9,692
Income taxes (Note 9)	6,929	4,333
Net income	$ 12,793	$ 5,359
Retained earnings (deficit) at beginning of year	(1,643)	(7,502)
Transfer of appraisal increment	500	500
Retained earnings (deficit) at end of year	$ 11,650	$ (1,643)
Earnings per common share [See **2** in Exhibit 5]	$3.17	$1.33
Average number of common shares outstanding	4,042,386	4,042,386

EXHIBIT 3

CANADIAN NEWS LTD.
Consolidated Statement of Changes in Financial Position
For the Year Ended December 31, 1991
(in thousands of dollars)

	1991	*1990*
Cash provided from (used for):		
Operations:		
Net income	$12,793	$ 5,359
Items not affecting cash:		
Amortization	5,672	4,744
Deferred revenue	337	(327)
Deferred income taxes	83	199
Loss on sale of capital assets	260	27
Gain on sale of investment	(11,263)	0
Cash flow from operations	7,882	10,002
Increase in accounts and loans receivable	(2,137)	(1,238)
Increase in inventories	(1,521)	(457)
Increase in accounts payable	156	1,357
Increase in income taxes	4,595	76
Decrease in long-term debt due within one year	(1,374)	(1,152)
Total	$ 7,601	$ 8,588
Financing activities:		
Long-term borrowing	$ 14,703	$10,793
Long-term debt repaid	(20,291)	(2,698)
Total	$ (5,588)	$ 8,095
Investment activities:		
Additions to capital assets	$(11,422)	$(6,922)
Proceeds from the sale of Lawrason Paper Limited	17,454	0
Proceeds from sale of capital assets	3,481	1,305
Total	$ 9,513	$(5,617)
Net cash provided	$ 11,526	$11,066
Cash and short-term investments less bank indebtedness at beginning of year	(4,086)	(15,152)
Cash and short-term investments less bank indebtedness at end of year	$ 7,440	$(4,086)

EXHIBIT 4

CANADIAN NEWS LTD.
Notes to the Financial Statements
December 31, 1991

1. *Summary of Significant Accounting Policies.*

The consolidated financial statements include the accounts of Plato Ltd., which is wholly owned. The accounts of Plato, which in prior years had been consolidated as at October 31, its fiscal year-end, have been consolidated on a December 31 year-end basis in 1991 as described in Note 2. Income from investments for the year ended December 31, 1991, was not material. [See **3** in Exhibit 5.]

Inventories are stated at the lower of cost, determined on the first-in, first-out basis, and market. Cost includes attributable direct costs and overheads other than amortization.

Land, buildings, machinery, and equipment and leasehold improvements are stated at cost. Amortization is provided primarily on a straight-line basis, using rates of 2.5 percent per annum for buildings and 4.0 to 14.0 percent per annum for machinery and equipment. Leasehold improvements are amortized over the term of the applicable lease.

Publishing rights are recorded at acquisition cost and are amortized over periods not exceeding 40 years. On the basis of annual reviews, any permanent impairment in the value of publishing rights is written off against earnings.

Net revenue from consumer magazine subscriptions is deferred and taken into income over the terms of the various subscriptions. These magazines derive a majority of their revenue from advertising and single copy sales. Current assets will not be used to discharge any obligations to subscribers and, therefore, no portion of such unearned revenue is included in current liabilities.

The company provides for income taxes currently payable and, in addition, provides for deferred income taxes resulting from timing differences between financial and taxable income. [See **4** in Exhibit 5.]

Pension costs related to current service are charged to income for the period during which the services are rendered. This cost reflects management's best estimates of the pension plan's expected investment yields, salary increases, mortality of members, termination and retirement ages. Adjustments arising from plan amendments, experience gains and losses, and changes in assumptions are being amortized over the expected average remaining service life of employees. [See **5** in Exhibit 5.]

Expenditure on new product development is expensed as incurred. [See **6** in Exhibit 5.]

EXHIBIT 4 (*continued*)

CANADIAN NEWS LTD.
Notes to the Financial Statements
December 31, 1991

2. *Consolidation of Plato Ltd.*

The accounts of Plato Ltd. have been consolidated on a December 31 year-end basis. In prior years, this subsidiary's accounts were consolidated on a two-month delay basis due to its fiscal year-end of October 31. As a result, these consolidated financial statements include the operating results of Plato Ltd. for the 14-month period to December 31, 1991. The operating income before interest and income taxes for the two-month period to December 31, 1991, has been disclosed separately in the income statement.

3. *Accounts and Loans Receivable.*

$75,000 (1990—$75,000) is due from employees under a common share purchase plan dated September 22, 1990. The loans are repayable over terms, the longest of which expires in 1995. If at the required repayment date the market price of the shares is less than $10, the company will absorb the difference.

4. *Inventories.*

	1991	*1990*
Materials and supplies	$ 9,133	$ 8,128
Work in progress	2,555	1,975
Finished goods	692	756
Total	$12,380	$10,859

5. *Capital Assets.*

	1991	*1990*
Land	$ 2,316	$ 2,296
Buildings	15,960	14,470
Machinery and equipment	58,080	53,497
Leasehold improvements and publishing rights	1,757	1,485
Less accumulated amortization	36,725	32,369
Total	$41,388	$39,379

EXHIBIT 4 (*continued*)

CANADIAN NEWS LTD.
Notes to the Financial Statements
December 31, 1991

6. *Long-Term Debt.*

Long-term debt of the company and its subsidiary is as follows:

	1991	*1990*
Short-term promissory notes at variable rates of interest *(a)*:		
Cdn. averaging 10.5%	$ 1,215	$20,925
U.S. averaging 9.6%	7,203	
Notes:		
Maturing 1993, at 12%	12,713	6,550
Maturing 1994, at 11.5% (U.S. $4,500) *(b)*	5,366	5,847
Other	818	955
Less current portion	1,164	2,538
	$26,151	$31,739

(a) The company's $40 million credit facility with banks provides committed revolving lines of credit to 1993 with automatic annual extensions from then on subject to bank approval. A term loan option provides for repayments in 1993 through 1996. The credit facility is available for general corporate purposes and support for issuance of short-term promissory notes. The amount of the credit facility not borrowed at December 31, 1991, was $39 million.

(b) The company's legal obligation in respect of the U.S. notes is for-12⅝% interest to June 15, 1994. This obligation was exchanged with a bank for the company's obligation to pay 11.5% to June 15, 1998.

(c) Approximate annual maturities of long-term debt using the term loan option for repayment in each of the next five years are 1992—$1,163,900; 1993—$3,920,000; 1994—$10,779,200; 1995—$3,789,300; 1996—$7,662,600.

The components of interest expense are:

	1991	*1990*
Long-term debt	$4,198	$2,919
Other	218	376
Total	$4,416	$3,295

EXHIBIT 4 *(continued)*

CANADIAN NEWS LTD.
Notes to the Financial Statements
December 31, 1991

7. *Capital Stock.*

Share constraint: The issue or transfer of the company's shares to non-Canadian persons or corporations is restricted to a maximum of 25 percent of the number of shares outstanding and the paid-up capital attributable thereto. This restriction ensures that the company will continue to have Canadian status so advertisers may deduct, for income tax purposes, the cost of advertising in any of its publications.

Common shares: The directors may determine whether to pay dividends in cash or by issuing fully paid common shares and which shareholders have the right to elect to receive such dividends in shares. The directors have determined that shareholders who come within the "constrained class" or who are indebted in respect of shares included in the common share purchase plan are ineligible to receive dividends.

8. *Appraisal Increment.*

The company's machinery and equipment were appraised on January 2, 1973, by Canadian Appraisals Limited of Toronto. As of January 31, 1973, the excess of appraised value of machinery and equipment over amortized cost was recorded in the company's books. This increment is being amortized over 20 years.

9. *Income Taxes.*

	1991	*1990*
Current	$6,846	$4,134
Deferred	83	199
Total	$6,929	$4,333

The following table reconciles the statutory federal and provincial income tax rate to the consolidated effective tax rate on income before income taxes:

	1991	*1990*
Income before taxes	$19,722	$ 9,692
Provision for income taxes based on combined basic Canadian federal and provincial income tax rate of 45.5% (1990 49.2%)	$ 8,974	$ 4,768
Decrease in taxes resulting from manufacturing and processing deduction	(413)	(435)
Nontaxable portion of capital gains	(1,632)	0
Total	$ 6,929	$ 4,333
Effective income tax rate	35.1%	44.7%

EXHIBIT 4 *(continued)*

CANADIAN NEWS LTD.
Notes to the Financial Statements
December 31, 1991

10. *Pension Plan.*

The company's defined benefit pension plan is a contributory plan that provides benefits based on length of service and final average earnings. The company has an obligation to ensure there are sufficient funds in the plan to pay the benefits earned.

The funded status of the plan at December 31 is as follows:

	1991	*1990*
Market value of assets	$36,003	$29,756
Projected benefit obligation	30,258	27,248
Assets in excess of projected benefit obligation	$ 5,745	$ 2,508
Pension expense	$ 1,336	$ 1,080

The measurement of the retirement obligation and expense involves estimating economic and demographic factors over an extended future period. The following provides the most significant assumptions:

	1991	*1990*
Rate of return	9.0%	9.0%
Inflation and salary progression	6.5%	6.5%

11. *Gain on Sale of Investment.*

The amount of $11,263,000 represents a gain on the disposition of a 47% interest in Lawrason Paper Limited.

12. *Commitments and Contingencies.*

The company has obligations under long-term operating leases extending for various periods to the year 2000. The minimum aggregate payments are as follows: 1992—$1,887,200; 1993—$1,708,900; 1994—$1,469,200; 1995—$1,285,600; 1996—$1,100,100 and $3,691,100 thereafter. [See 7 in Exhibit 5.]

Capital expenditures in 1992 are estimated at $9,600,000; the company has approved $4,000,000 of these expenditures.

13. *Segmented Information.*

The company considers that it operates principally in one geographic segment, North America, and in one industry segment, publishing.

14. *Related Party Transactions.*

Approximately 38% of the company's sales were to a major retailer (33% in 1990). Contracts over a four-year period have continued to increase and management believes that current contracts will be renewed indefinitely.

EXHIBIT 4 *(concluded)*

CANADIAN NEWS LTD.
Notes to the Financial Statements
December 31, 1991

15. *Subsequent Event.*
Subsequent to the year end the company acquired 100% of Hollings Press. The total cost of this investment was $4,600,000.

16. *Management Incentive Compensation.*
The company has a management incentive plan. Bonuses are based on a formula that considers consolidated earnings before income taxes. The board of directors may decide to pay additional amounts. Management incentive expense was $1,000,000 in 1991 (1990—$750,000).

EXHIBIT 5 Summary of Selected U.S. Generally Accepted Accounting Principles

1. Property, plant, and equipment are written up only in the case of a legal reorganization.

2. The denominator in the earnings per share calculation includes common share equivalents, securities that contain a provision that allows the holder to become a shareholder.

3. Year-ends within 93 days of each other require no separate measurement or disclosure of differences.

4. *APB Opinion 11* requires comprehensive tax allocation using the deferral method, with balance sheet disclosure as a deferred debit or credit. *SFAS 109* requires comprehensive tax allocation (on temporary differences) using the accrual method, with balance sheet disclosure as an aset or liability. *SFAS 109* is effective for fiscal years beginning after December 15, 1992.

5. Assumptions used include the discount rate at which the *projected* benefit could be effectively settled. The impacts of changes in assumptions and experience gains and losses are added together. If the total exceeds 10% of the greater of the market value of the assets or the projected benefit at the beginning of the year, the excess over the 10% is amortized over the "average remaining service life of active employees." Past service costs and the opening net asset or obligation position upon plan adoption are amortized over the "average remaining service life of active employees." An additional liability is recognized. This is the difference between the *accumulated* benefit (excludes

EXHIBIT 5 *(concluded)*

provision for future salaries) and the fair value of plan assets. An intangible asset offsets the liability. The plan assets should be valued at market. Average market value over not more than five years may be used in calculating the expected return on assets and experience gains and losses.

6. All costs classified as research or development are charged to income as incurred.

7. Similar characteristics that differentiate a capital versus an operating lease in Canada are presented in the United States as criteria, rather than guidelines.

Case 18

Canadian Products Corporation

You, Chester Grant, are the assistant to the controller at Canadian Products Corporation (CPC), a mid-size public company that manufactures industrial goods in Canada (in four plants in Alberta, Ontario, and Quebec), and in subsidiaries in the United States and Mexico.

Your boss, Jane Leung, has just left an audit committee meeting and has called you into her office.

"Chester, as you know, we're in the process of redesigning our annual report for next year. We're looking to float a new common stock issue over the next two or three years, and we want a report that really *sells* CPC. We've had a couple of rough years lately, but operating profits are starting to improve and we think the timing will be right. We've simply got to get rid of some of our debt load . . . so we'll issue equity and retire debt.

"Today in our audit committee meeting we began to discuss the form and content of the notes to the financial statements, because we want to take a fresh look at all our disclosures as part of this redesign project. We made some good progress, but we got a little bogged down on the pension note. That's where I thought you could help.

"I took a couple examples of pension disclosures to the meeting [see Exhibit 1]. At present, we have a pension note that is very similar to the Canadian Marconi example—except our pension plan is underfunded by about $6 million, a situation caused by prior service benefits awarded in our last round of collective bargaining. We'll be up to date again in about five years.

"The committee members were very impressed with the Moore Corporation Ltd. disclosures—but, really, few understood the meaning or significance of the information. They really didn't understand how both of

EXHIBIT 1 Financial Statement Extracts

Canadian Marconi Company, March 31, 1991

12. Pension Plans:

The Company maintains a number of pension plans to provide retirement income to its employees. The benefits provided to retiring employees under the plans are determined by calculations which include both defined benefit and defined contribution schemes. Based on actuarial evaluations of the defined benefit portion of these pension plans at March 31, 1991, the present value of the accrued pension benefits is $51,352,000 (1990—$45,653,000) and the pension fund assets are valued at $61,953,000 (1990—$56,848,000).

Moore Corp. Ltd., December 31, 1990

11. Retirement programs:

Defined benefit pension plan:

The Corporation and its subsidiaries have several programs covering substantially all of the employees in Canada, the United States, the United Kingdom, Australia, New Zealand, and Puerto Rico.

The following data are based upon reports of independent consulting actuaries as at December 31:

	Canada		*United States*		*International*	
	1990	*1989*	*1990*	*1989*	*1990*	*1989*
(in thousands)						
Funded status:						
Actuarial present value of:						
Vested benefit obligation	**$45,179**	$40,570	**$312,012**	$272,366	**$58,766**	$ 45,289
Accumulated benefit obligation	**45,498**	41,117	**337,016**	291,829	**60,281**	46,900
Projected benefit obligation	**$50,647**	$45,810	**$414,706**	$334,806	**$75,503**	$ 62,328
Plan assets at fair value	**60,588**	66,806	**383,143**	411,810	**96,494**	106,578
Excess of plan assets over projected benefit obligation	**9,941**	20,996	**(31,563)**	77,004	**20,991**	44,250
Unrecognized net loss (gain)	**8,760**	(964)	**(6,557)**	(38,258)	**10,564**	(15,633)
Unrecognized net obligation (asset)	**(13,132)**	(14,469)	**(30,490)**	(33,538)	**(21,441)**	(21,073)
Unrecognized prior service cost (credit)	**509**	244	**66,024**	5,453	**3,371**	(186)

EXHIBIT 1 *(concluded)*

	Canada		*United States*		*International*	
	1990	*1989*	*1990*	*1989*	*1990*	*1989*
(in thousands)						
Pension expense:						
Service cost	**$ 2,347**	$ 2,130	**$ 14,539**	$ 9,027	**$ 3,263**	$ 2,966
Interest cost	**4,283**	3,675	**32,386**	25,924	**5,560**	5,172
Actual return on assets	**2,244**	(6,435)	**8,486**	(71,350)	**16,538**	(22,918)
Net amortization and deferral	**(9,153)**	(129)	**(41,607)**	35,442	**(29,478)**	11,536
Net pension expense (credit)	**$ (279)**	$ (759)	**$ 13,804**	$ (957)	**$ (4,117)**	$ (3,244)
Other information:						
Assumptions:						
Discount rates:						
January 1	**9.0%**	9.0%	**8.5%**	9.0%	**8.7%**	8.9%
December 31	**9.0**	9.0	**8.8**	8.5	**9.1**	8.8
Rate of return on assets	**9.5**	9.5	**9.3**	9.5	**9.8**	9.9
Rate of compensation increase	**7.1**	7.1	**6.5**	6.5	**7.6**	7.6
Amortization period	**15 years**	15 years	**15 years**	15 years	**10 years**	11 years

In some subsidiaries, where either state or funded retirement plans exist, there are certain small supplementary unfunded plans. Pensionable service prior to establishing funded contributory retirement plans in other subsidiaries, covered by former discretionary noncontributory retirement plans, was assumed as a prior service obligation. In addition, the Corporation has entered into retiring allowance and supplemental retirement agreements with certain senior executives.

All of the retirement plans are noncontributory. Retirement benefits are generally based on years of service and employees' compensation during the last years of employment. However, in the United States the retirement benefit accrues each year based upon compensation for that year. At December 31, 1990, approximately 70% of the United States plans' assets, about 60% of the Canadian plans' assets, and approximately 85% of the international plans' assets were held in equity securities, with the remaining portion of the asset funds being mainly fixed income securities. The Corporation's funding policy is to satisfy the funding standards of the regulatory authorities and to make contributions in order to provide for the accumulated benefit obligation and current service cost. To the extent that pension obligations are fully covered by existing assets, a contribution may not be made in a particular year.

my very different examples could be GAAP, or what the ramifications of extensive disclosure might be for us.

"Chester, I want you to summarize the issues concerning pension disclosures, to give us a framework for discussion for our next meeting. Your recommendation might help us come to a faster resolution of the issues.

"You should go through the Moore Corporation note and explain what each and every item means. I guess you should explain what the components of their pension expense are, as well, since a few people on our committee were mystified by the negative pension expense Moore books.

"Make sure you consider the costs of this extensive disclosure, and how it would suit our circumstances!"

Required

Write the report requested by Jane Leung.

Case 19

Capilano Forest Company Ltd.

Capilano Forest Company Ltd. (CFCL) has been owned and managed by an experienced forester, Don Strom, for 20 years. The company has performed well in the last few years, but the industry is cyclical. In the interior of British Columbia, CFCL manufactures lumber of all grades from raw logs. A small lumber yard and sales office is located in Vancouver.

Your firm has been reappointed auditor for CFCL and you, CA, the senior on this engagement, have been going over some issues with the recently hired controller of the company, Everett Green. CFCL had been searching for a controller for several months. Green agreed to accept the position with the condition that his compensation package include a bonus based on net income. Strom finally agreed to this form of remuneration, despite initial resistance.

A large Japanese lumber importer has recently expressed an interest in purchasing CFCL. Therefore, Green proposes to make changes to CFCL's accounting policies, which he believes will maximize the value of the company.

During the year CFCL was granted, by the Ministry of Forests, the right to log a large area of standing timber on Crown land. Although CFCL does not own the land, it does have the right to log all the timber on it, not to exceed an allowable annual limit. This right was granted to the company at no initial cost. However, a fee is paid to the ministry based on the number of logs removed from the forest. Shortly after CFCL received

Adapted, with permission, from the *Uniform Final Examination Report,* 1990. Changes to the original question and/or suggested approaches to answering are the sole responsibility of the authors and have not been reviewed or endorsed by the CICA.

this right, the ministry announced that all holders of logging rights over Crown land are responsible for reforesting the lands at their own expense; the ruling applies to all rights granted in the last five years. After eight months of logging, CFCL has still not carried out any reforestation. The controller is proposing that CFCL record receipt of this right at fair market value. In addition, he would like to include in the financial statements the fair market value of rights received from the ministry two years ago. These rights do not currently appear on the company's balance sheet.

CFCL recently purchased the right to log the standing timber on a mine site. As part of the contract, CFCL agreed that it would cease logging in five years when mining would commence. Although CFCL would probably be unable to log all the timber in this period, the five-year rights were considered to be worth considerably more than the purchase price. Since logging operations began, however, it has become apparent that many of the trees are infested with insects and are, therefore, worthless. Green does not think that this presents a valuation problem for financial reporting. "These rotten trees are part of the cost of the good ones, and will be expensed as the good trees are sold. The purchase price will be allocated to all the good trees on the mine site."

With respect to the costing of trees on land that CFCL owns, Green contends that these trees really have no cost. "We paid for the land which produces the trees. The trees themselves do not have any cost. If anything, replanting and pesticide expenses are the only costs we have. The situation is similar to owning land on which we have a building and machinery producing widgets. When we sell the widgets, we don't expense the land, do we?"

Last year the company acquired a large tract of land and timber along the Pacific Coast for $2.9 million. This year 20 percent of this tract, along the shoreline, was sold to a resort developer. CFCL has assigned a cost of $25,000 to this parcel. At the date of original purchase, CFCL considered this parcel to be worthless from a logging standpoint. The rest of this land is abundant in timber. CFCL paid a premium for the land, with its rich soil and moist, coastal climate ideal for tree growth. Lately, however, the company has been having problems logging the area. Environmentalists have vowed that no one will be allowed to destroy its natural beauty. Roadways have been blocked on several occasions by these protesters. In addition, they have campaigned aggressively against the company and its products. In response, CFCL has spent large amounts on public relations advertising and on legal costs in order to obtain injunctions. These amounts, as well as the estimated costs of idle time related to the protests, will be capitalized as goodwill.

Green intends to include in goodwill costs relating to forest fires which are rampant in areas surrounding CFCL's land. Although none of CFCL's timber has been damaged by fire, the company did pay for resources to help control the fires. As the controller explained, "It was in our best interests to help combat the fires because they were headed towards our timber." The fires are continuing to burn, and CFCL has promised an additional $300,000 in aid.

The partner on this engagement has asked you to prepare a memo discussing the accounting alternatives and providing your recommendations for accounting policy choice.

Required

Prepare the requested memo.

Case 20

Carleton Company

Carleton Company is a major Canadian producer of high-quality glass and plastics packaging. The company's customers include most of the leading consumer-products companies in North America. Carleton operates 12 manufacturing facilities—5 glass-container plants in Canada and 7 plastics packaging plants, 5 in Canada and 2 in the United States.

Carleton Company was founded by Montreal's deGruchy family in 1917. A deGruchy grandson is now one of the company's vice presidents; otherwise the family is only a minor shareholder. The company is federally incorporated, and its common shares are traded on the Montreal and Vancouver stock exchanges.

The company operated a single glass-container plant near Montreal until 1954, when a second glass-container facility was constructed in Orillia, Ontario. This was followed by the acquisition of a plant in the Montreal area in 1967 and construction of plants in British Columbia and Alberta. Carleton Company has a long-established policy of keeping all its plants well maintained and technologically efficient, and each year most of the company's profit is reinvested in implementing this policy.

In 1966, Carleton Company expanded its range of packaging products beyond glass containers by entering the plastics packaging industry. Since then, it has grown to become a major fabricator of thermoformed, injection-molded, extrusion and injection blow-molded plastic packaging and of complete filling machine systems. The company holds licensing agreements with several of the world's most technologically advanced packaging companies.

Carleton Company has always rewarded its senior executives well. The compensation includes a generous salary and benefits package, as well as a share purchase plan. The share purchase plan permits the president and selected vice presidents to buy preferred shares of Carleton with the assistance of interest-free loans from the company. These loans have a 10-

year term, and 75 percent of all dividends received on the shares must be applied to the outstanding loans.

Extracts from Carleton's draft 1993 financial statements are included as Exhibit 1.

Required

Evaluate Carleton's valuation and disclosure policies for the loans receivable.

EXHIBIT 1 Extracts from the Draft Financial Statements of Carleton Company

	December 31	
	1993	*1992*
Current assets:		
Accounts receivable	$ 37,132,000	$ 30,553,000
Loans receivable from senior executives	12,860,000	12,630,000
Inventories	58,016,000	50,274,000
Prepaid expenses	3,568,000	2,621,000
Total current assets	111,576,000	96,078,000
Total assets	$253,588,000	$210,904,000
Shareholders' equity (Note 4):		
Preferred shares	$ 14,920,000	$ 13,780,000
Common shares	50,883,000	50,883,000
Retained earnings	67,167,000	60,520,000
Total shareholders' equity	$132,970,000	$125,183,000

Note 4: Capital Stock

Authorized

Unlimited numbers of common and preferred shares.

Issued

770,000 preferred shares
12,759,504 common shares

The preferred shares are redeemable in certain circumstances and, at the option of the holders, are convertible into an aggregate of 1.470 million common shares. They have been treated as common share equivalents for purposes of computing earnings per share, since they participate equally with the common shares as to dividends.

At the beginning of 1993 the company issued 70,000 convertible redeemable preferred shares for consideration of $1.140 million.

	1993	*1992*	*1991*	*1990*	*1989*
Net income ($ millions)	16.2	21.1	23.8	27.2	27.5
Dividends paid	9.6	10.7	11.3	11.6	12.1

Case 21

Carlyle Construction Corporation

The Carlyle Construction Corporation (CCC) is incorporated under the Ontario Business Corporations Act. It is a private company, controlled by Cyd Carlyle. Members of Cyd's immediate family and a few close business associates are also shareholders.

In the past, CCC has had its financial statements prepared by the company's head bookkeeper, and the bank and other creditors have accepted these statements without serious question. For the year ended July 31, 1993, however, the bank would like to have some assurance that the statements have been prepared in accordance with generally accepted accounting principles (GAAP). The bank's concern has arisen from the increase in the bank's lending to CCC; the operating loan increased from $1 million at the end of fiscal 1992 to $5 million at the end of fiscal 1993. In particular, the bank is concerned that the cash flow statement that CCC has been presenting does not coincide with its own analysis of CCC's cash flows.

Therefore, Cyd has approached you to review the financial statements for compliance with GAAP, in order to satisfy the bank. The draft statements as prepared by the head bookkeeper are attached. After some investigation, you learn the following information:

1. The net revenue shown on the income statement is the gross margin on the construction contracts, determined by use of the percentage of completion method. The costs incurred on contracts during fiscal year 1993 totaled $32.9 million.

Institute of Chartered Accountants on Ontario, adapted.

2. The contracts in progress as shown on the balance sheet are the total costs incurred to date on unfinished contracts, plus the gross margin earned to date, less amounts billed. For some contracts, CCC bills in advance, so the billings are in excess of costs plus profit to date. The $6.6 million shown on the balance sheet, therefore, is the excess of underbilled contracts, less the overbilled (or advance billed) contracts.

3. The note receivable arose from the sale of capital assets during the year and represents the gross sales price. The note is due on March 5, 1994, at which time the gain on the sale will be taxable at a 46 percent rate. The note is noninterest-bearing.

4. The current note payable is the bank operating loan. There are two long-term notes. One is a bank term loan of $5 million (1992—$6 million) that is the remaining principal amount of the loan that helped to finance

CARLYLE CONSTRUCTION CORPORATION
Balance Sheet (draft)
July 31
(in thousands)

	1993	*1992*
Current assets:		
Cash	$ 200	$ 100
Term deposits	1,300	1,000
Note receivable	1,600	—
Accounts receivable	18,000	16,600
Less bad debt allowance	(900)	(830)
Contracts in progress, net of billings	6,600	4,000
Total current assets	$26,800	$20,870
Furniture and equipment, net	11,000	13,000
Total assets	$37,800	$33,870
Current liabilities:		
Accounts payable	$ 7,000	$ 6,240
Accrued expenses	500	630
Bank loan	5,000	1,000
Total current liabilities	$12,500	$ 7,870
Long-term notes payable	13,000	13,000
Total liabilities	$25,500	$20,870
Shareholders' equity:		
Common shares	$ 1,000	$ 1,000
Retained earnings	11,300	12,000
Total shareholders' equity	$37,800	$33,870

CARLYLE CONSTRUCTION CORPORATION
Income Statement (draft)
July 31, 1993
(in thousands)

Net construction revenue	$4,100
Gain on assets disposal	600
Total revenue	4,700
Administrative expenses	1,100
Interest expense	2,100
Income tax expense	700
Total operating expenses	3,900
Net income before extraordinary item	$ 800
Extraordinary loss: write-off of contract costs	1,200
Net income (loss)	$ (400)

CARLYLE CONSTRUCTION CORPORATION
Cash Flow Statement (draft)
July 31, 1993
(in thousands)

Sources of cash:	
Operations, before extraordinary item	$ 800
Recovery of cost of capital assets sold	1,000
Increase in operating bank loan	4,000
Depreciation	1,000
Total inflows	$6,800
Uses of cash:	
Dividends	$ 300
Investment in working capital items	5,200
Contract costs written off	1,200
Total outflows	$6,700
Increase in cash during the year	$ 100

the capital assets. This loan is being paid down at the rate of $1 million per year plus interest at prime plus 1.2 percent. The second long-term note is a loan of $8 million (1992—$7 million) from Cyd Carlyle. This note is payable on call with 60 days' notice, but Cyd has no intention of calling the loan.

Notes to Financial Statements

Note 1: These statements are prepared in keeping with widely acceptable accounting practices and are unchanged from the preceding year.

Note 2: The $5 million bank loan carries interest at prime plus 1 percent.

Note 3: There are 1,000 common shares outstanding.

Note 4: The extraordinary item will not recur and therefore is not an operating expense and should not be considered when reviewing these financial statements.

Note 5: For the next fiscal year, the company will have to pay income tax of $276,000 on the gain on the capital asset sale, once the company has collected the note receivable.

Note 6: The retained earnings reflects the payment of dividends to the owners and the shareholders.

5. CCC uses the same rate for amortization for capital cost allowance for income tax purposes. The amortization expense is included primarily in the contract costs, with some amortization included in administrative expenses.

6. CCC's capital assets are low because the company rents most of its construction equipment on a short-term basis as it is needed for contracts.

7. In 1993 a major customer went into bankruptcy. The construction project that CCC was engaged in for this customer was 18 percent completed; the bankruptcy trustee suspended construction and canceled the contract. In view of the bank's refusal to include the costs incurred in the normal formula for operating loans and in view of the unlikely prospects of ever collecting the amounts owed, the outstanding billings and costs of $1.2 million were written off as a special charge.

Required

1. Review the draft statements and comment on any inappropriate presentation or disclosure and any apparent lack of conformity with GAAP. Briefly describe the more appropriate presentation or disclosure. Pay special attention to statement presentation.
2. Redraft the Cash Flow Statement, taking into consideration the points raised in part 1, so it is in accordance with GAAP.

Case 22

Cheer Radio

You are the assistant controller at Cheer Radio, an FM and AM operation in a large urban center. Your boss has just asked you to consider their policy for barter transactions. The station often enters into such barter arrangements with radio advertising time it cannot sell. It trades advertising time in exchange for gifts to be awarded to its listeners. (For example, the radio station will mention a store's products, services, hours, and so on in exchange for a dishwasher donated by the store as a "Jackpot" prize for a lucky listener.) To this point in the company's history, these barter transactions have not been recorded in the accounts, although they represent about 20 percent of commercial air time.

Your boss has pointed out that the transaction could be recorded at:

1. The market value of the air time.
2. The market value of the prizes.
3. The cost (to the client) of the prizes.
4. The cost (to Cheer) of the air time.
5. A nominal amount (e.g., $1.00).

He has also told you that, on the whole, he likes the current system the best, as it is simple and a change would involve a lack of consistency. Since Cheer is owned by one major shareholder and has very low debt levels, there is no particular reason to blindly follow the *CICA Handbook,* unless there is good reason. A qualified audit report would not upset the shareholder. The concern is, though, that the volume of the transactions is increasing. Your boss has asked you for a memo dealing with the issue, including your recommendations.

Required

Prepare the memo.

Case 23

Community Services Organization

Community Services Organization (CSO) is a nonprofit organization in St. John's, Newfoundland. The primary activity of CSO is to raise funds that are used to sponsor a wide variety of social, cultural, and educational programs within the local community. Many of the programs are actually conducted by other nonprofit organizations, but funded through grants (and a few loans) made by CSO. CSO's main sources of support revenue are from annual campaign pledges, grants, gifts, and investment revenue.

In CSO's most recent financial report, the following information was disclosed in the notes to the financial statements:

Recognition of Support and Pledges. Pledges are recognized as revenue in the year in which they are collected. Uncollected pledges are recorded as deferred revenue from pledges until they are collected. Receivables from pledges are reported in the balance sheet. No allowance is made for any portion that may not be collected.

Investments in Securities. Investments in securities are stated at fair market value. Unrealized gains and losses are included in income.

Loans to Affiliated Organizations. Loans to affiliated organizations amounted to $375,000 at the most recent year-end. Substantially all of the loans consist of unsecured noninterest-bearing loans to various constituent and beneficiary agencies due within one year. The collectibility of $68,000 of these loans is questionable; however, no provision for possible

Adapted, with permission, from the Atlantic School of Chartered Accountancy.

losses has been made in these financial statements. The amount would be written off only when collection is verified as impossible.

Property and Equipment. Both donated and purchased property and equipment are written off as acquired. Consequently, no allowance for depreciation is provided in the statements.

Contributed Services. A substantial number of unpaid volunteers have made significant contributions of their time in planning programs and in fund-raising campaigns of the organization. The value of this contributed time is not reflected in the financial statements, since it is not susceptible to objective measurement or valuation.

Required

Discuss the appropriateness of the accounting policies of CSO with reference to the requirements of the *CICA Handbook*. Include evaluation of alternatives and your recommendations regarding preferred treatment.

Case 24

Connect Air Limited

A recent graduate of an accounting program, you have just started work in the special accounting support group of a chartered bank. As one of your first assignments, you have been asked to analyze the liabilities of a public airline, a "feeder" to Air Canada. You've been told that your employer is negotiating a lending arrangement with the airline and is in the

EXHIBIT 1 Connect Air Limited Extracts from Financial Statements

CONNECT AIR LIMITED
December 31, 1994
(in millions)

Liabilities

	1994
Current:	
Accounts payable and accrued liabilities	$ 64
Unearned revenue—advance ticket sales	23
Current portion of long-term debt and capital lease obligations	34
Total	$121
Long-term debt and capital lease obligations (Note 6)	$135
Other long-term liabilities	89
Deferred credits (Note 7)	42
Total	$266
Minority interest	10
Subordinated perpetual debt (Note 8)	84

EXHIBIT 1 (*concluded*)

CONNECT AIR LIMITED
December 31, 1994
(in millions)

Shareholders' Equity

Preferred shares (Note 9)	25
Common shares	31
Retained earnings	43
Total	$ 99
Total	$580

EXHIBIT 2 Connect Air Limited Additional Information

CONNECT AIR LIMITED
December 31, 1994
(amounts in millions)

From the Notes to the Financial Statements

6. Long-Term Debt and Capital Lease Obligations

Long-Term Debt	*Final Maturity*	*Interest Rate (%)*	*December 31 1994*
U.S. dollar (*a*)	1995–2009	Various	$ 67
Canadian dollar:			
Government of Canada	1997	7.2	17
Other	1995–2004	Various	32
Swiss franc debt (*b*)	2000–2006	5.125–5.625	35
Deutsche mark bonds (*c*)	1996–2000	7.38/9.0	34
			$185
In-substance defeasance (*d*)			(16)
Net long-term debt			169
Current portion			(34)
Long-term debt and capital lease obligations			$135

a. Of the total U.S. dollar debt, U.S. $30 has a final maturity in the year 2009 and may be called by the Company with an indemnity until the year 2004 and at par thereafter.
Essentially all the U.S. debt is covered by long-term U.S. currency forward exchange and option contracts.

b. Swiss franc debt is comprised of 100 million Swiss francs maturing in the year 2000 and 200 million Swiss francs maturing in the year 2006.

EXHIBIT 2 *(concluded)*

CONNECT AIR LIMITED
December 31, 1994
(amounts in millions)

The 100 million Swiss franc debt may be called by the Company at a premium beginning in the year 1997, declining to par by the year 2000. The Company has entered into a currency swap agreement with a financial institution, which has the effect of extinguishing future exchange fluctuations on this debt and interest thereon. The 200 million Swiss franc debt may be called by the Company at a premium until 1997 and at par thereafter.

c. The interest rate on these notes will be reset in 1996 based on an interest rate index. These notes are unsecured and may be called by the Company at a premium until 1996 and at par thereafter.

d. In 1986 and 1987, the Company deposited government securities in irrevocable trusts, solely to satisfy the scheduled interest and principal repayment requirements of certain long-term debt and capital lease obligations. These obligations, which at December 31, 1994, amounted to $16 in long-term debt and capital lease obligations, are considered extinguished for financial reporting purposes and, together with the related securities, have been removed from the Company's balance sheet.

7. Deferred Credits

	December 31, 1994
Gain on sale and leaseback of assets	$18
Deferred income taxes	24
Deferred credits	$42

8. Subordinated Perpetual Debt

In November 1993, the Company concluded a Japanese yen subordinated perpetual debt financing. The interest rate is 6.55% until 1998, and it will be reset for each subsequent five-year reset period based on a capped spread over the Japanese long-term prime lending rate.

The Company has entered into currency swap agreements with certain financial institutions, which have the effect of extinguishing future exchange fluctuations for the five-year period until November 1998.

	December 31, 1994
60 billion Japanese yen at 6.55% until 1998:	
Callable in year 1998 and every fifth year thereafter at par	$59
300 million Swiss francs at 6.25%:	
Callable in year 2001 and every fifth year thereafter at 102% of par	25
Subordinated perpetual debt	$84

The maturity of this subordinated perpetual debt is only upon the liquidation, if ever, of the Company. Principal and interest payments on the debt are unsecured and are subordinated to the prior payment in full of all indebtedness for borrowed money. It is not probable that the Company will call the debt.

9. Preferred Share Capital

The authorized capital of the Company includes term preferred shares, which carry a cumulative dividend entitlement of $5 per share and must be redeemed at $107 on June 1, 2007. The shares may be redeemed at a higher price, at the option of the Company, on various dates starting on June 1, 2000. On December 31, 1994, 250,000 term preferred shares were outstanding.

process of drafting loan covenants to accompany the contract. At issue is the definition of "debt" for the "debt/equity" ratio. The company, Connect Air Limited, is reasonably profitable and has a healthy cash flow from operations, and it has a contribution margin on sales of about 70 percent (see Exhibits 1 and 2). Your task is to outline a debt definition that would be appropriate for your bank and to analyze the various balance sheet items with reference to your definition.

Required

Prepare an appropriate report.

Adapted, with permission, from the Atlantic School of Chartered Accountancy.

Case 25

Consolidated Holdings Inc.

Andrew Fleming, president and chief executive officer of Consolidated Holdings, Inc. (CHI), has quickly risen to prominence in the business community. Known as a shrewd dealmaker capable of spotting good quality opportunities in start-up and turnaround situations, he has recently built an impressive holding of investments.

Fleming started his career in 1976 with XL Corp. (XL), the Canadian subsidiary of a major U.S. multinational. As a manufacturer of precision components, such as timing chains and cam shafts for the automotive industry, XL encountered difficult times during the late 1970s and early 1980s. These problems were created primarily by a decline in the demand for less fuel-efficient six- and eight-cylinder engines, for which XL's products were targeted. Sensing a desire on the part of the U.S. parent to cut its losses, Fleming orchestrated a leveraged management buyout in 1986, which resulted in his ownership of 53 percent of XL's 6 million common shares outstanding.

Since that time, XL has invested in new product development and marketing, and it is now quite successful in supplying components for the new generation of V-6 engines used by both Big Three and Japanese automakers manufacturing here in Canada. Through CHI, which he formed as a holding company, Fleming has set out to invest in other business operations capable of being rejuvenated with proper management and financing.

Fleming has recently offered John Sheridan, a partner in a regional public accounting firm, the opportunity to provide audit services to his group of companies. Sheridan and his engagement manager, Tony Fer-

---

Institute of Chartered Accountants of Ontario, adapted.

rone, attended an initial meeting with Fleming on April 15, 1993. The following conversation took place at that time:

AF:

As you know, XL has a March 31 year-end. The current auditors have just commenced the 1993 audit, but once they're done I'll let them know that you'll be taking over the engagement from 1994 onward. Of course, I want you to take on the CHI audit right away.

JS:

That sounds fine to me. I understand that you have been busy turning CHI into far more than just a holding company for your investment in XL.

AF:

It has been a very exciting and challenge-filled year. We successfully outbid the competition for 100 percent control of Elliot Lake Mining Limited (EL), a former Crown corporation engaged in the uranium industry. EL was spun off by the federal government as part of its privitization program. We also acquired the lease financing subsidiary of PC Corp. Further details are contained in the notes prepared by my corporate controller [attached as Exhibit 1].

JS:

I'll have Tony review these notes in detail, and we'll get back to you on any significant implications they may have for our June 30 audit of CHI. Is there anything else we should know?

AF:

Given the substantial changes in CHI's operations that have taken place recently, it is important that CHI's financial statements reflect the unique nature of its holdings. I have had my controller draft a set of statements in the form we would like to see, based on March 31, 1993 figures [Exhibit 2]. A public offering of CHI is not more than two years down the road, so I'll be using the actual June 30 statements to attract interest in the investment community. Let me know if there is anything about the draft statements that you will not be able to live with.

EXHIBIT 1 CHI Corporate Structure

As at March 31, 1993:

Fleming — 76% → Consolidated Holdings Inc.

PC Corp. — 24% → Consolidated Holdings Inc.

Consolidated Holdings Inc.:

- 100% → Elliot Lake Mining Limited
- 100% → Equinox Finance Inc.
- 53% → XL Corp.

EXHIBIT 2

CONSOLIDATED HOLDINGS INC.
Balance Sheet
As at March 31, 1993
(in thousands)

Assets

Cash and short-term deposits	$ 2,348
Receivables (Note 2)	41,369
Inventories (Note 3)	28,741
Investments	4,676
Capital assets (Note 4)	29,505
Other assets (Note 5)	6,732
Total assets	$113,371

Liabilities and Shareholders' Equity

Trade payables and accrued expenses	$ 23,758
Secured creditors (Note 6)	63,214
Deferred credits (Note 7)	16,257
Share capital (Note 8)	4,474
Retained income	5,668
Total liabilities and shareholders' equity	$113,371

CONSOLIDATED HOLDINGS INC.
Statement of Income and Retained Earnings
For the nine months ended March 31, 1993
(in thousands)

Sales	$125,985
Cost of sales	111,509
Operating income	14,476
Finance income	727
Investment income	875
Total	$ 16,078
Selling, general, and administrative expenses	5,522
Interest expense	5,689
Total	$ 11,211
Net income before tax	4,867
Income taxes: current	1,856
deferred	(841)
Total	1,015
Total net income	$ 3,852
Less: minority interest	727
Income available to all common shareholders	3,125
Retained income, beginning of period	2,543
Retained income, end of period	5,668

See accompanying notes to financial statements.

EXHIBIT 2 (*continued*)

Notes to Financial Statements
For the nine months ended March 31, 1993
(all amounts expressed in thousands of dollars)

Note 1. Significant Accounting Policies

The accompanying financial statements have been prepared in accordance with the Recommendations of the Accounting Standards Board of the Canadian Institute of Chartered Accountants. Where such Recommendations are incomplete, management has applied those accounting principles which it considers to result in the most meaningful portrayal of the activities of the company.

Consolidation

The following majority-owned subsidiaries have been consolidated herein: XL Corp., Elliot Lake Mining Limited, and Equinox Finance Inc. All material intercompany transactions and balances have been eliminated.

Revenue Recognition

Revenue is recognized upon substantial completion of the earnings process.

Inventories

Manufacturing inventories are valued at the lower of cost and net realizable value. Refined minerals are valued at realizable value as established by forward sales contracts.

Note 2: Receivables

Trade receivables	$21,708
Lease receivables, net of unearned finance income	21,661
	43,369
Less doubtful accounts	(2,000)
Total	$41,369

Note 3: Inventories

Manufacturing inventories	$24,436
Refined materials	4,305
Total	$28,741

EXHIBIT 2 *(continued)*

Notes to Financial Statements
For the nine months ended March 31, 1993
(all amounts expressed in thousands of dollars)

Note 4: Capital Assets

	Cost	*Accumulated Amortization*	*Net Book Value*
Land	$ 2,500	$ —	$ 2,500
Buildings	6,000	2,986	3,014
Machinery and equipment	41,581	35,556	6,025
Mining properties	38,434	20,468	17,966
Total	$88,515	$59,010	$29,505

Amortization expense for the period totaled $2,951.

Note 5: Other Assets

Goodwill	$3,623
Deferred start-up costs	2,220
Prepaid expenses	889
Total	$6,732

Note 6: Secured Creditors

Consolidated Holdings Inc.:	
Noninterest-bearing notes payable to a shareholder, due February 1, 2003	$ 4,000
XL Corp.:	
Revolving bank line of credit, at prime plus 1½%	1,214
10-year debentures bearing interest at 12¾%, due April 1, 1998, convertible after April 1, 1994, into common shares of XL Corp. at the rate of 50 common shares per $1,000 debenture	48,000
Elliot Lake Mining Limited:	
Bank term loan, bearing interest at a floating rate of prime plus 2%; principal due in five equal annual installments commencing October 1, 1993	10,000
Total	$63,214

EXHIBIT 2 *(concluded)*

Notes to Financial Statements
For the nine months ended March 31, 1993
(all amounts expressed in thousands of dollars)

Note 7: Deferred Credits

Deferred income taxes	$13,887
Minority interest in a subsidiary	2,370
Total	$16,257

Note 8: Share Capital

Common stock, with no par value	
10,000 shares authorized	
5,000 shares issued and outstanding	$ 4,474

During the period, 1,200 common shares were issued in conjunction with the acquisition of Equinox Finance Inc. These shares have been recorded at a stated value of $4,094.

Note 9: Pension Plans

There are no significant unfunded liabilities in the defined benefit pension plans covering employees of the various subsidiaries consolidated herein.

Required

Assume the role of Tony Ferrone. Prepare a memorandum to John Sheridan that discusses the major accounting issues to be resolved with this new client.

Elliot Lake Mining Limited (EL)

EL is involved in the mining and refining of uranium for such nonmilitary uses as nuclear-powered generating stations and submarines. A federal Crown corporation since its inception in 1959, EL has had its share of ups and downs due to the political and social pressures that have shaped government policies directly affecting its marketplace.

The $10 million acquisition price for EL was financed by a term loan from XL Corp.'s bankers, bearing interest at a floating rate of prime plus 2 percent. For consolidation purposes, book values have been picked up directly from EL's internal statements, with the excess of EL's book value over the purchase price being recorded as additional accumulated depletion on EL's mining properties.

Uranium prices worldwide are established in U.S. dollars. EL's management regularly enters into U.S. dollar-denominated forward sales contracts covering approximately 50 percent of the total uranium refined each month. All defined uranium inventories are carried at the average realizable value established by these forward contracts, and are translated into Canadian dollars at the exchange rate prevailing at the end of the month in which refining is completed. Subsequent price and currency fluctuations are taken into income as incurred.

EL's year-end is June 30.

Equinox Finance Inc. (EFI)

Previously owned by PC Corp. (PC), a major publicly traded conglomerate, EFI provides long-term direct financing leases covering large-scale manufacturing equipment to various industrial customers, including XL Corp.

Under the terms of the EFI acquisition, CHI obtained 100 percent of EFI's common shares from PC in exchange for 1,200 common shares of CHI and 10-year noninterest-bearing notes payable. The common shares issued were recorded in CHI's books at $4,094,000, representing the amount by which the book value of EFI's net assets exceeded the $4 million face value of the notes payable.

Due to favourable income tax treatment of its leases, EFI has built up significant deferred income tax credits. CHI has booked on consolidation an adjustment of these deferred tax balances to reflect lower tax rates expected in the period of reversal. Income tax expense has been credited by the amount of this adjustment.

EFI's year-end is June 30.

XL Corp.

A major new production line is currently under construction at XL's Brampton facility. During the period of construction, all associated direct and indirect costs, such as interest and administrative overhead, will be capitalized as deferred start-up costs. XL's current intention is to amortize the deferred start-up costs on a straight-line basis over 10 years, commencing with the end of construction and the start of commercial production (expected to occur in the fall of 1993).

For consolidation purposes, CHI has historically picked up XL's March 31 year-end results.

Case 26

Constant Equipment Ltd.

Constant Equipment Ltd. is a heavy equipment dealer, selling road construction equipment, backhoes, bulldozers, and all types of farm equipment. Much of their volume is in construction equipment, a cyclical industry, and Constant accordingly suffers from volatile earnings and cash flows.

In 1993, such a cyclical downswing prompted the Charter Bank, Constant's primary secured creditor, to appoint a receiver. The receiver negotiated the sale of the company to Husky Equipment Ltd., a large equipment dealer in another province. The bank made some compromises, and a debt/equity financing package was structured to keep Constant in business. Husky Equipment Ltd. made some significant changes at Constant, reducing support staff positions considerably and replaced most of the top management. The new general manager, Walter Strong, has been charged with the responsibility to make the operation profitable as quickly as possible. He is paid a certain base salary, plus a bonus of 10 percent of operating income before tax. If the company has a loss, no bonus is paid, but future years' bonuses are unaffected. That is, each year stands on its own.

It is now July 17, 1994, and you are part of the audit team doing the fieldwork for the fiscal year ended June 30, 1994, Mr. Strong's first year as president. Preliminary results indicate that Constant will show an operating loss of $120,000 in fiscal year 1994. This loss position was expected both by the bank and by Husky, as 1994 was a rebuilding and restructuring year. Everyone has high hopes for 1995, however, as the company seems to be running efficiently and the construction industry is "heating up."

You have been put in charge of the current liabilities portion of the audit, and have collected the information in Exhibit 1. The chartered accountant in charge of the audit fieldwork has asked you to analyse

EXHIBIT 1 Constant Equipment Ltd Additional Information

Accounts Payable and Accrued Liabilities

Balance, June 30, 1994 . . . . . $337,974 cr

A review of invoices on and around June 30 reveals the following:

1. Two invoices for heavy equipment, for $71,200 and $47,900, were recorded on June 29. The equipment was received on July 4. Constant keeps a perpetual inventory system.
2. The following invoices were received and recorded in July 1994 and pertained to June 1994 or before:

Advertising	$ 1,200
Repairs and maintenance	4,120
Shop supplies	720
Parts inventory (periodic inventory)	34,200
Miscellaneous	300

Accrued Wages Payable

Balance, June 30, 1994 . . . . . . $17,400 cr

This amount relates to June 30, 1993. There was a weekly payroll on July 4, 1994, for $24,750, one fifth of which related to 1994. All payroll costs are charged to "Compensation Expense."

Demand Bank Loans

Balance, June 30, 1994 . . . . . $2,474,000 cr

This amount has been confirmed by the bank. While it is due on demand, or on 30 days' notice, there is a repayment schedule requiring $10,000 of principal, plus interest, each month. All parties seem to consider this debt to be long-term in nature, and management of Constant feels it should be disclosed as long-term debt.

Warranty Liability

Balance, June 30, 1994 . . . . . . $52,000 cr

This amount represents the expected warranty costs associated with new machinery sales, which carry a 24-month warranty on parts and a 12-month warranty on labour.

In the past, the warranty liability has been set up based on a percentage of sales, which would have resulted in a liability balance of $35,000 at June 30, 1994.

This year, Strong had his staff prepare an analysis of all equipment with warranties still outstanding and an estimate of cost per machine, which totaled the $52,000 above. You have checked this list and it appears accurate, although the cost estimate per machine is highly subjective.

You have checked with staff at your office who have done audits of other heavy equipment dealers, and all of them seem to set up a warranty liability based on sales, not specific identification.

EXHIBIT 1 (*concluded*)

Strong argues that, in their special circumstances, an average percentage based on sales is "not good enough," and specific identification is "much more accurate."

Coupon Liability

Balance, June 30, 1994 . . . . . . $10,000 cr

In April of 1994, Constant published an ad in a construction industry journal that gave customers a 5 percent discount if they mentioned the ad when buying new equipment. The journal is circulated to 70,000 subscribers, only 2 percent of which might be in the market for new equipment. Of these, only 10 percent might buy from Constant, and only half of them might mention the ad.

An average sale is $22,000. To June 30, 1994, 65 customers have mentioned the ad.

The $10,000 balance in this account was set up to be "on the safe side." This amount has been charged to Promotions Expense.

This is the first year this type of campaign has been undertaken by Constant.

Constant's accounts and policies and make any adjusting journal entries that are required. He has warned you to watch for overstatement of expenses, as he suspects Strong is trying to accrue as much as possible this year, as the company is already in a loss position.

Required

Carry out the assignment.

Case 27

David Technologies Limited

David Technologies Limited (DTL) is a privately held corporation; Wilf David holds 72 percent of the common shares, while family members and friends hold the remainder. The company was organized primarily to develop data base management systems and provide computer-related services. DTL has a calendar year-end.

In 1993, Wilf David entered into negotiations to sell 51 percent of the outstanding shares of DTL to Data Soft Limited, a public company specializing in development and marketing of software packages. David would be kept on as president and CEO. The price would be based on a multiple of average audited net income for 1991, 1992, and 1993.

It is now January 1994, and you, the CA in charge of the 1993 audit, have just reviewed the financial statements (Exhibit 1) and the notes prepared by your audit staff on various outstanding or incomplete issues (Exhibit 2).

A meeting between you and Wilf David is scheduled for tomorrow morning to discuss accounting policy decisions. Accordingly, you decide to prepare a report dealing with the issues to be discussed, outlining alternatives and your recommendations. You decide to calculate a corrected net income figure, after tax, incorporating your recommendations so the quantitative impact of the issues will be clearly understood.

Required

Adopt the role of CA and prepare the report.

Adapted, with permission, from the Atlantic School of Chartered Accountancy.

EXHIBIT 1 David Technologies Ltd. Financial Statements

DAVID TECHNOLOGIES LIMITED
Financial Statements

Draft
Income Statement

For the Year ended December 31, 1993
(in thousands)

Sales	$42,758
Cost of sales	27,008
	15,750
Selling expenses	3,107
Administrative expenses	2,570
Depreciation of fixed assets, amortization of product development expenses, etc.	1,920
	7,597
Operating income	$ 8,153
Interest on long-term debt	568
Other interest	492
Other expenses (income), net	(73)
	$ 987
Income before extraordinary item	7,166
Extraordinary item	241
Income for the year, before income taxes	7,407
Income taxes paid	200
Net income	7,207
Retained earnings, opening	6,626
	13,833
Dividends	560
Retained earnings, closing	$13,273

EXHIBIT 1 (*concluded*)

DAVID TECHNOLOGIES LIMITED
Draft
Balance Sheet

As at December 31, 1993
(in thousands)

Assets	
Cash	$ —
Accounts and notes receivable	16,041
Inventory	4,721
Prepaid expenses	401
	21,163
Long-term notes receivable	$ 7,350
Capital assets, net	3,144
Deferred development costs, net	3,301
Total assets	$34,958

Liabilities and Shareholders' Equity	
Bank loans	$ 1,642
Accounts payable and accrued liabilities	7,807
	9,449
Long-term debt	7,540
Deferred taxes	195
Total liabilities	17,184
Shareholders' equity:	
Share capital	$ 4,501
Retained earnings	13,273
Total equity	17,774
Total liabilities and shareholders' equity	$34,958

EXHIBIT 2 David Technologies Ltd. Additional Information

DAVID TECHNOLOGIES LIMITED
Additional Information

1. Early in 1993, DTL granted certain specific marketing rights for one of its products to Hessler Systems Inc. Subsequent to the grant, disagreements arose between the companies, and Hessler brought suit against DTL for breach of contract. On November 1, 1993, new agreements and understandings were settled and the lawsuit was dropped. The settlement resulted in DTL agreeing to sell 10-year distribution rights to Hessler for $5 million. The proceeds will be collected at the rate of $1 million per year over five successive years, with the first payment paid November 1, 1993. Hessler has the right to market certain of DTL's programs in specific geographic areas for 10 years. DTL will always provide Hessler with the current version of all programs covered by the arrangement. (The programs are regularly updated.) No royalty is payable to DTL on sales made by Hessler. The agreement was never reduced to writing by the parties, nor was interest specified on the payments. At the time of the agreement, prime rates were 12%, and DTL borrowed at prime plus 2%.

   Hessler Systems Inc. had always been a major customer of DTL. As of December 31, 1993, sales by DTL to Hessler, excluding the marketing agreement, were approximately 13% of total sales. Hessler has generally paid its accounts within a 60-day period and has a good credit rating, although they will not make any financial information available to DTL.

   The transaction has been recorded as a sale, in the amount of $5 million, in the 1993 draft financials. No costs were accrued.

2. The extraordinary gain was the result of a sale of land from DTL to Aqua Holdings on December 31, 1993. DTL sold a parcel of land adjacent to the DTL head office and took back a long-term note for the proceeds. The land had been bought in 1975 and never developed. Details of the transaction follow:

Land purchase price, 1975	$ 87,500
Real estate taxes 1975–1993	21,325
	108,825
Proceeds, long-term note	350,000
Difference (accounting gain)	$241,175

   The 10-year note bears an interest rate of 20%. However, interest only accrues starting from January 1, 1995, or when Aqua Holdings starts commercial operations on the site or resells it, whichever comes first.

   Aqua Holdings Ltd was incorporated in 1993 by Art David, Wilf David's younger brother, to manufacture bicycles and tricycles, garden furniture, and small pleasure craft.

3. Expenses include golf dues of $12,000 and interest on taxes of $1,500.
4. As of January 1, 1993, DTL instituted an employee pension plan with defined benefits. The plan is operated by a trustee. At the inception of the plan, the unfunded past service cost was $3 million. DTL agreed to fund this amount over 20 years and made the first payment on January 1, 1993. For 1993, the current service cost, using a "projected benefits prorated on services" actuarial cost method, was $650,000, earned evenly over the year. DTL paid all of this amount on July 1. A 10% interest rate is appropriate.

EXHIBIT 2 (*concluded*)

DAVID TECHNOLOGIES LIMITED
Additional Information

The expected average remaining service life of employees covered by the plan is 16 years. At year-end, the actuarial liability was calculated to be $3,727,000, and fund assets, $1,100,000. No payments were made to pensioners during the year. Experience gains or losses, if any, will be amortized starting in 1994.

All payments to the trustee were expensed and are tax deductible as paid.

5. The tax rate is 40%.

The provision for tax on the income statement reflects $200,000 of installment payments made. The following additional information is available:

1. Depreciation and amortization of product development expenses, $1,920,000.
2. Capital cost allowance for tax purposes, $476,000.
3. Expenditures on product development, $749,000 (capitalized on books, deductible for tax).
4. The extraordinary item will be a taxable capital gain when the proceeds are collected.
5. The sale to Hessler ($5,000,000) is taxable as regular income when collected regardless of the accounting method chosen.

Note: You realize you should first restate income for other items and then calculate the proper provision for tax.

6. The deferred tax balance of $195,000 on the 1993 balance sheet reflects no adjustments from 1992, when it consisted of the following:

Tax loss carryforward from 1990; $200,000 at $0.36	$ 72,000 dr.
Deferred tax credits arising from timing differences, $741,667 at $0.36	267,000 cr.
Total	$195,000 cr.

Thirty-six percent reflects the rate of accumulation.

Case 28

Develco

Develco Limited (DL) is a leading supplier of application software for computers used by hospitals and medical practitioners. DL went public shortly after its incorporation and has experienced rapid growth in sales over the last several years. For 1993 (DL has a December 31 fiscal year-end), audited net income was $3.2 million. During January 1994 the company returned to privately owned status by purchasing and cancelling all those shares not held by senior management.

Under an employee profit sharing plan, which was introduced in 1992, the company distributes 10 percent of audited operating income to its employees. Labour relations improved dramatically after introduction of the plan.

Prior to bringing a new software application to market, the company incurs two types of costs:

1. Costs for design, coding, and testing.
2. Costs, such as user documentation, that are incurred after commercial viability is established.

Once the software application has been developed and tested, manufacturing consists of reproduction using automated copying equipment. Thus, the manufacturing costs are relatively low. The disks, tapes, and diskettes produced are kept in inventory until ordered by a customer.

Promotional and selling costs include the following:

1. Preparation of salesman demonstration kits.
2. Initial media space to advertise the introduction of the application.
3. Ongoing advertising costs.

Society of Management Accountants, adapted.

The commercial life of a new application is difficult to ascertain, given the possibility of the development of similar software by competitors. The average life of a software product line has been five years, but this can vary by two or three years in either direction.

Now that DL is privately owned, senior management wants to take a fresh look at the company's accounting policies. As controller of DL, you recently attended a meeting with senior management to discuss the following issues related to the financial statements for 1994:

1. In prior years, DL has expensed previability costs (design, coding, and testing) but has capitalized and amortized costs, such as user documentation. Senior management proposes to expense all of these costs for 1994. It argues that the future benefit potential of such outlays is no longer objectively ascertainable because of the increasing threat of introduction of a competing product.

2. The company has a 90-day sales return policy. Sales returns for a new application are difficult to estimate and vary from 1 percent to 10 percent depending on the application. A sales return provision based on 5 percent (the historical average experienced by DL) was recorded in 1993 and prior years. For fiscal 1994, senior management has proposed two alternatives: to record a sales return provision using the 10 percent figure; or to delay revenue recognition until expiry of the sales return period.

3. In 1993 and prior years, the company used the percentage of sales method to estimate bad debts which occur mainly on receivables from medical practitioners. In 1994, senior management proposes to use the aging method and to provide an allowance for all receivables outstanding more than 30 days.

4. Management is planning to purchase new computers and systems software during 1994 for the software development process. This equipment (CCA rate 30 percent) will cost $750,000. Management estimates that the equipment will be technically obsolete within five years and is considering using the CCA rate for depreciation.

5. Currently, DL is suing one competitor for $1 million for copyright infringement. As well, DL itself is being sued for $2 million by another competitor for copyright infringement. This infringement was committed early in 1994 by a DL employee who was subsequently fired. The company's lawer has expressed the opinion that both lawsuits will be settled in 1995, the first one in favour of DL and the second against.

6. DL has had requests from several customers for financing assistance by leasing software, rather than selling it. The senior management is unsure what kind of lease and what terms would be most advantageous. DL would want the lease payments to cover the costs (plus a profit) of developing the software since in many cases the applications are customized. Also, DL normally guarantees to provide maintenance; for example, correcting problems and updating for a specific time period. It is difficult to estimate the cost of this service which is provided free of charge to the customer.

Senior management has asked you for a report discussing the issues considered at the management meeting. The report should include your recommendations.

Case 29

Dickens

Maureen Amerato is the sole owner of Dickens, a gift shop located in Toronto's exclusive Hazelton Lanes. The shop opened at the beginning of 1994; when Maureen started the business, she incorporated it. Maureen was able to finance the initial start-up costs by negotiating a large mortgage on her condominium. The shop premises are rented, so the company's major assets are inventory and store fixtures.

Business has increased rapidly. Operations are now completely self-financing, and Maureen is thinking of opening a second shop next year. The 1995 cash flow was so good that Maureen was able to purchase a computer and software to keep track of inventory levels and sales. However, to expand, Dickens will need financial assistance.

The only financial statement advice that Maureen has is from her brother Luke, who is taking an accounting course at university. Luke prepared the 1994 statements using GAAP. All assets were recorded at historical cost, and the inventory policy was FIFO. The fixtures were amortized at their Revenue Canada capital cost allowance rate. Luke prepared a full set of statements, including notes. Maureen has been talking to other retailers in the Lanes and has some questions about the 1995 statements.

1. Some of the other retailers use straight-line amortization for capital assets. The new computer cost $4,000. The Revenue Canada rate for computer hardware is 30 percent declining balance, with only one half the deduction allowed in the year of acquisition. The computer has a five-year useful life, with no salvage value. Maureen would like Luke's advice on whether to amortize the computer on a straight-line or declining-balance basis. She would like to know the impact over the next two years when the company may be expanding. Dickens's tax rate is 25 percent.

2. Maureen also would like to know the impact on the 1995 statements if the fixtures are amortized straight-line. She knows that last year Luke used declining balance but assumes that, if she chooses straight line for the computer, she will have to do the same for the fixtures.

3. During 1995, Maureen sold a cash register that she had used during the first year of operations. The proceeds from the sale were $500. The cash register's net book value at the time of sale was $100. Maureen hopes that Luke will not forget to include this item in sales and cost of goods sold; although 1995 has been a good year, the $400 will really help net income.

Required

Assume the role of Luke Amerato and respond to the above issues.

Case 30

Farmer John

You, CA, a sole practitioner, are sitting in your office when your most important agricultural client, John Plowit, walks in:

"I'm sorry to barge in like this, but I've just been to see my banker. He suggested that I ask you to explain to me some matters that affect my statements.

"You will recall that I needed to renew my loans this year. The new bank manager wants some changes made to my statements before he will process my loan application.

"The banker wants me to switch from a cash basis of accounting to an accrual basis. The cash basis provides me with the information I need to evaluate my performance for the year—after all, what I make in a year is the cash left in the bank once the harvest is sold.

"And I only use these statements for my banker and to pay tax! I know the tax department will accept either the cash or accrual basis.

"Also, the bank wants me to value all my cattle at their market value. Why do they want me to group all my cattle together when they aren't the same? Some are used for producing milk, some are sold as part of my beef operation, and some are used for breeding. Personally, I don't see the sense in valuing them at market when most of them won't be sold or replaced for a very long time.

"I realize that I must provide the type of information that the bank manager wants, but I am very interested in understanding why. After all, I'm the one who has to pay for all of this!

Required

Respond to John.

Case 31

Five Star Hotels Inc.

Five Star Hotels Inc. is a Canadian public company that owns and manages luxury hotels in cities and resorts throughout the world. The hotels are famous for comfort and service. They also are renowned for the quality of food available in the restaurants and for room service. Five Star Hotels Inc. recently has opened a new hotel in Tokyo to serve business travellers and tourists and to cater large banquets and weddings.

Five Star Hotels Inc. is the parent company, and it arranges most of the organization's financing. It has incorporated subsidiaries in many countries to manage the local properties.

For the year ended December 31, 1994, Five Star Hotels Inc. reported net income of $17,322,000, basic earnings per share of $0.86, and fully diluted earnings per share of $0.84. The number of outstanding common shares did not change significantly during 1994.

The company's debt at December 31 was ($000):

	1994	*1993*
Current:		
Bank indebtedness	$28,702	$26,907
Long-term debt due within one year	913	10,971
Long-term debt	39,215*	37,725

* The components are U.S. demand loans of $28,000,000 (Cdn), mortgages of $3,000,000 and other long-term liabilities, including capital leases, of $9,128,000. The current portion is $913,000.

Interest expense on long-term debt totalled $841,000 in 1994; other interest expense was $4,276,000.

In Five Star's 1994 financial statements, the subsequent events note disclosed that, effective February 14, 1995, Five Stars Hotels Inc. issued and sold 2 million special warrants. The proceeds were $14.65 per warrant, for a total of $29,300,000. Each special warrant entitles the holder to receive one common share without additional payment and may be exercised at any time. The net proceeds of the issue total $28 million and will be used to reduce outstanding indebtedness. The note contained no other description for the use of the proceeds.

Five Star's 1994 effective tax rate is:

Combined basic Canadian federal and provincial income tax rate	41.5%
Lower foreign income tax rates	(11.9)
Earnings not subject to tax	(7.8)
Total	21.8%

Required

Calculate Five Star Hotel Inc.'s 1994 pro forma basic and fully diluted earnings per share. State any assumptions that you have to make.

Case 32

Flossy Co.

Flossy Co. is a chain of ice cream shops located in several southwestern Ontario cities. The company is 100 percent owned by its founder, Cassie O'Neill. In addition to Cassie's equity, the company has long- and short-term bank financing. The bank requires audited financial statements annually.

It is now the first week of February 1994. You are about to complete the audit work for Flossy's December 31, 1993, financial statements and are considering whether any adjustments will be required for the following items:

1. During 1993, Flossy Co. was sued by a competitor for patent infringement; the competitor charges that Flossy Co. copied one of its flavours, including the name. The competitor is claiming $30 million damages and legal fees. Unfortunately, Flossy Co.'s lawyer thinks that the suit has a good chance of succeeding. However, awards in cases of this type have typically ranged from $100,000 to $300,000, with the average settlement being $250,000 (plus legal fees).

The case is scheduled to be heard this month, but this depends on whether the judge's current case is finished. You must decide what statement presentation will be required if a judgment is rendered in the next few weeks, and what will be required if the outcome is still unknown.

2. On January 1, 1993, Flossy Co. rented a machine that makes sugar cones and made the first of four annual payments of $5,000 on the same day. Flossy Co. has the option to renew the lease for two more years at a rental of $5,000 per year and then to purchase the machine for $1. The machine has a useful life of 10 years with no salvage value. Flossy Co. could have purchased the machine on January 1, 1993, for $24,000. Flossy Co's incremental borrowing rate is 12 percent; Cassie O'Neill knows that the rate implicit in the lease is 10 percent. On the date the machine was rented, Cassie recorded rent expense of $5,000 for the cheque that was written. No other entries were made regarding the rental in 1993.

Required

Assume the role of Flossy Co.'s auditor. What impact, if any, will the two items above have on the December 31, 1993, financial statements of Flossy Co. How will they be disclosed?

Case 33

Forest City Church

Forest City Church was founded in Brandon, Manitoba, in 1908 by several of the town's wealthy families. The initial membership was 200; it grew over the decades to a high in the early 1960s of over 1,500 but since then has fallen to 1988's level of 1,000. In Forest City's years the members shared the premises of a neighbouring church; in 1911, a spectacular building on two acres of land in what became downtown Brandon was constructed after several years of fund-raising. The design of the church included 10 magnificent stained glass windows, a chapel, a small kitchen and auditorium to provide for meetings and wedding receptions, and office space for the ministerial and support staff. In 1958, an addition was built, which contained a larger kitchen and auditorium. The church's property included one manse until 1950, when a second house was purchased to accommodate an additional full-time ministerial appointment.

From the time the church was founded, members have received an audited set of financial statements. The statements show a balance sheet, statement of revenue and expense, and details of changes in each of the church's funds during the preceding year. The statements are prepared on a cash basis.

Clare Langley, the church treasurer, is aware that the *CICA Handbook* now covers not-for-profit entities, and she is concerned about Forest City's accounting policies concerning capital assets and amortization. Accordingly, she has contacted you, the auditor, and asked to be advised on the situation.

Specifically, Langley wants to understand any options that may be open and the impact each would have on the various financial statements and the users. Finally, she would like your opinion of the most appropriate alternative.

FOREST CITY CHURCH
Extracts from the Financial Statements
For the Year Ended December 31

	1992	*1991*
Assets:		
Church capital fund:		
Church buildings	$10,392,000	$10,467,000
Furniture, fixtures, and equipment	1,187,000	1,209,000
Total assets	$11,579,000	$11,676,000
Liabilities and capital:		
Church capital fund:		
Replacement cost of capital assets	$11,579,000	$11,676,000
Church capital fund, statement of revenue, and expense:		
Revenue:		
Interest	$ 90,683	$ 95,443
Dividends	20,810	19,235
Gain on sale of investments	7,612	2,871
Total	$ 119,105	$ 117,549
Expense:		
Miscellaneous expense	$ 4,950	$ 6,226
Excess of revenue over expense for the year	$ 114,155	$ 111,323
Treasurer's general fund, statement of revenue and expense:		
Revenue (details omitted)	$ 463,920	$ 426,910
Expense:		
Worship	$ 35,517	$ 30,833
Pastoral care	7,046	6,843
Education	4,514	4,344
Communications	33,108	31,086
Occupancy cost	107,726	107,188
Salaries, honoraria, and benefits	197,656	199,598
Administration	25,853	26,931
Total expenses	411,420	406,823
Excess of revenue over expense	$ 52,500	$ 20,087

FOREST CITY CHURCH (*concluded*)
Extracts from the Financial Statements
For the Year Ended December 31

Significant Accounting Policies

Capital Assets

Buildings, furniture, fixtures, and equipment are carried at replacement value as determined for insurance purposes.

Capital assets do not include any amount in respect of land.

Amortization is not provided on church buildings, furniture, fixtures, and equipment.

Required

Prepare a report that addresses the concerns raised.

Case 34

Frank & William

In early 1994, Frank Williams and his half brother, William Franks, set up a limited company to invest some of their personal wealth. They chose the vehicle of a limited company for these investments for a number of reasons: both extremely wealthy, there were no tax advantages to personal ownership. They wanted to make some investments "anonymously," as their personal investment activity was closely monitored by the investment community. Finally, they were both convinced that future tax reform left their personal wealth a bit vulnerable and wanted to "cover the bases" of legal investment vehicles.

Accordingly, South Shore Investments was incorporated in 1994. Under corporate law, the shareholders could waive the requirement for an audit, and Frank and William did this at the first shareholders' meeting, which was held in the back of Frank's limousine. Both men were directors, too.

Frank and William each contributed $4 million to the company and agreed on a certain investment portfolio balance; that is, *X* percent in bonds, *X* percent in safe blue-chip stock, *X* percent in risky stock, *X* percent in precious metals, and so on. The percentages were ranges, as holdings would be dependent on market conditions.

These parameters were communicated to two stockbrokers, each of whom was "in charge," subject to the approval of either Frank or William, of $2 million of the company's funds. The remaining $4 million stayed under the direct management of Frank and William and has been invested in real estate.

The real estate bought includes a piece of vacant land, which the two men have reason to believe will be a prime development site within the next decade. They were able to buy this land privately from a business associate. They paid an amount in excess of its appraised value, but they believe the appraisal did not consider the possibility of development of which they are aware. The remaining real estate consists of a few rental properties, apartment buildings, bought through real estate brokers.

Apartment buildings are commonly valued based on their expected cash flow, discounted at current market interest rates.

Frank and William want an annual financial report that will help them evaluate the performance of their investment decisions and the performance of the two stockbrokers. They will prepare separate accounting statements for tax purposes.

Frank is emphatic that he wants the statements to tell him if he made money—"real money—after inflation." (The high inflationary period of the 1970s left a deep impression on Frank.) William is more doubtful on this issue; he argues that inflation is low right now, so adjustments are not worth the bother. He does not really understand how the statements could be altered to reflect inflation or what items would change.

Both men agree that they want to see "relevant" information and values in the financial statements. They have asked you to discuss problems you foresee in obtaining "relevant" information. They want to know, though, where those relevant numbers would come from and what degree of reliability, especially for the real estate portfolio, could be expected.

Both also agree that they do not plan to take much out of the company, either in salaries or in dividends, over their lifetimes. They will simply reinvest company money in whatever appears to have the best income-earning potential in the market.

Required

Respond to the requests of Frank and William. Suggest a financial reporting system that would meet their needs. Make sure you explain it and respond to the questions they have raised.

Case 35

Georgia McGuinness

Georgia McGuinness is the owner of one of Toronto's most prestigious art galleries, located in the Yorkville district of the city. Revenues and commissions approach $1 million per year.

In the spring of 1992, while visiting the Tate Gallery in London, Georgia was impressed with the work of a Spanish painter, Juan Allende, who had painted during the same period as Picasso and whose work had been greatly influenced by the master. Allende's works were included in the collections of several European royal families, further attesting to his importance, and Georgia decided to try to obtain a painting while overseas. Through her contacts in London, Georgia was introduced to an auctioneer in Paris who had recently been hired to sell an important French estate. Among the estate's possessions was a small oil painting by Allende, which Georgia was able to acquire for her gallery for $75,000.

In early 1993, the art world was shaken by rumors of the discovery by the Louvre of a forgery among its Spanish collection. The rumors persisted; world news reports spoke of a sophisticated network of artists and dealers who had been able to duplicate and distribute "masterpieces" allegedly by Picasso, Dali, and El Greco, among others, which fooled even the experts.

In December 1993, Georgia met with her accountant, Katherine Dickson, to discuss the year-end financial statements. The following conversation ensued:

KD:

I've been hearing sporadic reports about a scandal involving the Louvre and its Spanish collection—something to do with forgery. Have you ever been afraid you might accidentally acquire a painting which wasn't authentic?

GM:

Well, actually the small Allende oil I bought over a year ago is the only piece in my current stock which could conceivably have been produced by this ring of forgers, but the public doesn't seem to think so—I was offered $80,000 for it last week; but I feel Allende's stature will increase, so I said no. I'm sticking to my $95,000 selling price for now.

KD:

If it were a forgery, would it have any value, maybe as a collector's item of a historic event in the art world?

GM:

No—I might be able to sell it at the City Hall outdoor art sale for $400. It's a lovely painting regardless of the identity of the artist. However, this discussion is absurd! I'm paying insurance premiums based on its true market value of $95,000.

Katherine Dickson left her client's gallery feeling somewhat uneasy. She was concerned that the Allende painting should no longer be carried at cost due to the risk of a potential loss. That evening she pondered the alternatives available for the valuation and disclosure of part of Georgia's inventory and came to a decision.

Required

Should the painting be written down even if the appraisal is favourable? What disclosure, if any, would be appropriate? If it has to be written down, evaluate the following alternative treatments for the write-down: cost of goods sold, extraordinary item, and prior period adjustment.

Case 36

Golden Co.

Golden Co. is a closed-end investment company, which has been listed on the Toronto and Montreal stock exchanges since 1983. A closed-end investment company is one where the owners must deal through a stock exchange if they wish to buy or sell shares in the company, as opposed to dealing with the company directly. In addition to stock prices, an investment company's net asset value per share is public information. This value is published each week but is also available daily from the company.

Golden Co.'s investment policy requires that at all times at least 75 percent of the market value of the noncash assets are invested in gold-related investments. Cash resources of the company are invested in short-term obligations issued by the governments of Canada and the United States.

The price of gold has fluctuated widely since Golden Co. became a public company. During the same period, the prices of gold shares as measured by various stock exchange gold indexes have exhibited much greater volatility than the price of gold. The political condemnation of South Africa's apartheid policies and the associated regulated disinvestment of South African assets has squeezed gold investors into smaller and less liquid markets. The prices of Canadian, American, and Australian gold shares have risen dramatically as gold investors avoided South Africa. The emergence of large North America-based gold mining companies has increased the number of gold investment alternatives for institutional investors.

In the first few weeks of 1988, the price of gold fell. The October 1987 stock market crash was causing fears of global economic recession. There was concern that the new gold production from Australia and North America would create an oversupply problem. The increasing use of gold loans and forward sales by gold producers had impacted the spot price of gold.

EXHIBIT 1

GOLDEN CO.
Consolidated Statement of Net Assets (draft)
December 31
(in thousands except for value per share)

	1987	*1986*
Assets		
Investments at market value (cost $187,017; 1986–$167,800)	$211,450	$181,478
Cash, including Treasury bills of $10,282 (1986–$5,199)	10,719	5,494
Receivables from investments sold	662	99
Accrued income	789	491
Total assets	$223,620	$187,562
Liabilities		
Payables for investments purchased	1,792	1,584
Accounts payable and accruals	225	182
Income taxes payable	3,227	—
Deferred income taxes	6,186	709
Total liabilities	11,430	2,475
Net assets	$212,190	$185,087
Represented by:		
Share capital	183	183
Surplus:		
Contributed surplus	$171,014	$168,067
Retained income	3,286	2,216
Accumulated realized gain on sale of investments	19,460	1,653
Unrealized appreciation in the value of investments	18,247	12,968
Total surplus	212,007	184,904
Total	$212,190	$185,087
Net asset value per share	$ 12.10	$ 10.55

EXHIBIT 1 (*concluded*)

GOLDEN CO.
Consolidated Statement of Income (draft)
Year Ended December 31
(in thousands except for earnings per share)

	1987	*1986*
Income:		
Dividends	$ 2,348	$ 2,464
Interest	1,562	613
Total income	3,910	3,077
Expenses:		
Management fee	1,834	1,375
General and administrative	408	382
Total expenses	2,242	1,757
Income before income taxes	1,668	1,320
Provision for income taxes	598	638
Net income for the year	$ 1,070	$ 682
Earnings per share	$ 0.06	$ 0.04

GOLDEN CO.
Consolidated Statement of Charges in Net Assets (draft)
Year Ended December 31
(in thousands)

	1987	*1986*
Net income for the year	$ 1,070	$ 682
Reduction of income taxes on the application of prior year's noncapital loss for income tax purposes	2,971	1,107
Purchase of shares for cancellation	(24)	(110)
Realized gain on investments for the year	17,807	1,314
Unrealized appreciation in the value of investments for the year, net of deferred income taxes	5,279	33,951
Increase in net assets	27,103	36,944
Net assets at beginning of year	185,087	148,143
Net assets at end of year	$212,190	$185,087

As is the practice for investment companies, Golden Co. carries its marketable securities at market value. It is now the third week of March 1988, and the audit of the 1987 financial statements is coming to an end. As the auditor, you are concerned about fair presentation of Golden Co.'s position at the year-end and are pondering the valuation of the marketable securities.

Golden Co.'s draft financial statements are presented in Exhibit 1.

Required

What is the impact on Golden Co.'s financial statements of carrying marketable securities at market value, rather than cost? If an amount less than market value were to be used for the valuation, what would the alternatives be for calculating this amount? What is your opinion about the carrying value of Golden Co.'s marketable securities at December 31, 1987?

Case 37

Habitant Inc.

Habitant Inc. is a federally incorporated entity engaged in the merchandising business. Its retail department stores sell an extensive range of products. Habitant has never issued shares to the public or obtained debt financing through a public offering. The company's long-term debt was equal to approximately 26 percent of its total assets at January 31, 1994.

The head office of Habitant was located in Toronto and the chain included 93 stores in Ontario, Quebec, and the four western provinces. The Habitant stores were either operated by the company or franchised to dealers. Recent expansion had been by way of franchises, and as of January 31, 1994, 31 of the Habitant stores were franchised.

The terms of a typical franchise agreement are summarized in Exhibit 1.

EXHIBIT 1 Terms of Franchise Agreement

1. The initial fee ranges from $70,000–$150,000, depending on the location. Twenty percent of this is to be paid in cash on signing the contract. The remainder is financed with noninterest-bearing notes, due in equal installments over four years, with the first payment due 12 months after the franchise is opened.
2. Habitant is entitled to an additional 2.75 percent of gross revenue of the franchisee, for advertising, product development, and so on.
3. The franchisee buys most of its inventory from Habitant. Habitant does not wholesale goods to any other ''outside'' retail outlets. Corporate head office believes that their prices to franchisees are about 5 percent lower than they (the franchisees) could otherwise get. This is due to the bulk buying power of Habitant. An average franchise buys $750,000 of merchandise from Habitant in a year.

EXHIBIT 1 (*concluded*)

4. The initial franchise fee paid is refunded (except for a $5,000 flat fee) by Habitant Inc., if, for some reason, the deal "goes sour" and the franchisee does not open a Habitant outlet.
5. The franchise agreement commits Habitant to do the following for the franchisee:
   a. Assist in location choice.
   b. Help negotiate a lease.
   c. Provide building plans and specifications.
   d. Help choose a contractor.
   e. Provide and finance store fixtures.
   f. Supervise construction.
   g. Provide assistance for the start-up period.
   h. Set up accounting records.
   i. Provide expert advice over the first five years in merchandise control, training, and promotion.

   These services mentioned in item (*i*) would cost the franchisee on average $8,000–$9,000 in total if they were done on a fee-for-service basis.
6. Store fixtures are sold to franchisees on a delayed payment scheme. They are paid for over six years, and Habitant keeps title to the fixtures until the last payment is made, at which time they belong to the franchisee.
7. All franchisees would be able to borrow at 10 percent from chartered banks. To date, there have been no defaults on notes payable from franchisees.

EXHIBIT 2 Accounting Guideline, Franchise Fee Revenue, *CICA Handbook*

Introduction

1. This Accounting Guideline provides guidance on the recognition and disclosure of franchise fee revenue.[1]
2. A franchise is a contractual privilege, often exclusive, granted by one party (the franchisor) to another (the franchisee) permitting the sale of a product, use of a trade name, or rendering of a service in a single outlet at a specified location (individual franchise), or in a number of outlets within a specified territory (area franchise). The rights and responsibilities of each party are usually set out in a franchise agreement, which normally outlines specific marketing practices to be followed, specifies the contribution of each party to the operation of the business, and sets forth certain operating procedures.
3. Most franchise agreements require the franchisee to pay an initial franchise fee as consideration for establishing the franchise relationship and for initial services provided by the franchisor. The initial services may include as-

EXHIBIT 2 (*continued*)

sistance in site selection; in obtaining facilities and related financing, architectural, and engineering services; in advertising; in personnel training; in administration and record-keeping; and in quality control programmes. Occasionally, the initial fee includes consideration for tangible assets, such as initially required equipment or inventory. These items, however, are usually the subject of separate consideration.

4. Continuing franchise fees represent the consideration for the continuing rights granted by the franchise agreement and for general or specific services to be provided by the franchisor during the life of the franchise.

Revenue Recognition

Initial Franchise Fees

5. Revenue from initial franchise fees relating to the sale of an individual franchise or an area franchise would ordinarily be recognized, with an appropriate provision for estimated uncollectible amounts, when all material conditions relating to the sale have been substantially performed by the franchisor. Substantial performance is considered to have occurred when:
   a. The franchisor has performed substantially all of the initial services required by the franchise agreement or volunteered by the franchisor as a result of normal business practice.
   b. The franchisor has no remaining obligation or intent—by agreement, industry practice, or legislation—to refund amounts received or forgive unpaid amounts owing.
   c. There are no other material unfulfilled conditions affecting completion of the sale.

   In practice, these conditions will not normally be met before the franchisee commences operations.

* * *

7. Franchise agreements may be structured so that the consideration received by the franchisor for establishing the franchise relationship and for providing initial services includes notes receivable. If the notes receivable bear an interest rate below the market interest rate at the date of sale, discounting may be considered as an aid in their valuation and, hence, in the determination of the amount of franchise fee revenue to be recognized. If the notes are receivable over an extended period of time and there is no reasonable basis for estimating collectibility of the notes, revenue would be recognized using either the installment or cost recovery method.[2]

8. When an initial franchise fee includes consideration for tangible assets, such as initially required equipment and inventory, it would be appropriate to recognize the fair value of the tangible assets as revenue when title to them has passed. The balance of the fee, relating to services, would be recognized as revenue when the conditions in paragraph 5 have been met.

EXHIBIT 2 *(concluded)*

9. Sometimes, the initial franchise fee is large but continuing franchise fees are small in relation to future services. When it is probable that continuing fees will not cover the costs of the franchisor's continuing services and provide a reasonable profit on those continuing services, it would be appropriate for a portion of the initial franchise fee to be deferred and amortized over the life of the franchise. The amount deferred should be sufficient to cover estimated costs in excess of continuing franchise fees and provide a reasonable profit on continuing services.

* * *

Continuing Franchise Fees

12. Continuing franchise fees would be recognized as revenue in the period in which the services are rendered.

Agency Sales

13. A franchisor may engage in transactions in which the franchisor is, in substance, an agent for the franchisee by placing orders for inventory, supplies, and equipment, which are then sold to the franchisee at no profit. Such transactions would be accounted for as receivables and payables and not as revenues and expenses in the financial statements of the franchisor.

Franchising Costs

14. Costs directly related to the sale of a franchise for which revenue has not been recognized would be deferred until the related revenue is recognized. The amount of costs deferred would not exceed expected revenue in excess of estimated additional related costs. Indirect costs of a regular and recurring nature that are incurred regardless of the level of franchise sales would be expenses as incurred.

* * *

Disclosure

17. The notes to the financial statements would disclose the method of accounting for revenue from franchise fees.
18. Initial franchise fees would be segregated from continuing franchise fees. If it is probable that revenue from initial franchise fees will decline in the future, because sales of franchises predictably reach a saturation point, it may be appropriate to disclose this fact in the financial statements.
19. Revenue and costs related to franchisor-owned outlets would be distinguished from revenue and costs related to franchised outlets. The number of franchises sold and acquired during the period, and the number of franchisor-owned and franchised outlets in operation at the end of the period would also be disclosed.

EXHIBIT 2 (*concluded*)

20. The following disclosures would also be appropriate:
    a. The amount of revenue deferred and related deferred costs; and
    b. The particulars of any significant commitments and obligations resulting from franchise agreements.

[1] *Revenue,* Section 3400, issued in September 1986, sets out the general principles governing recognition and disclosure of revenue. The guideline governs franchises.
[2] Under the installment method, the gross profit related to the sale is recognized proportionately with actual cash collections of the notes receivable. Under the cost recovery method, equal amounts of revenue (cash collected) and expense are recognized as cash collections are made until all costs have been recovered, thus postponing any recognition of gross profit until that time.

Habitant has asked you, their new chief accountant, to examine the issue of revenue recognition associated with the franchise agreements. Your report is to be used for discussion at the next board of directors meeting, and should analyse the issues with reference to the *CICA Guideline,* ''Franchise Fee Revenue.'' (Exhibit 2.) It must discuss the concepts underlying revenue recognition behind the guideline, and provide recommendations.

Required

Prepare the report.

Case 38

Harrison Auto Inc.

On January 1, 1993, Harrison Auto Inc. (Harrison) of Sault Ste. Marie purchased an auto parts manufacturer, Maple Ltd. Maple Ltd. had a defined contribution pension plan, which it had negotiated with its union several years earlier. There was no credit for past service in the plan agreement, and Maple Ltd. funded its current service obligation annually. Harrison's management wanted their own and Maple Ltd.'s pension benefits to be based on the same formula and changed Maple Ltd.'s plan to a defined benefit plan, with credit for past service.

The change was effective January 1, 1993. On that date the market value of Maple Ltd.'s pension plan assets was $200,000. The actuary informed Harrison management that the obligation for past service, based on Harrison's benefit formula and using an interest rate of 10 percent, was $350,000 on January 1, 1993. The actuary suggested that the past service component of the plan be funded at a rate of $33,000 per year. Harrison's management agreed to this funding but decided to amortize the past service obligation over the expected average remaining service life of 20 years.

During 1993 and 1994, the current service benefits earned by Maple Ltd.'s employees were $55,000 and $60,000, respectively. This was accrued and funded at the end of each year. The past service contribution also was funded at the end of the year. There had not been any retirements from Maple Ltd. to date.

On December 31, 1994, Harrison's board of directors asked the actuary for a valuation. The valuation showed that the market value of the plan assets was $400,000 and the present value of the obligation was $550,000. The board decided to begin the amortization of experience gains or losses in 1995.

Institute of Chartered Accountants of Ontario, adapted.

On January 2, 1995, the board of directors of Harrison Auto Inc. confirmed rumours by announcing a plan to reduce Maple Ltd.'s staff 15 percent by the end of the first quarter. The cuts would be at all levels of the company. New estimates would be required for the pension plan incorporating the 15 percent cutback effective immediately.

Required

Calculate the December 31, 1994, balance sheet and income statement amounts relating to the pension plan. Ignore the impact of deferred taxes.

Case 39

Hartford Mills Corporation

Recently, as the auditor for Hartford Mills Corporation, you sat in on a board meeting where the presentation of the current year financial statements was being discussed. Jim MacInnes, the president, started the discussion about the income statement (Exhibit 1): "Well, gentlemen, we

EXHIBIT 1

HARTFORD MILLS CORPORATION
Income Statement and Statement of Retained Earnings
For Year Ended December 31, 1994

Sales	$5,440,000
Cost of goods sold	2,920,000
Gross margin	2,520,000
Selling expenses	600,000
General and administration expenses	1,960,000
Other income:	
Gain on settlement of litigation	80,000
Investment income	160,000
Net expenses	2,320,000
Income before income tax and extraordinary items	200,000
Provision for income tax	80,000
Income before extraordinary items	120,000
Extraordinary loss on bankruptcy of a major customer (net of applicable income tax of $40,000)	60,000
Net income	$ 60,000
Retained earnings, January 1	325,000
Retained earnings, December 31	$ 385,000

sure haven't met our net income target this year. Net income of $60,000 is well below our budget figure of $100,000."

Frank Harvey, the corporate secretary, added: "That's certainly true. I notice one of the items on the income statement is an $80,000 gain from settlement of litigation. If it weren't for that, we'd have done much worse."

Jim replied, "If you remember, we sued one of our suppliers when material they shipped turned out to be defective. That was back in 1990, but you know how slow the courts are. At least they came through in a year when we needed it!"

Another board member spoke up. "What about this extraordinary item? It says 'Loss on the bankruptcy of a major customer—net of applicable income tax of $40,000.'"

"Yes, that's the result of the Hardley Company bankruptcy. When they went into receivership, they owed us a lot of money. We've classified the loss as extraordinary because we feel it's a nonrecurring item in the evaluation of our business. After all, major customers don't go bankrupt every day!"

Frank added, "We got a good price for that piece of land, though."

"Indeed!" smiled Jim. "When we bought that piece of land we never had any intention of reselling it. It was to be used for our factory expansion program. But it was expropriated this year by the provincial government as part of a landfill program. We got a good price for it, though—$220,000 for land that cost $70,000 isn't bad!"

"Where's that gain?" someone asked. "I don't see it here anywhere."

"Oh," replied Jim. "It's part of 'investment revenue' on the income statement. The land was a long-term investment, so it seemed logical to put the gain there."

"Well, I guess that about covers it, unless our auditor here has anything to say. And listen, if you do, I'd like to see how any change you suggest would affect this statement."

Required

Assume the role of the auditor. Identify the financial reporting issues raised by the above discussion. Provide an analysis of each issue, concluding with your recommendations. If your recommendations differ from the current presentation, redraft the statement(s).

Case 40

Helena Cosmetics Corporation

In the early 1980s, Helena Cosmetics Corp. (HCC) had acquired some land in Rockville intending eventually to build a warehouse on it. Over the years, however, the company's distribution had changed, and by 1993 management concluded that a warehouse would never be needed at Rockville. Consequently the company sought to sell the land, for which it had paid $60,000. The best cash offer for the land was $170,000 in June 1993; but since an independent appraiser hired by HCC had appraised it in April 1993 at $200,000, management was unwilling to accept the cash offer.

The Rockville land was next to a warehouse owned by the Xenon Chemical Company (XCC), one of HCC's regular suppliers of chemicals used to make cosmetics. This company expressed an interest in buying the property to expand its own facilities. XCC was unwilling to pay cash, but offered instead to exchange 250 tons of Type X chemical, to be delivered at the rate of 50 tons per year for five years. The first delivery would be October 1, 1993. The going market price for this chemical was $1,000 per ton.

HCC typically used slightly more than 50 tons a year of Type X chemical in the manufacture of their normal product line. Normally, orders were placed for delivery not more than six months in the future, unless there were firm contracts from customers that required specific products. HCC had no such contracts in the autumn of 1993. After considerable discussion as to the risk involved in the unusually large commitment for this chemical, HCC management finally decided to accept XCC's offer. Type X chemical is a fairly standard, if very expensive, ingredient of many items in the HCC product line.

Used with permission from Tim Sutton.

The contract was signed on September 13, 1993, and on that day HCC's accountant made the following journal entry, recording the chemical at its market price and showing the difference between this amount and the book value of the land as profit:

Inventory due from supplier	$250,000	
Land		$ 60,000
Gain on sale of land		190,000

On October 1, 1993, 50 tons of the chemical were received from XCC as promised, and the entry made was as follows:

Chemical inventory	$ 50,000	
Inventory due from supplier		$ 50,000

When examining the accounts of HCC for the year ending December 31, 1993, the company's auditor raised questions about this transaction. He pointed out that the net effect of the above entries was that the entire profit on the transaction was shown in 1993, although only 50 tons of chemical had been delivered. Of the 50 tons delivered, 6 tons had actually been used in production.

He suggested alternative treatment: to split the profit into two parts. One part, $110,000, was the difference between the book value of the land and the best cash offer; this was to be called *profit on price level changes* and shown in the 1993 income statement. The remainder, $80,000, was to be called "gain on sale of land" and divided one fifth to 1993 and four fifths to subsequent years, as the chemical was delivered. The auditor stated that such a separation was not usually made, but neither was this an ordinary transaction.

HCC management disliked the implication in the above treatment that they had not made the $190,000 profit in 1993, especially since the price of Type X chemical had risen to $1,200 per ton by December 31, 1993.

You have been hired by the management of HCC to examine this issue, and present your analysis and recommendations in a report that can be used by the audit committee in discussions with the external auditor.

Required

Carry out the assignment.

Case 41

High Flyer

Pauline Inc. is a company that holds various investments. Most of these investments are in shares of stable corporations with low debt levels, but the company added some real estate to the portfolio in 1991 and was delighted with the constant and guaranteed cash flow it was receiving from the rental proceeds. Pauline Inc. decided to expand the real estate component of the portfolio. Effective January 1, 1993, Pauline signed an agreement with High Flyer to rent land and a building. Pauline Inc. felt that the lease terms were very attractive and was delighted with how the leased assets would improve its balance sheet.

High Flyer's Board signed with a sigh of relief, because business conditions were worsening and it was becoming difficult to pay the mortgage.

The terms of the agreement were as follows:

Selling price: $48 million.

Appraised value of the land: $25.1 million.

Lease term: 20 years; at the end of the lease term High Flyer will have the opportunity to repurchase the property at a bargain purchase.

Annual lease payments, due on January 1: $5,128,205; the parties negotiated these payments to equal the fair market value of the property.

Institute of Chartered Accountants of Ontario, adapted.

Required

1. For the year ended December 31, 1993, show the impact of this agreement on High Flyer's balance sheet, income statement, and notes. Show details of all calculations. Ignore deferred tax implications.
2. Without doing any calculations, describe the impact of this agreement on the statements of Pauline Inc. for the year ended December 31, 1993. Ignore deferred tax implications.

Case 42

Holiday Hotels Limited

Holiday Hotels Limited (HHL) is a small Canadian company continued under the Canada Business Corporations Act. The company was formed in 1973 but has only been marginally profitable. Recent severe losses have significantly reduced its equity base and made HHL the subject of close scrutiny by lenders. Secured creditors have requested audited statements for the first time in 1993. Company management is convinced that the operation is viable. A description of operations is presented in Exhibit 1.

EXHIBIT 1 Holiday Hotels Limited, Operations Information

HOLIDAY HOTELS LIMITED
Operations Information

HHL owns four resorts, each with the capacity of 100–250 guests. HHL strives continually for quality service and customer comfort. HHL provides package vacations to singles, couples, and families. Packages include all accommodation, meals, beverages, and entertainment for a one-week period. Rooms are only available under these packages and cannot be booked for shorter visits.

HHL owns one resort in Atlantic Canada, one in southern Ontario, and two in Florida. Each has a two to three month busy season and less busy shoulder-seasons. Several resorts shut down in the off-season.

Customers book in advance and make a deposit of 60 percent of the vacation fee in advance. If a customer cancels more than 30 days prior to the vacation date, 80 percent of the deposit is refunded. Less than 5 percent of customers cancel more than 30 days prior to the vacation. If cancellation is made less than 30 days prior to the vacation, all the deposit is forfeit. The balance of the fee is paid as the

Adapted, with permission, from the Atlantic School of Chartered Accountancy.

EXHIBIT 1 (*concluded*)

HOLIDAY HOTELS LIMITED
Operations Information

customer checks in. At December 31, 1993, prepayments totalled $50,000, down $15,000 from December 31, 1992.

HHL advertises heavily during September to January in travel magazines catering to upper-income consumers. In addition, promotional offers are given to travel agents when facilities are not fully booked 30 days in advance. Travel agents pay only for the cost of meals. HHL feels this is an effective form of advertising and promotion.

Every three years the "common areas"—lounges, restaurants, and reception rooms—are redecorated. This is done, if possible, when the resorts are closed for the off-season. If time out of service is necessary (as it is for the Florida resorts) then bookings are refused for the redecoration period. Individual rooms are redecorated every five years, when the rooms are not in use (during off-season or shoulder-season). Expenditures for room renovations were $40,000 a year in each year from 1987 to 1992. Common area renovations amounted to $60,000 in 1991 and $75,000 in 1992.

During 1993, HHL experienced a most unfortunate incident. One of the Florida resorts was severely damaged by a hurricane. Fortunately, all customers were evacuated safely to other hotels. The insurance carried by HHL paid for the alternative accommodations and for a $3 million replacement value on the HHL premises. HHL plans to rebuild the premises shortly, about 25 percent larger than the facility destroyed, for $4,200,000. Meanwhile, the resort is closed; some bookings were transferred to the other Florida resort while others had to be refunded in full.

The hotel employees in the two Canadian locations have recently unionized. Terms of their first contract call for a pension plan with past service benefits (PSC). The PSC is to be funded over 10 years, with payments made, in advance, of $6,500 per year. Current service cost, payable at the year-end, will amount to $32,700 this year, using a "projected benefit prorated on services" actuarial cost method. Employees covered have an expected average remaining service life of 17 years, and an interest rate of 5 percent is considered appropriate.

Vacation packages for the Florida properties are priced in U.S. dollars. Most expenses for these properties are also in U.S. dollars. The U.S. operations keep a central bank account for collections and disbursements; monies are remitted quarterly to the Canadian main bank account, at which time the underlying revenues and expenses are recorded using the exchange rate in effect at the end of the quarter. For example, assume revenues collected were $100,000 and expenses paid, $75,000, and the resulting cash balance of $25,000 was remitted when $1 U.S. equalled $1.15 Cdn. Revenues and expenses also would be recorded at $1.15, even if the average exchange rate for the period was $1.19. No exchange gains or losses need be recorded using this method. The U.S. branches keep complete records throughout the year. Receivables and payables of the branches are recorded by HHL in Canadian dollars only at year-end. In the last year, the Canadian dollar has strengthened relative to the U.S. dollar.

As a public accountant, you have been appointed auditor. You have scheduled a meeting to discuss the 1993 draft financial statements as prepared by HHL, with the HHL controller (see Exhibit 2 for extracts from these statements). You wish to discuss the appropriateness of accounting policies but you are aware that you must quantify, if possible, the earnings impact of your recommendations and be sensitive to HHL's financial position.

EXHIBIT 2

HOLIDAY HOTELS LIMITED
Financial Statement Extracts

Income Statement
December 31, 1993

Revenues:	
Rooms	$ 375,659
Food and beverage	226,083
Gain on insurance proceeds	1,140,000
Total revenues	$1,741,742
Direct operating expenses:	
Rooms	115,027
Food and beverage	194,027
Other	241,048
Depreciation and amortization	94,386
Total expenses	644,488
Operating income	1,097,254
Interest	289,516
Income before tax	807,738
Provision for tax (recovery):	
Current	—
Deferred	502,000
Provision for loss recovery	(151,500)
Total provision	350,500
Net income	$ 457,238

Notes to financial statements:

1. Revenue is recognized as cash is received.
2. U.S. funds received from the U.S. bank account are recorded at the Canadian equivalent on the day of transfer.

EXHIBIT 2 *(concluded)*

HOLIDAY HOTELS LIMITED
Financial Statement Extracts

Income Statement
December 31, 1993

3. The following expenses are included in "other operating expenses" as paid:
   a. Advertising ($60,000 in 1993, $58,000 in 1992).
   b. Renovations ($70,000 in 1993, all for room renovations).
   c. Pension expenditures.

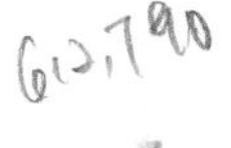

4. HHL had loss carry-forwards in the amount of $600,000 at the end of 1993. These loss carry-forwards expire starting in 1995. The benefit of the loss carry-forward has been recognized as an asset in the financial statements.
5. The gain in insurance proceeds was calculated as follows:

Net book value, destroyed property . . .	$1,860,000
Proceeds	3,000,000
Gain	$1,140,000

   The corporate tax rate is 40%. For tax purposes, all the gain is a timing difference, and $456,000 of the deferred taxes reported on the income statement relate to this item.
6. No accounting recognition is given to the "bargain" price given to travel agents. Cash received is reported as revenue.
7. For the last year, housekeeping services in the Ontario resort have been subcontracted to Housekeeping Services Ltd., a company owned by one of the shareholders of HHL. This was meant as a cost-cutting move, but actual expenses of $76,200 were 10% higher than last year, when HHL did it themselves.
8. At the end of 1993, there was a credit balance of $421,200 in Deferred Taxes on the Balance Sheet.

Required

Prepare a report dealing with accounting policy choice as a basis for the upcoming discussion. If changes in accounting policy are advised, your recommendations should include guidance on how to treat the changes in the financial statements and revised 1993 net income.

Case 43

Hydro Thames Ltd.

Hydro Thames Ltd. is a publicly owned Canadian utility that is heavily debt-financed. The organization needs new funds to expand into a remote area of Ontario and has been offered a favourable floating interest rate for new Canadian debt. However, Hydro Thames's management anticipates rising interest rates and would prefer to fix the rate of the new borrowing. Hydro Thames's banker knows of a company that is also about to borrow in Canada. This company is able to negotiate a reasonable fixed interest rate but would prefer to take the risk of a floating rate. All terms of the two debt issues, other than the interest rates, are identical. Hydro Thames's banker has negotiated an interest rate swap between the two borrowers.

Required

In situations such as this one the substance of the transaction often dictates the accounting treatment and financial statement disclosure, especially where there is little authoritative guidance. Explain the substance of the transaction and suggest appropriate financial statement treatment, including disclosure, for Hydro Thames.

Institute of Chartered Accountants of Ontario, adapted.

Case 44

Investco Corporation

Investco Corporation is a Canadian-based, multinational, multi-industry corporation. On January 1, 1993, Investco formed Foreign Sub Limited in Montavia. It was financed by Investco's equity and 10-year long-term debt, borrowed in Montavian currency and guaranteed unconditionally by Investco.

Montavia was chosen because its social and physical infrastructures lend themselves well to foreign investment. Wage rates are low and raw materials cheap. Montavia has no personal income tax, so the Canadian manager who was moved to Montavia has a high standard of living. Corporate tax is at a 35 percent rate, but new companies enjoy an eight-year tax holiday. Earnings during that period are entirely tax free, unless repatriated to a (foreign) parent company.

Investco moved a Canadian domestic operation to Montavia, but continues to sell, in Canadian dollars, to the same Canadian/North American customers from the new location. Increased shipping costs are more than offset by reduced production costs. In fact, Foreign Sub Limited already has accumulated respectable cash balances that Investco cannot touch without paying the 35 percent corporate tax. As a result, Investco is evaluating other investment opportunities in Montavia.

During the current year, the exchange rate for Montavian currency declined in relation to the Canadian dollar, from $0.12 to $0.10. The exchange rate had been $0.145 when Foreign Sub Limited was formed. Slippage was due to the perceived strengths of Canada's natural resource base and not faults in the economy/management/political stability of Montavia.

Adapted, with permission from the Atlantic School of Chartered Accountancy.

EXHIBIT 1 Foreign Sub Limited. Financial Statements

FOREIGN SUB LIMITED
Financial Statements
December 31, 1994
(in thousands)

		Canadian Dollar	
	FC	*Temporal*	*Current Rate*
Cash	FC 22,000	$ 2,200	$ 2,200
Accounts receivable	10,000	1,000	1,000
Inventories	8,000	960	800
Plant and equipment (net)	60,000	8,700	6,000
Total assets	FC 100,000	$12,860	$10,000
Current liabilities	FC 20,000	$ 2,000	$ 2,000
Long-term liabilities (8 years until maturity)	40,000	4,000	4,000
Common shares	30,000	4,350	4,350
Retained earnings	10,000	2,510	1,270
Exchange adjustment		—	(1,620)
Total equities	FC 100,000	$12,860	$10,000
Sales	FC 95,000	$10,925	$10,925
Cost of goods sold	76,000	9,240	8,740
Depreciation expense	8,000	1,160	920
Other expenses	5,000	575	575
Total expenses	89,000	10,975	10,235
Operating income		(50)	690
Exchange adjustment		510	
Net income	FC 6,000	$ 460	$ 690

You, the assistant to the VP Finance for Investco, have been asked to assess the foreign currency translation method used for Foreign Sub, the temporal method. As a starting point, you have been provided with the financial statements of Foreign Sub Limited, in Montavian currency (FC) and translated Canadian dollar statements, using both the current rate and temporal methods (Exhibit 1). You have noticed, however, that none of the exchange adjustment calculated under the temporal method has been deferred; this calculation must be done.

You wish to discuss the impact that consolidation of each of the alternatives (temporal and current rate) would have on the financial position and operating results of Investco.

In order to properly analyze the foreign currency translation policy, you have decided to compare the economic exposure and the accounting exposure created by the Montavian subsidiary. This includes a classification of the subsidiary as self-sustaining or integrated according to Section 1650 of the *CICA Handbook*.

Required

Prepare a report that deals with the issues raised and concludes with your recommendations.

Case 45

J. J. Ltd.

J. J. Ltd. was incorporated in January 1994 by John Jamieson and Allan MacKenzie, computer science graduates who had met while working in the New Product Division at IBM. J.J.'s initial financing included a low-interest loan from Jamieson's wife, Margaret, of $80,000. In addition, each of the two partners purchased one share for $10,000 per share, and the Royal Bank extended the company a working capital loan of $10,000 (a total of $110,00).

Jamieson and MacKenzie had left IBM after 10 years' employment there for several reasons. One of them was the desire to enjoy the challenge of running their own business, but more important was their wish to complete a project on which both had worked at IBM. This project had been dropped from further development by the computer giant.

The product, Inter Act, was a program which people with little computer training could use to write their own programs—it was a question and answer format which converted nontechnical responses into computer code, thereby eliminating the need to hire a programmer.

Because John and Allan had worked on Inter Act for so many years there was very little development work left to do. The partners felt that IBM had tried to produce a product for sophisticated business and scientific usage when in reality potential purchasers would come from smaller firms which could not afford to support a computer department. By October 1994 five contracts had been signed between J.J. Ltd. and purchasers to buy Inter Act early in 1995 for $6,000 each; the contracts would be void if Inter Act was not delivered by March 31, 1995.

During 1994 J.J. Ltd. incurred the following costs:

Salaries for John and Allan, $2,000 per month each, starting May 1	$32,000
Promotional literature and mailing costs	2,000
Attendance at computer shows in Toronto, Montreal, and Vancouver (registration fees, hotels, meals, travel)	5,000
Temporary office help, miscellaneous (telephone, etc.)	3,750
Interest	900
Rental of premises	24,000
Rental of computer equipment	15,000
Total	$82,650

From January to September, John and Allan had worked on developing Inter Act. The proportion of time spent on various stages was as follows:

Product design	15%
Detail program design	20%
Coding and testing	50%

The remaining time was spent at conferences and making contacts with potential customers; J. J. Ltd. now has a mailing list of over 400 firms which have indicated interest in Inter Act.

In December 1994, John met with Katherine Dickson, CA, to obtain some assistance in preparing J. J.'s 1994 financial statements. During the conversation John said:

> Our company has had no operations this year so I'm just preparing a balance sheet. What I want to discuss with you is Al's and my salaries. As you know, we lived on our savings for the first four months, then started paying ourselves below-market incomes. We feel that a more accurate monthly salary would have been $5,000 each (I expect this to increase substantially in 1995 as we sell Inter Act). As a result, I'm going to include $120,000 ($5,000 × 2 people × 12 months) in the balance sheet amount for "Unamortized Computer Software Costs" and add the difference to capital. I'll show the software development as a long-term asset; we're going to need an increase in our working capital loan next year, and I want the bank to see that we intend to be around for a long time!

Required

Present your recommendations for fair presentation of J. J. Ltd.'s position and results during its first year. Suggest any accounting policies that you feel J. J. Ltd. may wish to adopt.

Case 46

Jaded Jeans Limited

Jaded Jeans Limited operates a nationwide chain of clothing stores that cater to young men and women. Jaded Jeans has been trying to obtain space in a new downtown shopping development which is extremely popular with young people. The management of Jaded Jeans feels that it is important for Jaded Jeans to have a presence in this development, even if the cost of obtaining a sublease offsets the potential profits for this location.

Recently, Jaded Jeans was able to negotiate a sublease with Pencil & Paper Ltd. (PP), an office supply firm, which leased a 2,000 square foot store in the development. To induce PP to sublet, Jaded Jeans agreed to pay $100,000 to PP immediately. Jaded Jeans is to make the lease payments directly to the mall owner. None of the $100,000 paid to PP will go to the mall owner; the $100,000 will be retained by PP.

Jaded Jeans accounted for the $100,000 payment by charging it directly to expense for the current period. CA, the auditor of Jaded Jeans, objected to Jaded Jeans's treatment of the item and insisted that the payment be capitalized and allocated to the remaining five years of the sublease, preferably by the declining-balance method. CA argued that treating the payment as a current expense would result in mismatching revenue and expense.

The vice president, finance (VP), has countered by arguing that, although Jaded Jeans made the payment in expectation of large future revenues and profits from the new location, there was no way that the profits could reliably be predicted (if indeed, they materialized at all). The VP felt that, just as the *CICA Handbook,* Section 3450 requires research

---

costs should be charged to expense due to the uncertainty of future benefits, so should Jaded Jeans's payment be charged to expense. The VP also stated that this payment could be written off immediately for income tax purposes and wondered why he could not do the same for accounting purposes.

In addition, the VP cited arguments from accounting literature that financial accounting allocations are inherently arbitrary. Since allocations are arbitrary, he argued, they must therefore be useless at best and misleading at worst.

The VP indicated that he had just finished cleaning up his balance sheet last year by writing off the balance of intangibles, and he was not anxious to introduce a major amount again. He indicated that bankers and financial analysts "discount" intangibles anyway.

Finally, the VP pointed out that, although CA argued about the importance of matching as an accounting principle, he could not even find it in the topical index of the *CICA Handbook*.

Required

Discuss the arguments presented and state your conclusions.

Case 47

Kent Helicopters Ltd.

"We've just had a call from Ottawa! The Department of Defence wants a bid on the manufacture of 36 helicopters. Fortunately we've got four in inventory and, with our normal production capacity of two aircraft per month, we can just make the first deadline if we're awarded the contract by the end of January 1993. The inventory was designed for our construction company clients, so the instrument panels will have to be modified according to the government's specifications, but this shouldn't be a problem."

Paul Kent, president of Kent Helicopters Ltd., was speaking to his vice president of manufacturing. Paul had heard rumours of a potential war that could have international repercussions, but this was his first evidence the rumours might have some basis. The rumours had placed the timing of trouble anywhere from early summer to the end of 1993.

The two men spent the next few days preparing Kent Helicopters' bid (Exhibit 1). Within two weeks Paul was informed that Kent had been awarded the contract, and the nonrefundable deposit of $7,710,000 was received the day the contract was signed. The terms of the contract are summarized in Exhibit 2.

The first shipment, on February 28, 1993, consisted of the four modified aircraft from inventory and two newly manufactured helicopters. The second shipment was made according to schedule on May 31. Payments were received from the government on delivery, as per the progress payments schedule in Exhibit 2.

In August 1993, a missile attack was launched by an aggressor, and war was declared. The government of Canada agreed to send troops, planes, and provisions to the war zone.

Institute of Chartered Accountants of Ontario, adapted.

EXHIBIT 1

KENT HELICOPTERS LTD.
Calculation of Contract Price for a Tender to the Government of Canada Department of Defence
(date of tender: January 12, 1993)
(dollars in thousands)

Contract price:	
4 helicopters from inventory, at $4,300	$ 17,200
32 helicopters to be built, at $4,300	137,600
Total	$154,800
Costs:	
Raw materials, labour, variable overhead*	$109,520
Physical modification of aircraft in inventory	180
Development costs for client specifications†	9,700
Interest‡	20,000
Amortization of manufacturing facilities*	3,800
General and administrative*	2,400
Total costs	145,600
Profit before tax	$ 9,200

* The figures for raw materials, labour, variable overhead, amortization, and general and administrative include costs for all 36 helicopters, regardless of when they were manufactured.
† This applies to the government work needed on all 36 helicopters.
‡ Interest on debt raised specifically for this contract will be incurred evenly over the 16 months of the contract.

Kent Helicopters Ltd.'s August 31 and November 30 shipments and receipt of payment occurred according to the contract, and, by December 31, two more helicopters were ready for the next delivery. The company had correctly calculated the cost of the four helicopters, with modifications, which were sent in the first shipment. However, there had been a cost overrun of $85,000 per aircraft on the subsequent manufacturing.

Required

For each scenario described below, select appropriate accounting policies for revenue and expense recognition and for inventory valuation on this contract. Determine the impact your policies will have on the revenue and expense recognition and on the inventory valuation of Kent Helicopters

EXHIBIT 2

KENT HELICOPTERS LTD.
Summary of the Terms of the Contract with the Government of Canada Department of Defence (dollars in thousands)

Term of the contract:	February 1, 1993, to May 31, 1994 (16 months).
Contract price:	$154,800.
Nonrefundable deposit:	5% ($7,710), due the day the contract is signed.
Delivery dates:	Six helicopters on each of February 28, May 31, August 31, and November 30, 1993, and February 28 and May 31, 1994.
Progress payments:	$26,322 [1/5 of ($154,800 − $7,710 nonrefundable deposit − $15,480 payment on May 31, 1994)] due on delivery on February 28, May 31, August 31, and November 30, 1993, and February 28, 1994.
Final payment:	10% ($15,480) of total contract price due on delivery on May 31, 1994.
Cancellation clause:	The government of Canada may cancel this contract with six weeks' written notice; there is no cancellation penalty and no refund to the government of any portion of the $7,710 deposit.

Institute of Chartered Accountants of Ontario, adapted.

Ltd. at December 31, 1993. Round all calculations to the nearest thousand.

1. By December 1993, the war had escalated beyond all previous predictions. Your work on Kent Helicopters Ltd.'s financial statements was scheduled to begin the third week of January 1994 and continue to the end of February.

2. By late November 1993, it appeared that the war might end soon; hopes were high that the forces could start coming home by Christmas. On January 15, 1994, the government of Canada cancelled the contract with Kent Helicopters Ltd. Peace was declared in February.

Case 48

Kerr Addison Mines Limited

North American mining companies have flexibility in deciding how to account for their reserves. The profession has had to balance the need for relevant information on reserves with lack of reliability in estimating reserves.

Accounting for reserves is important for a number of reasons. Proven reserves are frequently the basis for negotiating sales of properties and companies, for arranging financing, for assessing equity securities, and for evaluating managerial and corporate performance.

The "value" of mineral reserves in excess of capitalized exploration and development costs is an "off-balance-sheet" asset; however, reserve estimates impact net income. Depletion of deferred exploration and development costs is calculated by units of production. Thus, the reserve calculations are also vital in writing off capitalized costs and in establishing limits on the extent of capitalization. These calculations are complicated by the fact that reserve estimates are constantly being revised.

Estimating mineral reserves and classifying them according to their likelihood of recoverability is a job that requires the training of a mining engineer or geologist. The quality of the estimate depends on such factors as changes in technology and market conditions affecting either production costs or selling prices (which are volatile). The estimate must also take into consideration likely future changes in recovery rates, dilution rates, and inefficiencies during extraction, processing, and transportation of the metals. Opinions among geologists and engineers will inevitably vary.

Before its retraction, reference to the measurement and disclosure of mining company reserves was found in Section 4510, "Reporting the Effects of Changing Prices." The recommendations stated:

Mining

.56 Supplementary information about the effects of changing prices for enterprises that have interests in mineral reserves, other than oil and gas, should include, except in the situation outlined in paragraph 4510.67, the following additional information:

a. Quantities of mineral reserves as at the beginning and the end of the period or as at disclosed dates as close to the beginning and the end of the period as is practicable. Mineral reserves should be computed on a proved basis, or a proved and probable basis, consistent with the basis used for cost amortization purposes.

b. Quantities expressed in physical units or in percentages of reserves, of each significant mineral product contained in the reserves included under subparagraph (*a*).

c. Changes in the quantities of mineral reserves during the reporting period, separately disclosing changes attributable to each of the following factors:

i. Revisions of previous estimates.
ii. Discoveries.
iii. Purchases of reserves in place.
iv. Sales of reserves in place.
v. Reserves used in production.

d. Quantities of each significant mineral product produced during the period.

e. The amount of each of the following types of costs for the current period, whether such costs are capitalized or charged to expense at the time incurred:

i. Cost of acquiring mineral rights.
ii. Exploration costs.

.57 When important economic factors or significant uncertainties affect particular components of an enterprise's mineral reserves, it is desirable that management provide an explanation of those factors. Many such factors can arise as a result of the geographic location of the reserves and, therefore, an analysis of the reserve quantities by location or geographic area may provide an improved understanding of the nature of reserves and changes in reserves.

.58 In respect of the requirements for disclosure of reserve quantities, as set out in paragraph 4510.56, the following definitions apply:

Proved mineral reserves are the estimated quantities of commercially recoverable reserves that, on the basis of geological, geophysical, and engineering data, can be demonstrated with a reasonably high degree of certainty to be recoverable in the future from known mineral deposits by either primary or improved recovery methods.

Probable mineral reserves are the estimated quantities of commercially recoverable reserves that are less well defined than proved reserves and that may be estimated or indicated to exist on the basis of geological, geophysical, and engineering data.

* * *

.67 The reserve quantity and cost information required by paragraphs 4510.56, .59, and .65 need not be disclosed in those rare circumstances when, in the opinion of management, such disclosures would be harmful to the enterprise.

Kerr Addison Mines Limited is a Canadian mining company whose predecessor company was founded over 50 years ago. During its history, the company has owned and operated mines in Canada, the United States, and Ireland and has also diversified into the oil and gas business. At December 31, 1991, Kerr Addison reported total assets of $588,836,000. Net sales in 1991 were $160,986,000 and net income was $3,207,000.

Kerr Addison's 1991 "Review of Operations" for Mining and Exploration and Development is presented below.

The mining operations achieved or exceeded most of their production goals in 1991. Contained metals amounted to almost 42,000 tonnes of copper; 57,000 tonnes of zinc; 104,000 ounces of gold; and 4.3 million ounces of silver. Unit operating costs were reduced at all the operations. Revenues, however, declined significantly because of lower metal prices and the strength of the Canadian dollar. All of the divisions recorded a cash operating profit contribution.

Lac Dufault Division

The Ansil mine, located near Rouyn-Noranda, Quebec, completed its second full year of production at record levels. The division contributed a cash operating profit of $41.5 million, compared to $51.4 million in 1990.

As expected, underground conditions deteriorated because of the high rock stresses in the mine. The problems with the ore pass that were encountered during 1990 recurred in the second half of 1991 due to these increasing stresses. Production, however, was not significantly affected while repairs were made. As a result of good rock mechanics analyses, engineering design, and mining practice, the mine achieved total recovery of the ore while maintaining safe working conditions.

The Norbec mill achieved record high copper and gold recoveries of 97.9 percent and 89.4 percent, respectively, to produce 118,805 tonnes of copper/gold concentrates. In 1992, zinc concentrates will also be produced as a result of mining in the zinc-rich portion of the Ansil orebody. The tailing pond capacity was increased during the year to enable it to hold all future Ansil tailings. Rehabilitation and revegetation of the former Millenbach mine site was completed successfully.

Winston Lake Division

The Winston Lake Division, situated near Schreiber, Ontario, once again met all its operational targets. The division's reduced cash operating profit in 1991 of $16.3 million, compared to $36.3 million in 1990, was due solely to lower average metal prices throughout the year. The lower revenues were partially offset by reduced operating costs achieved as a result of productivity improvements in all areas of the operation. Development of the lower ore zone has commenced, which will permit the operation to maintain its 1,000 tonnes per day production rate from 1993 onwards.

The mill produced 101,643 tonnes of zinc concentrates and 13,714 tonnes of copper concentrates. A particle size monitor was integrated into the process control system along with an Expert Systems computer package. This will assist in improving zinc recovery and in decreasing reagent and power consumption. High environmental standards were maintained in all facets of the operation. Concentrate handling facilities and practices were modified to eliminate any further problems with dusting.

Lac Shortt Division

The Lac Shortt gold mine, located west of Chapais, Quebec, performed as planned in spite of the difficult conditions resulting from the highly stressed ground in the mine. The division achieved a cash operating profit of $1.4 million, compared to $1.7 million in 1990.

By year-end, the stoping and surface pillar extraction were nearing completion, with 73,000 tonnes of ore remaining to be mined. Closure of the mine is planned for March 1992. A minesite closure and rehabilitation plan has been submitted to the provincial government for approval.

Samatosum Division

At the Samatosum operation, near Barriere, British Columbia, the underground exploration program at the base of the open pit, started in 1990, was completed by mid-year and required a major readjustment of the stated ore reserves. As a result, the year-end ore reserves at Samatosum have declined by the quantity mined during the year as well as from a further negative adjustment of 197,000 tonnes. A decision was made in mid-1991 to extract the remaining ore by underground mining methods.

The development of the underground mine began in August 1991, and ore was being supplied to the mill through the fourth quarter. A total of 83,000 tonnes of ore will be extracted from underground, and the life of the operation will now be

Financial Review

	Lac Dufault		*Winston Lake*		*Lac Shortt*		*Samatosum*		*Opemiska*	
	1991	1990	**1991**	1990	**1991**	1990	**1991**	1990	**1991***	1990
Average price received:										
Copper ($ per pound)	**1.17**	1.31	**1.16**	1.37			**1.14**	1.38	**1.23**	1.35
Zinc ($ per pound)		0.63	**0.58**	0.79			**0.58**	0.83		
Lead ($ per pound)							**0.28**	0.42		
Gold ($ per ounce)	**412**	438	**405**	494	**413**	489	**408**	438	**410**	434
Silver ($ per ounce)	**4.57**	5.20	**4.55**	4.93			**6.58**	5.83	**4.72**	5.20
Net sales ($000s)	**$62,355**	$73,619	**$39,080**	$60,696	**$18,754**	$20,899	**$21,733**	$34,406	**$13,123**	$17,150
Cost of production:										
Mining	**11,618**	14,085	**11,729**	13,376	**8,249**	10,062	**6,929**	11,141	**3,842**	9,362
Milling	**4,845**	4,385	**5,533**	5,451	**3,683**	3,772	**3,461**	3,785	**693**	1,358
Plant	**1,331**	1,457	**1,402**	1,343	**2,246**	2,108	**362**	406	**1,834**	3,444
General	**3,069**	2,255	**4,114**	4,224	**3,139**	3,199	**1,732**	1,607	**2,068**	3,511
Total operating costs	**20,863**	22,182	**22,778**	24,394	**17,317**	19,141	**12,484**	16,939	**8,437**	17,675
Operating profit (loss)	**41,492**	51,437	**16,302**	36,302	**1,437**	1,758	**9,249**	17,467	**4,686**	(525)
Minority interest					**62**	96	**1,014**	4,420		
Royalties							**830**	1,667		
Underground exploration		453			**53**	390				429
Depreciation and amortization	**18,934**	19,799	**10,818**	10,235	**6,879**	11,283†	**6,047**	9,873	**234**	934
Profit (loss) before tax	**$22,558**	$31,185	**$ 5,484**	$26,067	**$ (5,557)**	$(10,011)	**$ 1,358**	$ 1,507	**$4,452**	$ (1,888)

* Based on six months' production.
† Excludes write-down of $10 million.

Production Review

	Lac Dufault		*Winston Lake*		*Lac Shortt*		*Samatosum*		*Opemiska*	
	1991	1990	**1991**	1990	**1991**	1990	**1991**	1990	**1991***	1990
Tonnes milled (000s)	**440**	425	**347**	346	**367**	349	**178**	169	**198**	340
Grade:										
Copper, %	**7.5**	8.2	**1.2**	1.1			**0.8**	1.2	**3.0**	1.8
Zinc, %			**16.4**	17.7			**2.2**	2.9		
Lead, %							**1.1**	1.6		
Gold, grams per tonne	**2.7**	2.4	**1.7**	1.4	**4.1**	4.1	**1.3**	1.9	**2.0**	1.7
Silver, grams per tonne	**28.2**	29.9	**38.7**	36.6			**690.0**	1,072.0	**21.4**	13.4
Production:										
Copper, pounds (000s)	**70,703**	75,091	**7,582**	6,698			**2,555**	3,225	**12,589**	12,915
Zinc, pounds (000s)		520	**119,161**	128,960			**5,554**	7,099		
Lead, pounds (000s)							**2,822**	5,831		
Gold, ounces	**34,474**	30,032	**7,768**	6,954	**45,448**	42,855	**5,319**	8,998	**10,870**	16,542
Silver, ounces (000s)	**299**	325	**192**	160			**3,673**	5,342	**117**	121
Operating cost:										
$ per tonne milled	**47.41**	52.14	**65.61**	70.43	**47.20**	54.78	**70.29**	100.14	**42.52**	52.02
Number of employees, December 31	**190**	199	**177**	174	**111**	154	**47**	51	**43**	214
Lost time accident frequency per 200,000 hours worked	**2.9**	4.6	**2.7**	1.3	**3.2**	0.7	**3.9**	0.0	**1.6**	5.9

* Based on six months' production.

extended to September 1992. Production from the open pit will be concluded in April 1992.

The company's share of this division's cash operating profit was $7.4 million, compared to $11.4 million in 1990. The mill produced 4,763 tonnes of copper concentrates; 4,962 tonnes of zinc concentrates; and 2,673 tonnes of lead concentrates. The precious metals are contained chiefly in the copper concentrates.

Opemiska Division

With the exhaustion of its ore reserves, the Opemiska operation was closed at the end of June after an illustrious 38-year mine life. It was very profitable in its final months, generating a $4.7 million cash operating profit, compared to a loss of $0.5 million in the previous year.

The company's comprehensive communication program with its employees and the community of Chapais, Quebec, combined with a fair severance package, helped the community manage the impact of the closure. Dismantling of the facilities is now underway and site reclamation will commence in 1992.

Ore Reserves (diluted) at December 31, 1991

Deposit	*Category*	*Tonnes*	*Percent Copper*	*Percent Zinc*	*Percent Lead*	*g/t Silver*	*g/t Gold*
Ansil	Proven	428,000	6.3	1.4	—	22.4	1.2
	Probable	118,000	3.3	1.3		13.0	0.4
	Total	546,000	5.6	1.4		20.4	1.0
Winston Lake	Proven	870,000	1.2	15.5	—	33.5	1.5
	Probable	755,000	0.9	12.6		25.1	1.0
	Possible	201,000	0.9	10.6		21.2	0.6
	Total	1,826,000	1.0	13.8		28.7	1.2
Lac Shortt	Proven	73,000					4.1
Sama-tosum	Proven	108,000	0.8	1.8	1.1	703.0	1.2

Note: g/t means grams per tonne.

Exploration and Development

Exploration expenditures declined in 1991 to $19.7 million from the 1990 level of $23.9 million. This reflects the substantially decreased expenditures on the Mobrun 1100 lens and on underground exploration at the mining operations. Exploration for base and precious metals continued throughout the year in the

Canadian Shield areas of Quebec, Ontario, and Manitoba; in British Columbia; and in the southwestern United States, principally in Nevada. In addition, an office has been established in Panama City, and exploration programs are underway in Panama and Bolivia.

Izok Lake

In November, Minnova announced that it was acquiring several base metal properties in the Northwest Territories, the most significant of which is the Izok Lake deposit.

The Izok Lake, Hood River, and Gondor polymetallic sulphide deposits were acquired after year-end for U.S.$20 million and certain capped royalties. An exploration program in 1992 is being designed to increase the tonnage and confidence of the reserves at Izok Lake. The deposit is located about 360 kilometres north of Yellowknife. At present, the drill-indicated reserves are 13.4 million tonnes at a grade of 3.2 percent copper, 14.4 percent zinc, 1.3 percent lead, and 74.1 grams of silver per tonne. Engineering and environmental baseline studies to define project parameters and costs will also be undertaken.

The major challenge to the project is in the development of infrastructure to support a remote operation and to enable seasonal trucking of large quantities of metal concentrates on winter roads to an Arctic port. A mine could possibly be developed for start-up in 1997.

RFC Resource Finance Corporation

Kerr Addison owns a 46 percent equity interest in RFC Resource Finance Corporation, which is evaluating its Pend Oreille zinc-lead property located in northeastern Washington. A 19,000-foot, 13-hole underground diamond drilling program was carried out during the year to extend the limits of the known mineralization of the northeast zone in the Yellowhead horizon. This highly successful program confirmed the continuity and the increasing grade and thickness of the deposit in this area. Drill-indicated geological reserves were increased to 3.9 million short tons at 10.4 percent zinc and 1.7 percent lead, which represents a 24 percent increase of contained zinc metal over previous reserves. RFC is now attempting to secure the financing necessary to complete a feasibility study.

Mobrun

Studies of the Mobrun 1100 lens, in the Lac Dufault area of Quebec, continued throughout the year examining several scenarios at various operating rates. Minnova completed the requirements of earning into a 50 percent joint venture interest in the deposit. At year-end, all work had stopped while Audrey secures its financing.

Frotet

A prefeasibility study is nearing completion on this large gold-copper deposit located 120 kilometres north of Chibougamu, Quebec. Open-pittable, drill-indicated geological reserves are 36 million tonnes at a grade of 1.6 grams of gold per tonne. Substantial additional mineralization has been identified both within and beneath the outlines of a 200-meter-deep open pit. A decision to undertake a feasibility study is pending.

Pick Lake

Additional drilling at Pick Lake, situated 1.5 kilometres southwest of the Winston Lake mine, failed to locate any substantial additional tonnage. Several studies are in progress to determine if additional work should be carried out.

Required

Evaluate the 1991 disclosure by Kerr Addison Mines Limited of its reserves. Suggest other information that would be useful to an investor in predicting the company's future results.

Case 49

Kett Brothers

It is a sunny day in April 1993, and you have just sat down to work when the phone rings. George Gainsborough, one of your original clients and the president of Kett Brothers, is calling for some advice. He is not happy with the earnings per share reported by Kett in 1992 and has two ideas on how to improve the figures in 1992 and in the future.

One of George's ideas is to change Kett's amortization policy from declining balance to straight line on some of the company's capital assets. Last year Kett had some major acquisitions which were unlike the capital assets previously owned by the company, and George feels that adopting the old amortization policy for the new assets was a mistake.

George's other idea is to defer the planned purchase of a building. He feels that the additional amortization expense will further impair the 1993 earnings per share reported, and he would like to have at least 1992 and 1993 showing improved results before increasing the expenses.

You completed the audit of Kett Brothers' 1992 financial statements at the end of February this year. On checking them you note that they show net income before extraordinary items of $34,000 and net income of $29,800. Kett's share capital at January 1, 1992, consisted of:

1. 6,000 Class A common shares.
2. 1,000 Class B noncumulative convertible shares with an annual dividend of $1, which had most recently been declared and paid in December 1991. One Class B share was convertible into two class A shares.
3. 500 Class C cumulative preference shares paying a fixed dividend of $4 per annum.
4. 1,000 Class D noncumulative preference shares with a fixed dividend of $2.25 per annum; this dividend was declared in 1992.
5. 100 options giving the holder the right to purchase any time during the next two years one Class A share for one option and $350 cash.

Kett's tax rate is 45 percent, and the company expects to earn 12 percent before tax on its assets.

No options were exercised in 1992. However, the following events took place during the year for Class A shares:

March 1	Sold for cash	600
July 1	Issued for converted Class B shares	2,000
Sept. 1	Purchased and cancelled	300
Dec. 1	Issued in return for equipment	3,000

The capital assets George referred to during the telephone call cost $50,000. They had a useful life of 10 years and no salvage value. In 1992 Kett Brothers had amortized these assets at a rate of 20 percent declining balance, which was the rate allowed by Revenue Canada.

Required

What earnings per share figures were reported on Kett Brothers' 1992 financial statements (ignore 1991 comparative figures). What earnings per share figures will be reported this year for the 1992 comparative figures if the company changes its amortization policy for the new capital assets?

Advise George Gainsborough on the wisdom of changing the amortization policy. Also advise him about the deferral of the building purchase.

Case 50

LAC Minerals Ltd.

LAC Minerals Ltd. is a Canadian company engaged in gold mining and oil and gas exploration. The current company ("LAC") was created by an amalgamation in 1985 of Lac Minerals Ltd., Lake Short Mines Limited, Wright-Hargreaves Mines Limited, Little Long Lac Gold Mines Limited, and two wholly owned subsidiaries of these companies.

In 1986, the company held five producing gold mines and mills in Ontario and Quebec, and a limestone quarry, in addition to oil and gas and mineral interests in Canada, the United States, and Australia.

In May 1981, representatives from Lac Minerals Ltd. and another mining company, International Corona Resources Ltd., were engaged in negotiations toward a joint venture operation to develop an area adjacent to Corona land holdings in Hemlo, Ontario. The area had been staked in 1945 by Dr. Jack K. Williams, a physician who spent several summers making claims and prospecting in the Hemlo area. Reports about the area's gold potential were written between 1945 and 1947 by Trevor Page, a geologist. After Dr. Williams's death in 1953 his family continued to pay the taxes necessary to maintain the claims.

During the 1981 Lac/Corona discussions the Lac representatives were able to examine maps, drill core, and cross sections of drilling that Corona had done. There was also publicly available documentation about drilling in the area and on Corona's property, which Lac was able to use in its assessment of the area's worth.

In July 1981, Lac representatives approached Dr. Williams's widow and acquired the claims for Lac. A feasibility study on the development of the Hemlo project was carried out in 1983, and, on December 6, 1985, Ontario Premier David Peterson and LAC president Peter Allen poured the first gold bar at a ceremony held at the Page-Williams Mine. Extracts from LAC's financial statements before and after the opening of the Page-Williams Mine are presented in Exhibit 1.

EXHIBIT 1 Extracts from Annual Reports (in thousands)

	1986	*1985*	*1984*	*1983*	*1982*
Mining interests	$388,532	$327,821	$164,753	$ 94,047	$ 68,588
Oil and gas interests	27,046	31,264	35,370	37,380	35,033
Total assets	597,229	463,759	397,751	221,368	122,261
Hemlo component of mining interests	233,485	194,077	75,464	14,314	512
Revenue	229,657	142,363	169,673	157,232	130,398
Hemlo component of revenue	112,121				
Net income before extraordinary items	19,118	6,128	39,307	27,969	21,928
Hemlo component of net income before extraordinary items	12,558				
Ounces of gold produced, total	478,394	265,925	299,571	257,064	201,181
Ounces of gold produced from the Page-Williams Mine	204,034	1,900			

In October 1981, International Corona Resources Ltd. launched a lawsuit against Lac Minerals Ltd. charging breach of a confidential relationship in LAC's acquisition of the Williams claims. Reference to the lawsuit first appeared in Lac's 1983 statements as a note, "Commitments and Contingencies" (Exhibit 2).

On March 7, 1986, Mr. Justice Richard E. Holland of the Supreme Court of Ontario ruled that Lac had breached a fiduciary duty it owed to Corona and had used confidential information acquired from Corona. Ownership of the Page-Williams mine was awarded to Corona, upon payment to LAC of $153,978,000 plus interest from the date of judgement to the date of payment to compensate LAC for amounts spent to develop the site. LAC immediately appealed the judgement.

LAC's 1985 audit report was dated March 11, 1986, with regard to the reporting of the trial. In addition, the audit report included "Comments on Differences in Canadian–United States Reporting Standards" (LAC shares trade on the New York Stock Exchange as well as in Paris, Brussels, and Antwerp) in accordance with the requirements of a CICA *Auditing Guideline*. The "Comments" indicated that if the audit report had been prepared according to U.S. reporting standards the opinion would have been qualified as being subject to the outcome of significant uncertainties described in Note 14(*c*). The "Comments" explained that Canadian reporting standards do not include such a qualification when the uncertainty is adequately disclosed in the financial statements. The 1986 statements contained a similar audit report and note disclosure. In addition, the 1986 results were reported on two bases—including and excluding the Page-Williams Mine.

EXHIBIT 2 Commitments and Contingencies Notes

1983

9(a). In October of 1981, International Corona Resources (Corona) commenced an action against, among others, a predecessor of the Company in which it now claims general damages of $500,000,000 for breach of a confidential relationship which precluded the acquisition of certain patented mining claims in the Hemlo area of Ontario, a declaration that the Company's interests in the subject mining claims are held in trust for Corona and an order directing their transfer to Corona, an injunction to prevent the Company from dealing with the claims, and an accounting for profits from the claims. Based on evidence provided by the Company and subject to any evidence revealed by further examinations for discovery that must be conducted, counsel for the Company is of the opinion that Corona should not succeed in its claim.

1984

11(a). In October of 1981, International Corona Resources Limited (Corona) commenced an action against, among others, a predecessor of the Company in which it now claims general damages of $3 billion for breach of a confidential relationship which precluded the acquisition of certain patented mining claims in the Hemlo area of Ontario, a declaration that the Company's interests in the subject mining claims are held in trust for Corona and an order directing their transfer to Corona, an injunction to prevent the Company from dealing with the claims, and an accounting for profits from the claims. Based on evidence provided by the Company and subject to any evidence revealed by further examinations for discovery that must be conducted, counsel for the Company is of the opinion that Corona should not succeed in its claim.

1985

14(c). Judgement was rendered by the Supreme Court of Ontario on Friday, March 7, 1986, in the action against LAC by International Corona Resources Ltd. ("Corona") with respect to certain patented mining claims in the Hemlo area of Ontario owned by LAC, now the location of the Page-Williams Mine.

The Court held that in acquiring the claims on which the mine is now located, LAC had breached a fiduciary duty it owed to Corona and had used confidential information it had acquired from Corona.

The Court ordered that the Page-Williams Mine be transferred by LAC to Corona upon payment by Corona to LAC of $153,978,000 plus interest on such amount from the date of the judgement until payment, together with all sums, other than royalties, paid by LAC to the vendor of the property. The Court also gave judgement in favour of Corona for the

EXHIBIT 2 *(concluded)*

amount of profits, if any, obtained by LAC from the operation of the Page-Williams Mine from the date on which the production of gold commenced, and its cost of the action.

LAC has reviewed the judgement and completely disagrees with the findings and considers them to be contrary to the evidence at trial. It therefore has filed an appeal of the judgement to the Ontario Court of Appeal.

It is believed that the appeal could be heard as early as September 1986.

Any adjustments arising from the resolution of this matter will be recorded in the year the case is finally determined.

1986

14(d). Judgement was rendered by the Supreme Court of Ontario on March 7, 1986, in the action brought against LAC by International Corona Resources Ltd. ("Corona") with respect to 11 patented mining claims in the Hemlo area of Ontario owned by LAC, now the location of the Page-Williams Mine.

The Court held that in acquiring the 11 patented claims LAC had breached a fiduciary duty it owed to Corona and had used confidential information it had acquired from Corona.

The Court ordered that the Page-Williams property be transferred by LAC to Corona upon payment by Corona to LAC of $153,978,000 plus interest on such amount from the date of the judgement until payment, together with all sums, other than royalties, paid by LAC to the vendor of the property.

The Court also gave judgement in favour of Corona for the amount of profits, if any, obtained by LAC from the operation of the Page-Williams property from the date on which the production of gold commenced, and its cost of the action. LAC reviewed the judgement and completely disagreed with the findings and considered them to be contrary to law and the evidence at trial. It therefore filed an appeal of the judgement to the Ontario Court of Appeal. The appeal was heard during November 1986; the decision of the court of Appeal has not yet been published.

Any adjustments arising from the resolution of this matter will be recorded in the year the case is finally determined.

On October 2, 1987 the Ontario Court of Appeal upheld the 1986 Supreme Court decision.

Toronto Stock Exchange share prices of LAC and Corona before and after the 1987 ruling are presented in Exhibit 3.

EXHIBIT 3 Selected Share Prices, Toronto Stock Exchange

	High	*Low*	*Close*
LAC Minerals Ltd.:			
53 weeks ended September 25, 1987	18.50	7.87	18.25
October 2, 1987			18.00
October 5, 1987			15.12
53 weeks ended October 9, 1987	20.00	7.87	16.25
International Corona Resources Ltd.:			
October 2, 1987			47.50
October 5, 1987			79.00

Required

Evaluate LAC Minerals Ltd.'s disclosure of International Corona Resources Ltd.'s lawsuit from 1983 to 1986 inclusive.

Case 51

John Labatt Limited

John Labatt Limited (Labatts) is a Canadian management holding company that produces, distributes, and sells beer, packaged food, and processed agricultural products. In 1985, Labatts's principal shareholder was Brascan Limited, which has significant interests in some of Canada's largest financial services and in mining, forestry, and real estate companies. Brascan owned 38 percent of the outstanding voting shares and had two members on Labatts's board of directors.

The other significant shareholder, at 11 percent of outstanding voting shares, was Caisse de depot et placement du Quebec, a pension fund created in 1966 to invest the Quebec pension plan contributions.

Labatts's production and sales activities were conducted primarily in Canada. However, at the end of 1985, the U.S. market contributed 25 percent of the company's sales and 20 percent of its earnings. The stated objective was to double the contribution of the U.S. business by 1990. The company's two fastest growing groups—Agri-Products and Packaged Food—have extensive U.S. manufacturing and sales operations. The Agri-Products group is represented in several other international markets.

Recent Developments

As a result of diversification, Labatts had insulated itself from economic fluctuations and the business cycle. Selected consolidated financial information is provided in Exhibit 1. The six-month brewing earnings were moderately ahead of the previous year's earnings. The Packaged Food group showed the most significant growth in 1985. The Agri-Products group showed an increase in both sales and earnings.

This case is used with the permission of its author, Dr. George Athanassakos, School of Business and Economics, Wilfrid Laurier University, Waterloo, Canada.

EXHIBIT 1

JOHN LABATT LIMITED
Selected Consolidated Financial Information
(in millions of dollars except per share amounts)

	Six Months Ended October 31		*Year Ended April 30*				
	1985	*1984*	*1985*	*1984*	*1983*	*1982*	*1981*
Net sales	$1,629.4	$1,268.0	$2,426.5	$2,132.9	$1,928.7	$1,821.4	$1,296.9
Earnings before bottle write-off and extraordinary items[a]	56.2	54.0	81.7	86.4	72.7	57.4	44.6
Net earnings	56.2	54.0	81.7	66.7	69.2	53.9	41.4
Earnings per common share before bottle write-off and extraordinary items:[a,b]							
Basic	1.82	1.81	2.74	3.04	2.66	2.14	1.74
Fully diluted	1.56	1.53	2.35	2.51	2.26	1.85	1.61
Net earnings per common share:[b]							
Basic	1.82	1.81	2.74	2.35	2.53	2.01	1.61
Fully diluted	1.56	1.53	2.35	1.99	2.16	1.75	1.49
Dividends per common share[b]	0.495	0.465	0.945	0.873	0.778	0.720	0.650
Total assets	1,596.7	1,328.2	1,548.1	1,185.6	953.3	905.5	723.0
Total long-term debt[c]	414.2	318.5	285.7	289.2	249.2	255.0	177.1

Notes:
[a] Earnings before bottle write-off and extraordinary items for 1984 are prior to a $19.7 million bottle write-off provision. (Up to 1984, the brown stubby beer bottle was the industry standard. In 1984, companies started to pursue marketing strategies that differentiated their products from other brands. As a result, in 1984 there was a one time write-off in going from stubby bottles to differently shaped bottles.)
[b] All per share amounts have been adjusted to reflect the 2 for 1 stock split effective September 1983.
[c] Before conversion into common shares of the 11% Convertible Subordinated Debentures (approximately $77.9 million outstanding on October 31, 1985).

EXHIBIT 2

JOHN LABATT LIMITED
Selected Extracts from the Five-Year Review
(in millions except per share and other data)

	Year Ended April 30				
	1985	*1984*	*1983*	*1982*	*1981*
Operating results:					
Gross sales [$, (Y to Y%)]	$ 2,802.6 (14.4%)	$ 2,449.5 (10.1%)	$ 2,225.0 (7.1%)	$ 2,077.3 (38.9%)	$ 1,495.7 (11.5%)
Depreciation and amortization	51.9	42.5	38.4	34.7	29.1
Interest expense	40.3	32.7	30.4	37.9	25.7
Income taxes	52.5	58.2	51.3	47.6	29.6
Funds from operations	165.7	123.1	131.1	118.1	82.1
Common share dividends	28.2	24.9	21.3	19.4	16.6
Capital expenditures	111.1	70.7	53.1	50.7	39.4
Acquisitions and additional investment in partly owned businesses	$ 194.8	$ 95.4	$ 23.9	$ 101.3	$ 17.1
Financial position:					
Working capital	$ 71.6	$ 241.5	$ 253.1	$ 192.2	$ 151.6
Fixed assets	637.9	418.2	333.8	328.1	270.6
Short-term debt	209.1	101.9	39.3	74.1	84.0
Shareholders' equity	518.1	449.3	383.2	330.8	282.6
Total capitalization	$ 1,010.3	$ 798.8	$ 674.0	$ 674.5	$ 604.0
Data per common share:					
Shareholders' equity	17.05	15.29	13.92	12.22	10.93
Price range—high	$25\frac{3}{4}$	$25\frac{1}{8}$	$22\frac{1}{8}$	$14\frac{5}{8}$	$14\frac{3}{4}$
—low	$ $17\frac{5}{8}$	$ $17\frac{5}{8}$	$ $12\frac{1}{8}$	$ $11\frac{5}{8}$	$ $10\frac{5}{8}$

EXHIBIT 2 *(concluded)*

JOHN LABATT LIMITED
Five-Year Review
(in millions except per share and other data)

Other data:					
Return on average shareholders' equity	16.9%	16.0%	20.3%	18.7%	16.6%
Earnings before bottle write-off and extraordinary item as a percent of sales	2.91%	3.53%	3.27%	2.76%	2.98%
Working capital ratio	1.11	1.67	2.08	1.79	1.75
Total debt to equity ratio	0.96	0.87	0.75	0.99	0.92
Long-term debt to equity ratio	0.55	0.64	0.65	0.77	0.63
Total debt as a percent of total capitalization	32.0%	33.0%	30.2%	36.4%	36.1%
Common shares outstanding (in thousands)	30,392	29,377	27,533	27,073	25,868
Number of shareholders	11,648	11,727	10,325	11,146	11,410
Number of employees	13,000	10,500	9,000	11,000	10,400

Growth, Diversification, and Financing

Labatt's diversification increased after 1967. One result was that gross sales from Packaged Food and Agri-Products amounted to 59 percent of total gross sales by 1985 versus 48 percent in 1978.

The company had continued its program of long-term capital investment to enhance its existing facilities, to increase capacity, to develop new markets, and to improve productivity in each of its major business areas. As a result, capital spending was $111.1 million in fiscal 1985, more than double 1983 (Exhibit 2).

All this growth, however, was not without cost. The company's cash flows (net of dividends) provided financing for internal growth. However, bank loans and long-term debt were used for acquisitions. As a result, the amount of total debt in the company's capital structure was well above optimal levels and did not compare favourably with the main competitors or the industry. Labatt's desired level of total debt to equity was 0.82. In fiscal 1985, the ratio had reached 0.96. Long-term debt to equity was still above 50 percent. To maintain its Aa bond rating and financial flexibility, Labatts had to reverse the current trends.

Also, the company wanted to maintain flexibility for future capital investments in case the equity markets, which had been performing so well, suddenly soured. Labatt's stock had appreciated by close to 100 percent over the past three years, from a low of $18 in the first quarter of 1983 to a closing price of $32⅝ on February 14, 1986. Analysts were predicting continued stock market improvement, despite the fact that long-term bond yields were still historically high at over 10.50 percent.

An equity issue at this time would be difficult, because Brascan Limited was opposed to this financing.

Plans for Future Growth

Labatts was committed to continued growth through capital spending and diversification.

The Brewing group was expected to continue to increase market share by building on its momentum in the Canadian markets. In addition, the company planned further development in the United States and outside North America through direct investment or management contracts. Non-brewing growth was expected to come from acquisition of closely related operations, new product development, and new worldwide markets.

The Economy

The Canadian economy had experienced its third consecutive year of economic growth in 1985. Real GNP was increasing, while inflation was at its lowest levels in years. Interest rates and unemployment, while low as based on recent history, were still high by historical standards.

Projected economic growth for the next two years was fairly steady. Real GNP was expected to increase by 2.6 percent and 3.2 percent in 1986 and 1987 and prices measured by the CPI were expected to increase by 4.4 and 3.9 percent. The reduction in inflation was expected to lower long-term interest rates below 10 percent by the end of 1987.

Nevertheless, consumer sentiment was beginning to show some signs of deterioration. Consumers did not foresee a recession, but they also did not expect any positive changes in the economy.

Industry and Government Regulation

Labatt's Canadian industries were heavily influenced by marketing boards, which controlled pricing, distribution, and imports. They also were influenced by federal and provincial government regulations and practices. Consolidation and rationalization of the Canadian industry had occurred to improve economies of scale and competition; yet the industry remained regionally organized. The ongoing consolidation had led to the domination of the industry by three main players: Labatt Brewing Company Ltd., Molson Breweries of Canada Ltd., and Carling O'Keefe Breweries of Canada Ltd. While no one was immune to a takeover, Labatts was the least possible candidate for a hostile takeover attempt, because Brascan and Caisse de depot effectively controlled 49 percent of the company's outstanding shares.

Under the proposed Free Trade Agreement (FTA) with the United States, the elimination of tariffs on Labatt's products was not expected to have a major impact on the company. Brewery products and marketing boards were to be exempt from all provisions of the FTA. Hence, changes to existing Canadian government practices for listing, distribution, and pricing would not be required under the FTA.

Proposed Financing

Labatts proposed to issue an innovative convertible debenture, packaged to resemble equity. The company would try to record this issue as equity. If recorded as equity, this new issue would solve Labatt's capital structure problem and would satisfy Brascan Limited.

Exhibit 3 summarizes the proposed Adjustable Rate Convertible Subordinated Debentures. The debentures would be issued under a trust indenture dated February 28, 1986, and would mature on February 28, 2006. The gross proceeds of $125 million would be used primarily to reduce short-term bank indebtedness. The issue's underwriting fees and expenses would be paid from Labatts's general funds.

EXHIBIT 3

JOHN LABATT LIMITED
Summary of the Offering

Issue:	1986 Adjustable Rate Convertible Subordinated Debentures, due February 28, 2006 (the Debentures).
Amount:	$62.5 million.
Concurrent sale:	$62.5 million.
Price:	100 plus accrued interest, if any.
Interest:	Adjustable rate payable semiannually on March 1 and September 1. The rate of interest per annum for each six-month period will be equal to the greater of (*i*) 6% and (*ii*) the percentage that two times the dividends paid on the common shares in the previous six months is of the conversion price, plus 1%. The first payment of interest on the Debentures will be September 1, 1986, and will be $30.33 per $1,000 principal amount being the foregoing adjustable rate for the six-month period commencing March 1, 1986, applied for a period of six months plus two days.
Conversion:	Convertible at the holder's option into common shares on or before the earlier of February 27, 2006, or the last business day prior to redemption, at a conversion price of $35.75 per common share, being approximately 27.972 common shares per $1,000 principal amount of Debentures, subject to adjustment in certain events.
Interest rate and conversion price adjustment:	At any time after February 28, 1990, the Corporation may, on not less than 30-day notice, adjust the conversion price to $40 provided that the Corporation also fixes the interest rate at 7% per annum.
Redemption:	Not redeemable on or before February 28, 1990. If at any time on or prior to February 28, 1990, at least 85% of the original principal amount of the Debentures has been converted, redeemable at any time at 106% of the principal amount plus interest, if any. At any time after February 28, 1990, redeemable at the principal amount plus accrued interest, if any.
Subordination:	Direct unsecured obligations of the Corporation ranking equally with the 9.5% Convertible Subordinated Debentures and the 1983 Adjustable Rate Convertible Subordinated Debentures but subordinated to all other indebtedness of the Corporation for borrowed money.
Use of proceeds:	The net proceeds of this issue will be used to reduce short-term bank indebtedness and for general corporate purposes.
Interest and asset coverages:	Interest coverage on long-term debt[a]: . . . . 4.2 times Net tangible asset coverage of long-term debt[b]: Including deferred income taxes . . . . 2.3 times Excluding deferred income taxes . . . . 2.1 times
Closing Date:	On or about February 27, 1986.

Notes:

[a] Based on consolidated earnings of John Labatt before interest on long-term debt (including capital lease obligation) and income taxes.

[b] Based on estimated net proceeds of this issue to John Labatt plus total tangible assets less current liabilities (excluding current portion of long-term debt).

Brascan Limited agreed to purchase 50 percent of the convertible issue, and other major shareholders and institutional investors agreed to buy the balance. The purchasers had given "reasonable assurance" that they would ultimately convert their holdings to common shares.

Reaction

The Ontario Securities Commission questioned Labatt's proposed classification of the convertible debentures issue. The commission wondered whether the accounting complied with Canadian generally accepted accounting principles. The commission also wondered whether the convertible debentures issue represented permanent capital, whether John Labatt Limited had the ability to force conversion of debt into shares and intended to exercise this right, and whether there existed significant retraction privileges. Also, the issue's security, subordination, and its coupon rate and the conversion rights of the holders had to be analyzed to determine whether the convertible debentures possessed more attributes of equity than debt.

Dominion Bond Rating Service Ltd. (DBRS), has recently disclosed that it considers three criteria in determining whether a financial instrument is deemed to be equity equivalent. These are: (*a*) permanence (e.g., the security could not be redeemed for at least 10 years); (*b*) subordination (e.g., the security had to be subordinated to all other debt); and (*c*) conversion (e.g., the holder of the security had to have the right to convert to share equity at any time).

Canadian brokerage firms did not believe that convertible debentures were equity. They indicated that they were going to treat the issue as debt and calculate financial ratios accordingly.

Required

Assume the role of a vice president of finance at Labatt's. Prepare a presentation to the auditors and to the Ontario Securities Commission to convince them that the issue of convertible debentures resembles equity, rather than debt.

Case 52

Laidlaw Inc.

Laidlaw Inc. (Laidlaw) was incorporated as a trucking company in 1968. In 1969, the company entered the waste services business. The company is now the second-largest hazardous waste disposal business and the third-largest waste operation in North America. By 1992, 65 percent of Laidlaw's revenue was from waste services, and 69 percent of the company's revenue came from the United States.

Waste Services

Laidlaw provides waste collection, treatment, and disposal services to commercial, industrial, and residential customers in 22 states and seven provinces. The company operates 29 waste landfill sites in the United States and 11 in Canada. Laidlaw owns 25 of these sites; 3 others are leased and 12 are operated for local government units. Hazardous waste services are provided in 12 states and six provinces.

Regulation

In its Securities and Exchange Commission Form 10-K, Laidlaw describes local, state, provincial, and federal regulations for the collection and disposal of solid and chemical wastes and the operation of sanitary landfills. The regulations govern disposal activities and the location and use of facilities and impose restrictions prohibiting or minimizing air and water pollution. Laidlaw states that it complies in all material respects with the regulations.

Regulations require that Laidlaw demonstrate financial assurance for sudden and accidental or nonsudden and gradual pollution occurrences and financial assurance for future closure and post closure expenses. U.S. legislation requires companies that are responsible for the release of hazardous substances be liable for remediation costs and environmental damage (this requirement is called "Superfund").

Recent Events

In 1990, Laidlaw wrote down the value of a treatment site in Cleveland, Ohio. The site was closed after a court injunction to cease operations due to legal and safety violations. The state of Ohio withdrew its charges in return for the closing.

In 1990, the state of South Carolina ruled that Laidlaw establish a $114 million (U.S.) trust fund for 10 sites identified for potential environmental accidents. Laidlaw responded that its $30 million (U.S.) insurance coverage was sufficient.

In 1991, the state of South Carolina demanded that Laidlaw put aside $133 million (U.S.) cash for potential problems at the Pinewood, South Carolina, hazardous waste landfill. The landfill's lining had a tear in it. The state threatened to close the site in three years. The site's capacity is:

Hazardous waste deposits: 135,000 tons per year for 12 years **plus** nonhazardous waste deposits: 150,000 tons per year for 15 years.

In 1991, the Quebec Ministry of the Environment conducted a search based on allegations that a subsidiary, before acquisition by Laidlaw, had illegally buried up to 600 barrels of industrial waste. The search located barrels, and the subsidiary submitted a restoration plan. The Quebec government ordered the subsidiary to collect all the contaminants dumped, emitted, issued, or discharged into the environment.

The U.S. Environmental Protection Agency has announced new rules effective in 1993. All landfills will have to monitor ground water to detect leakage of lead, plastics, or other contaminants. Garbage must be covered with soil each day. Landfill operators will have to check methane levels to ensure that the gas does not build up and explode. Dump sites will have to be monitored for 30 years after closure.

August 31, 1992, Annual Report

Extracts from the Legal Proceedings of the Management Discussion and Analysis follow:

> As of August 31, 1992, subsidiaries of the Company had been notified that they are potentially responsible parties in connection with 14 locations listed on the Superfund National Priority List under the Comprehensive Environmental Response, Compensation, and Liability Act in the United States. The Company periodically reviews the role, if any, of each subsidiary with respect to each such location, considering the nature and extent of the subsidiary's alleged connection and the accuracy and strength of evidence connecting the potentially responsible parties at the location.
>
> The majority of these proceedings are based on allegations that certain Company subsidiaries (or their predecessors) transported hazardous substances

to the facilities in question, often prior to acquisition of such subsidiaries by the Company. Based on the results of the review of the various sites, expense accruals are provided by the Company for its anticipated share of future costs associated with remedial work to be undertaken and existing accruals are revised as deemed necessary.

The Legal Proceedings Note to the Consolidated Financial Statements follows:

> The business of the Company's solid waste and hazardous waste services segments is continuously regulated by federal, state, provincial and local provisions that have been enacted or adopted, regulating the discharge of materials into the environment or primarily for the purpose of protecting the environment. The nature of the Company's business results in it frequently becoming a party to judicial or administrative proceedings involving all levels of government authorities and other interested parties. The issues that are involved generally relate to applications for permits and licenses by the Company and their conformity with legal requirements and alleged technical violations of existing permits and licences.
>
> In June 1992, the Ministry of Environment of the Province of Quebec requested a subsidiary of the Company to advise the Ministry of its intentions concerning the carrying out of certain characterization studies of soil and water and restoration work with respect to certain areas of the subsidiary's property in Ville Mercier. In 1968, the Quebec government issued two permits to an unrelated company to dump organic liquids into lagoons on this property. By 1971, groundwater contamination had been identified. The Company believes that its subsidiary is not the party responsible for the lagoon and groundwater contamination or for the restoration of the property.
>
> While the final resolution of these proceedings may have an impact on the financial results for a particular period, the Company does not believe that these matters are material to its business or financial condition.

There were no references in the financial statements to the matters described above. Newspaper reports estimate the Quebec liability at $150 million to one billion dollars.

Events after the Year End

In October 1992, Laidlaw gave the South Carolina government a $100 million (U.S.) financial guarantee. The guarantee covers reparation for any problems at the Pinewood landfill site during the next 100 years. Laidlaw will deposit into a trust fund $5 per ton of hazardous waste and $2 per ton of nonhazardous waste that it deposits at the landfill. Corporate guarantees cover any shortfall from the $100 million. A spokesperson for Laidlaw said that the company will not have to make a financial provision for the settlement.

Laidlaw's most recent results are ($000 U.S.):

	1992	*1991*	*1990*
Net income (loss)	$ 132,392	$ (344,361)	$ 214,506
Total assets	3,658,935	3,595,316	3,894,939
Total liabilities	1,698,981	1,913,253	1,841,072

Required

Discuss the accounting issues raised above and Laidlaw's treatment of them.

Case 53

Leisure Time Ltd.

"This economy is killing us!" Sam Spalding was complaining to Leisure Time's auditor, Glenda James. Leisure Time Ltd. is a retailer of patio furniture; the company was founded by Sam and his brother Paul in the mid-1970s. The company had good results for most of its seasons. A few rainy summers and the economic downturn in the early 1980s had put a damper on earnings, but most years were very profitable. Sam and Paul have been able to retain ownership, and both run the business. The company has an audit only at the bank's request.

It is now February 1993, and Glenda James is having a chat with Sam before beginning her audit work. "You've had a bad year, Sam. What happened?"

"Glenda, you wouldn't believe it. Nothing went right last year. We knew that sales of patio furniture might be bad, so last summer we decided to start selling children's toys. We figured that these sales would be heavy during the Christmas season and would help offset any setbacks in patio furniture. We also hoped that people coming in for the toys would look at the summer inventory and buy it, too. We had space, so we installed a few shelves and placed orders for inventory. No problem, right? Wrong! The inventory didn't arrive until the third week of November. We knew were were in trouble, so we advertised heavily in both daily newspapers. We'd ordered lots of the newest and most popular children's toys; with the inventory arriving so late, we were lucky that we'd stocked the trendy items. Even so, we have a lot left. The patio furniture didn't move at all; I guess people don't think about summer in December. Last month we advertised heavily for the January sales, but I've never seen such a terrible response."

"I see you've put together some preliminary figures for me to look at, Sam [see Exhibits 1, 2, and 3]. We'll talk about taxes and note disclosure

---

Institute of Chartered Accountants of Ontario, adapted.

EXHIBIT 1

LEISURE TIME LTD.
Draft Balance Sheet
January 31, 1993

	1993	*1992*
Cash and short-term investments	$135,985	$110,425
Accounts receivable	62,350	55,935
Inventories (see Exhibit 2)	173,000	136,685
Total	$371,335	$303,045
Capital assets	$120,970	$118,580
Deferred advertising*	$ 8,420	
Total assets	$500,725	$421,625
Bank loan	$ 65,000	$ 25,000
Accounts payable and accruals	44,820	31,555
Income taxes payable	10,250	7,945
Current portion of long-term debt	1,750	1,750
Total	$121,820	$ 66,250
Long-term debt	$ 17,700	$ 18,620
Shareholders' equity:		
Capital stock	$ 30,800	$ 30,800
Retained earnings	330,405	305,955
Total	$361,205	$336,755
Total liabilities and equity	$500,725	$421,625

* This is advertising for the toys; it will appear in the newspapers in February and March.

LEISURE TIME LTD.
Draft Income Statement
For the Year Ended January 31, 1993

	1993	*1992*
Sales	$560,410	$570,070
Cost of goods sold, selling, and administration	$521,875	$485,095
Amortization	11,870	11,495
Interest on long-term debt	2,215	2,580
Total	$535,960	$499,170
Net income before tax	$ 24,450	$ 70,900

EXHIBIT 2

LEISURE TIME LTD.
Analysis of Inventories at January 31

	1993		1992	
	Cost	*January Sale Price*	*Cost*	*January Sale Price*
Patio furniture:				
Tables	$ 53,500	$ 58,200	$ 59,820	$ 67,500
Chairs	42,350	46,300	47,400	50,200
Umbrellas	14,250	12,250	29,465	27,500
Total	$110,100	$116,750	$136,685	$145,200
Toys:				
VCR Checkers Game	$ 20,400	$ 21,000		
"Orphan Ella" dolls*	27,000	13,200		
Assorted board games	10,300	9,900		
Total	$ 57,700	$ 44,100		
Interest on the increase in the demand loan to finance the toys	5,200			
Total	$173,000	$160,850	$136,685	$145,200

* "Orphan Ella" was a children's film that came out in the summer of 1992. There are no plans to release it in video.

EXHIBIT 3

LEISURE TIME LTD.
Selected Pension Plan Information at January 31

	1993	1992
Estimated average remaining service life:		
Employees earning past service benefits	12	15
Current work force	27	26
Current year's experience loss on the present value of the obligation	$ 1,800	$ 1,680
Current year's pension expense	$ 18,000	$ 15,000
Current year's funding payments	$ 12,000	$ 15,000
Market value of plan assets	$712,000	$847,000

Because business was so bad in 1993, the company funded only the current service cost and a small portion of the normal funding for past service. This is the first year that Leisure Time Ltd. has not funded the amount calculated for the pension expense.

another time, but there are a couple of items I'd like to look at now. The deferred advertising caught my eye. Also, I attended the inventory count, so I know that you're heavily stocked; I want to take a closer look at your numbers. And last week I received a letter from the administrator of the pension plan you set up a few years ago. There are some changes to last year's estimates and funding, and I want to look at the impact these items will have on your financial statements."

Required

Assume the role of Glenda James. Decide how you will deal with the advertising and inventory issues for the year ended January 31, 1993. In addition, explain to Sam the impact that the letter from the pension administrator will have on the statements.

Case 54

LOTT Ltd.

LOTT Ltd. is a supplier of fully digital telecommunications switching equipment. The company has subsidiaries, most of which are wholly owned, in Canada, the United States, the United Kingdom, South America, Germany, eastern Europe, Malaysia, and Japan. LOTT Ltd. operates 21 manufacturing plants worldwide and conducts research and development at 10 of these facilities.

The company's common shares trade on the Toronto, Montreal, Vancouver, New York, London, and Tokyo stock exchanges. The preferred share listings are only on Canadian exchanges.

LOTT Ltd. has worldwide operations to enhance its presence in markets that are not receptive to imported goods. In some countries, government regulations require the establishment of an operating company. In addition, overseas subsidiaries ease LOTT's access to local debt and equity sources. Long-term debt is issued in the United Kingdom and France.

At December 31, 1992, LOTT Ltd.'s (consolidated) assets were $3.4 billion ($3.2 billion at December 31, 1991). Long-term debt was $447 million ($492 million). Sales were $3.2 billion ($2.9 billion), cost of goods sold was $2.0 billion ($1.8 billion), and net income was $230 million ($188 million).

LOTT Ltd.'s financial statements are prepared in accordance with Canadian generally accepted accounting principles.

Below are details of three of LOTT Ltd.'s intercorporate investments.

Tundra Satellite Inc.

Ten years ago, LOTT Ltd. was one of the first backers of a new Canadian company, Tundra Satellite Inc. (Tundra). LOTT Ltd. purchased the long-term notes payable of Tundra. LOTT Ltd. and Tundra's bank still provide all the long-term financing.

Tundra's initial business was the provision of television and radio signals by satellite to remote communities throughout the country. The company's operations have expanded over the years to include cross-border transmission. Recently Tundra has entered into negotiations to set up a business arrangement in the Confederation of Independent States.

LOTT Ltd. found Tundra an attractive operation, because it predicted that more efficient satellite communication would soon replace land lines in data transmission. Receiving dishes are now less than two metres in diameter. Uses of these dishes include the transmission of stock market information and cellular telephone communication.

When Tundra became a public company three years ago, LOTT Ltd. purchased $600,000 of the preferred shares as part of its long-term investment strategy. Tundra has never declared dividends on these shares.

LOTT Ltd. and Tundra have cooperated on several projects in the development of specialized voice and data digital networks. Tundra's reputation for innovation and quality has developed quickly, and requests for development proposals are being received from all over the world.

After five years of start-up losses, Tundra began to generate profits; these profits have grown steadily during the past five years. Tundra's common share price has ranged from $10.50 to $13.75 in 1992. (Refer to Tundra's most recent comparative balance sheet and income statements in Exhibit 1.)

During the last quarter of 1992, LOTT Ltd., through several of its subsidiaries, began acquiring common shares of Tundra. The acquisitions stopped in late November; by that time, the LOTT group had acquired 46 percent of Tundra's outstanding common shares for cash. There are no plans to acquire any of the remaining common shares.

Most of the other outstanding shares are in small lots; the next largest block after LOTT Ltd. is 10 percent. Tundra's 12-member board of directors holds a total of 28 percent of the outstanding common shares (there is no representative from LOTT Ltd. on Tundra's board).

Las Palmas

LOTT Ltd. founded Las Palmas, a wholly owned South American company, 16 years ago. The country's government provided substantial low-cost debt financing to help in Las Palmas's establishment, because the

EXHIBIT 1

TUNDRA SATELLITE INC.
Balance Sheet
December 31

	1992	*1991*
Assets		
Current:		
Accounts receivable	$ 4,976,000	$ 4,594,000
Prepaid expenses and deposits	565,600	826,100
Inventories	1,787,800	2,030,800
Notes receivable—current portion	36,000	231,000
Total current assets	7,365,400	7,681,900
Notes receivable	1,835,400	1,517,400
Capital assets	13,091,000	18,112,200
Development projects	9,434,200	7,659,200
Investments	2,296,600	1,696,600
Total assets	$34,022,600	$36,667,300
Liabilities and Shareholders' Equity		
Current:		
Accounts payable and accrued liabilities	1,869,200	2,013,500
Notes payable—current portion	175,000	150,000
Total current liabilities	2,044,200	2,163,500
Unearned revenue	881,700	708,000
Long-term debt:		
Bank term loan	7,395,600	18,524,000
Notes payable	800,000	750,000
Total liabilities	8,195,600	19,274,000
Shareholders' Equity		
Capital stock:		
Preferred shares, 8 percent, nonvoting, noncumulative	715,000	715,000
Common shares	38,000,000	37,814,100
Deficit	(15,813,900)	(24,007,300)
Total shareholders' equity	22,901,100	14,521,800
Total liabilities and shareholders' equity	$34,022,600	$36,667,300

EXHIBIT 1 *(concluded)*

TUNDRA SATELLITE INC.
Income Sheet
Years Ended December 31

	1992	*1991*
Revenues	$40,178,200	$36,431,000
Direct costs	16,393,600	17,192,400
Administration and selling expenses	9,918,400	8,480,100
Total	$26,312,000	$25,672,500
Operating income	13,866,200	10,758,500
Interest on long-term debt	1,604,000	2,584,800
Amortization	4,068,800	4,192,800
Income before income taxes	8,193,400	3,980,900
Income taxes:		
Current	4,602,000	2,945,600
Deferred	(1,028,300)	(1,225,600)
Reduction of income taxes due to application of prior years' losses	(3,573,700)	(1,720,000)
Net income	$ 8,193,400	$ 3,980,900
Net income per common share	$0.80	$0.39
Weighted average number of common shares outstanding during the year	10,300,000	10,204,000

new enterprise would provide jobs and training for many citizens. The Las Palmas factory does all the manufacturing and sells to numerous South American governments and businesses.

Over the years, LOTT Ltd.'s senior managers from all over the world have accepted three-year postings to Las Palmas. The government is stable, inflation is under control, the lifestyle is appealing, and the managers benefit from the experience of working in another language and culture.

The host country government placed some restrictions on LOTT Ltd. when Las Palmas was incorporated. The restrictions were in return for the low-cost debt and for favourable tax treatment.

The most significant restriction was that 85 percent of annual income had to stay in the country. The company could either reinvest the funds to benefit the employees or could use them for other purposes that would further the government's social objectives. LOTT Ltd. has always complied with this requirement. There have been many years when LOTT

Ltd. has not repatriated any funds. The investment in Las Palmas has never been consolidated with LOTT Ltd.'s results, nor has equity accounting been used.

The People's Union

In November 1992, LOTT Ltd. acquired a 60 percent interest in The People's Union, a company located in eastern Europe. The host country's government retained 40 percent of the ownership. The government was eager to attract international capital, and it placed few restrictions on the company's activities. LOTT Ltd. wanted to establish a base to participate in the increasingly open eastern European economy.

The host country had a history of strong government, supported by the military. In mid-1992, there were rumours of discontent in the country. LOTT Ltd.'s board of directors believed that the government could deal with any threats. In January 1993, the military overthrew the existing government and assumed power. The new leaders assured LOTT Ltd.'s board that the situation was "business as usual." However, the board decided reduce their exposure and quickly adopted a formal plan of disposal, with the intention to sell the investment in The People's Union and withdraw from the country.

Required

As LOTT Ltd.'s new controller, you have been asked for advice on the appropriate December 31, 1992, financial statement presentation for the investments in Tundra Satellite Inc., Las Palmas, and The People's Union.

Case 55

MacDonald Limited

MacDonald Ltd. (ML) is controlled by the Harnish family and has been in operation for seven years, manufacturing and selling blank tapes for use in VCRs. Presently, the Harnish family owns 70 percent of the shares, with the remaining 30 percent owned by a wealthy entrepreneur, David MacIntosh. The shareholders judge the success of the company on its cash flow available for salary and dividend distribution. Harold Harnish, the largest shareholder, is ML's president. The tapes have been well received in the marketplace due to their quality, price, and shrewd marketing. To break into the large U.S. market, ML has just set up a subsidiary in the United States called MacDonald U.S. Ltd. (MUSL). While Canadian operations have been quite successful, MUSL is not expected to be profitable for two to three years due to fierce competition in their chosen market.

Bill Countway, an assistant to the controller, noted the following:

1. Tape packaging material is purchased from Packing Unlimited, a company in which Harold Harnish has a 40 percent interest. Packaging material costs amount to 6 percent of the cost of production.
2. ML provides data processing services to MUSL. Further, ML's controller, Dave Corkum, goes to Buffalo, New York, once a week to review the accounting records. MUSL is not charged for these services. Dave explained to Bill that there is no point in doing so because MUSL is expected to be in a tax-loss situation for several years.
3. MUSL purchases all its tapes from ML. It also sells cassette tapes (35 percent of its sales) but it buys these from a Japanese supplier.
4. Of MUSL's sales, 50 percent are to one department store chain. MUSL's management are confident about increasing sales to this chain at a pace faster than sales to other retail outlets.

Adapted, with permission from the Atlantic School of Chartered Accountancy.

EXHIBIT 1 MacDonald U.S. Limited, Trial Balance

MACDONALD UNITED STATES LIMITED
Trial Balance
December 31, 1994
(U.S. dollars)

	Dr	*Cr*
Cash	$ 40,000	
Accounts receivable	329,000	
Allowance for doubtful accounts		$ 10,000
Inventory (closing)	200,000	
Plant and equipment	539,000	
Accumulated depreciation		18,000
Accounts payable		410,000
Long-term debt		500,000
Common shares		300,000
Retained earnings		—
Sales		1,040,000
Cost of goods sold	860,000	
Expenses	310,000	
Total	$2,278,000	$2,278,000

Other Information

1. The subsidiary commenced business on July 1, 1994, at which time its only assets were an inventory of $100,000 and cash of $200,000, and the common share investment of the parent for $300,000.
2. Fixed assets and the 10-year term loan were acquired on July 15, 1994.
3. Purchases, sales, and other expenses were incurred evenly over the third and fourth quarters. Closing inventory related primarily to fourth quarter purchases.
4. $300,000 of MUSL's accounts payable are to ML. ML has recorded these at $370,000.
5. Selected exchange rates:

	$1 U.S. =
July 1, 1994	$1.43 Cdn.
July 15, 1994	$1.41 Cdn.
December 31, 1994	$1.33 Cdn.
3rd quarter average, 1994	$1.39 Cdn.
4th quarter average, 1994	$1.35 Cdn.

5. MUSL has borrowed U.S. $500,000 from a U.S. bank. The loan has a 10-year term. ML has guaranteed the loan for its subsidiary.

The company controller has asked Bill to consider the foreign currency translation policy that should be adopted to account for the U.S. subsidiary. The trial balance for the subsidiary is given in Exhibit 1. Regardless of your conclusion, he has asked you to translate the trial balance into Canadian dollars using both the temporal method and the current rate method, explaining the likely impact of the differences.

Required

Assume the role of Bill Countway and respond to the requests of the controller.

Case 56

Macintosh Ltd.

On February 1, 1992, Macintosh Ltd., a Canadian company, purchased shares in Overseas Co. for Foreign Currency (FC) 10,000. At the time of the acquisition 1 FC = $1 Cdn. Although Macintosh Ltd. frequently exports and imports goods, this is the only time that the company has invested overseas. There are no business transactions with this particular country. Macintosh Ltd. acquired the shares as a temporary holding, since management was predicting a sudden and dramatic increase in Overseas Co.'s share price; hence, the investment was classified as a current asset. On March 1, 1992, when the exchange rate was still 1 FC = $1 Cdn., Macintosh Ltd. entered into a futures contract to sell 10,000 FCs. The contract matures on March 1, 1993, and the rate in the contract is 1 FC = $1.10 Cdn. The proceeds from the sale of shares will be used to discharge the contract.

Macintosh Ltd.'s year-end is December 31. Unfortunately, Overseas Co. had a bad year, and the market value of Macintosh's shares is 8,000 FC at year-end. Financial analysts are very pessimistic about the share price ever recovering, and Macintosh Ltd.'s board of directors has approved a policy of no further speculative investments for the company.

The exchange rate at December 31, 1992, is 1 FC = $0.90 Cdn.

Required

Discuss the measurement and disclosure issues for Macintosh Ltd., including calculations where necessary.

Institute of Chartered Accountants of Ontario, adapted.

Case 57

Maple Farm

Jason Thomas, the owner of Maple Farm, has recently asked you to reconsider one of the bases on which you prepare his annual financial statements. You have always valued his herd at purchase price, recognizing revenue when the cattle were sold. However, Jason is approaching retirement and will be putting his operation up for sale within the next five years as he has no heirs. He wishes to show the most favourable history possible to prospective buyers.

Maple Farm is a feedlot operation located in southwestern Ontario. A feedlot farm is one which buys cattle from beef cow farms and fattens them for slaughter. The operation may also use part of the herd for breeding, then fatten their own calves, but the primary source of revenue is the sale of younger animals (heifers and steers) which bring higher prices than those which have been bred and are, therefore, older (cows and bulls). Cattle are purchased from the beef cow farms when they are 6 to 12 months old and are sold for slaughter at between 18 and 24 months. Occasionally a heifer will have been used to produce one calf before sale.

Several events have changed the competition in the livestock industry. In 1984, Alberta experienced its worst drought in 50 years, resulting in a sell-off of cows because of a lack of feed for the winter months. The Alberta beef cows were purchased by feeder operations in provinces where government subsidies designed to protect producers from unfavourable market conditions have actually stimulated entry into the feeding business. In spite of this activity, overcapacity exists in slaughter houses. (Cow slaughter in western Canada fell 22.1 percent between 1984 and 1986.) In addition, consumers have become more aware of the risk of high-fat diets, particularly with the publication of studies linking these diets with the incidence of cancer and heart disease. In 1985, the beef industry began an information campaign to address some of the concerns and misconceptions about beef consumption.

Thomas's draft balance sheet and income statement are attached (Exhibit 1). He has requested that the increase in the value of his herd be recognized as the cattle are fattened, rather than having to wait until the stockyard sales. Thomas points out that all cattle are sold. The only variance may be the price per pound, which is dependent on the age and grade of the animal and market conditions. The market is guaranteed, as

EXHIBIT 1

MAPLE FARM
Balance Sheet (draft)
December 31, 1991

Assets	
Current assets:	
Cash	$ 5,781
Accounts receivable	7,357
Market livestock	186,722
Home-grown crops	53,315
Purchased feed and supplies	7,256
Intermediate assets:	
Field machinery	110,880
Barn equipment	9,011
Long-term assets:	
Land	226,555
Farm buildings	105,653
Total farm assets	$712,530
Liabilities	
Accounts payable	$ 6,736
Other current debt	126,495
Intermediate debt	35,147
Long-term debt	84,198
Total farm liabilities	252,576
Equity in farm business	$459,954

MAPLE FARM
Selected Statistics for Year Ended December 31, 1991

Average selling price per head	$942
Average selling weight per head	1,133 lb.
Average buying price per head	$642
Average buying weight per head	681 lb.
Average rate of gain per day	1.87 lb.
Death loss	5 head

EXHIBIT 1 *(concluded)*

MAPLE FARM
Income Statement (Draft)
Year Ended December 31, 1991

Revenue:	
Cattle	$390,264
Crop sales	47,468
Total cash revenue	$437,732
Change in receivables	1,298
Inventory change:	
Home-grown crops	(7,027)
Supplies and purchased feed	2,535
Market livestock	(5,643)
Total farm revenue	$428,895
Expenses:	
Livestock expenses:	
Purchased livestock	$247,291
Purchased feed	27,861
Veterinary and medicine	2,537
Marketing and trucking	4,770
Stable supplies	2,231
Crop expenses:	
Seed and plants	6,999
Fertilizer and pesticides	18,995
Crop insurance	243
Crop drying	348
Allocated expenses:	
Hired labour	12,251
Gas, oil, and fuel	9,964
Repairs	14,226
Hydro, telephone	2,091
Taxes, insurance	6,845
Car and house expenses	1,551
Interest (term)	10,092
Interest (operating)	12,882
Total cash expenses	$381,177
Change in current payables	nil
Amortization	18,673
Total farm expenses	$399,850
Net farm income	$ 29,045

provinces with government subsidies will buy Ontario cattle if the Ontario price weakens. In addition, falling herd sizes will assist in price maintenance.

Required

Describe how a change in the timing of revenue recognition would affect Thomas's statements. Present your recommendation.

Case 58

Maxicon Steel Corporation

"Well, I'm confused!" With this disgusted comment, your roommate dumped the 1989 Maxicon Steel Corporation annual report on your desk. "These tax amounts don't make sense to me. Can you explain them?" (See extracts, Exhibit 1.) As an intelligent and industrious accounting student, you cheerfully agree to explain everything—you hope!

"What bothers me is the provision for taxes. How can a company that has a loss of $3,310 recover $7,516 in tax? That's $2.27 in tax saving for every $1.00 of loss! And how much of the $7,516 is an actual refund to Maxicon, anyway? Maybe you should show me a journal entry!

EXHIBIT 1 Maxicon Steel Corporation Financial Statement Extracts

MAXICON STEEL CORPORATION
December 31, 1989
(all amounts in thousands)
from the Statement of Earnings

	1989	*1988*
Earnings (loss):		
Before income taxes	$ (3,310)	$ 52,264
Income tax expense (recovery)	(7,516)	11,657
Net earnings	$ 4,206	$ 40,607

EXHIBIT 1 (*continued*)

MAXICON STEEL CORPORATION
December 31, 1989
(all amounts in thousands)
from the Statement of Financial Position

	1989	*1988*
Other liabilities:		
Long-term debt	$248,847	$315,964
Deferred income taxes	47,902	57,765
Accrual for pension and other post-employment benefits	15,778	6,534
Provision for relining blast furnaces	16,623	5,498
Unamortized exchange gains on foreign currencies	1,410	4,198
Total	$330,560	$389,959

from the Statement of Changes in Financial Position

	1989	*1988*
Cash provided from (used for) operating activities:		
Operations (note 14)	33,472	64,939
Decrease (increase) in operating working capital	$ 47,064	(51,271)
Total	$ 80,536	$ 13,668

from the Summary of Significant Accounting Policies

Income taxes — The Corporation follows the tax allocation method of providing for income taxes. Under this method, timing differences between reported and taxable income result in deferred income taxes.

from the Notes to the Financial Statements

1. Changes in Accounting Policies and Restatement of Prior Years' Financial Statements

Effective January 1, 1989, the Corporation changed its accounting policies as follows:

(4) The Corporation adopted the revised recommendations of the Canadian Institute of Chartered Accountants respecting extraordinary items. Accordingly, income tax benefits from loss carry-forwards not previously recorded by United States subsidiaries, of $1.0 million and $3.7 million in 1989 and 1988, respectively, are included with income taxes in the Statement of Earnings. Previously, such tax benefits were disclosed as extraordinary items. There is no effect on net earnings.

EXHIBIT 1 *(continued)*

MAXICON STEEL CORPORATION
December 31, 1989
(all amounts in thousands)
from the Statement of Financial Position

2. Income Taxes

The provision for income taxes in the Statement of Earnings (in thousands of dollars) is comprised of:

	1989	*1988*
Current	$ 2,879	$ 2,215
Deferred—provision for current year	(9,378)	13,103
Benefit resulting from application of prior years' losses	(1,017)	(3,661)
Total	$ (7,516)	$ 11,657

A reconciliation of the provision for income taxes to amounts computed by applying the income tax rates of the various jurisdictions in which the Corporation operates to earnings and losses before income taxes is as follows (in thousands of dollars):

	1989	*1988*
Income taxes computed at statutory income tax rates	$ (3,149)	$ 22,203
Increases (decreases) resulting from:		
Nonrecognition of tax benefit of current year's losses for tax purposes	748	—
Interest expense on income debentures	1,456	1,480
Application of prior years' losses	(1,017)	(3,661)
Manufacturing and processing allowance	308	(1,500)
Federal and provincial resource allowances	(8,306)	(5,582)
Canadian and United States minimum taxes	1,772	543
Other	672	(1,826)
Total	$ (7,516)	$ 11,657

As at December 31, 1989, a Canadian subsidiary of the Corporation had operating losses of approximately $1.8 million, the income tax benefit of which has not been reflected in these financial statements.

EXHIBIT 1 *(concluded)*

MAXICON STEEL CORPORATION
December 31, 1989
(all amounts in thousands)
from the Notes to the Financial Statements

14. Cash Provided from Operations

	1989	*1988*
Net earnings	$ 4,206	$ 40,607
Items not affecting cash:		
Depreciation and amortization	42,628	40,674
Other noncash operating costs	5,670	1,156
Deferred income taxes	(9,378)	13,103
Other (net)	(5,293)	(3,456)
Blast furnace reline expenditures	(13,615)	(20,325)
Pension and other post-employment benefit expense in excess of funding	9,254	(6,820)
Total	$ 33,472	$ 64,939

"While you're at it, you could tell me what Maxicon has done with their loss carry-forwards. Why do they show up on the 1989 income statement when they relate to prior years? And what is the change in accounting policies all about? What's different?"

"I'd like you to explain the rationale behind tax allocation and tax-loss accounting."

Gamely, you pick up the financial statements and begin to frame an answer to these questions.

Required

Respond to your roommate's questions.

Case 59

McBeans Ltd.

McBeans Ltd. was incorporated in Canada in 1982. It was a private company closely held by the Burton family. The company owned fast-food outlets; the main dish on the menu was chili. Customers could order hot, medium, or lightly spiced servings so all members of a family could enjoy the meal. Sales increased rapidly, and by the end of 1983 the company had over a dozen outlets and was taking steps to expand across the country. All outlets were company owned and the board of directors felt that McBeans would benefit from having the majority of the subsequent outlets operated as franchises; this would take the day-to-day, on-site operating pressures off head office and help develop a team of highly motivated managers, while promoting a consistent image for the company and the product. It would also allow for expansion without having to issue shares to the public. During the next four years almost all the McBeans opened were franchises. The units were primarily located along major roads and highways, rather than in shopping centres; customers could park on the unit's property and eat in the restaurant or use the take-out service. With the increase in meals eaten away from home and the tasty, reasonably priced product, the large bright McBeans sign became well known along Canadian roads.

In July 1994, Catherine Anderson, the manager in charge of the McBeans audit, was called to a meeting at the Winnipeg head office to discuss the upcoming 1994 audit, some possible changes in the financial statements, and preparation of a prospectus for a public share offering. The following is an excerpt from the remarks made at the meeting by Bob Stewart, McBeans VP of finance:

> Catherine, there's an accounting treatment required by Section 3450 that has been applied to our results more strictly than I believe was the *Handbook's* intention. I'm referring to the section on research and development, of course. Certain of our costs are being defined as research and are being expensed immediately, while others are treated as development and aren't expensed until the new menu item is introduced in the outlets.

Our development process actually begins much earlier than the point at which we're accumulating costs that can be deferred. You and the members of the audit team have all been on a tour of our test kitchen here at head office so you've seen the type of activities that go on. Our staff tries various levels and types of preservatives in the chili to ensure that each batch will taste freshly cooked. They also experiment with different spices to produce a varied menu. They test the flavour and consistency effect of cooling the mix and reheating it, and they also blend various ratios of the meat, beans, peppers, tomatoes, and spices to minimize cooking time for the product. Of course, we also do menu planning here so all ages of customers can eat a balanced, nutritious meal at any McBeans. When we've decided on a particular blend of ingredients we hold dinners for our staff and invited guests to get their reaction to the item.

We've had to expense the costs of all the test kitchen activities as they were incurred, and this seems unreasonable. Every product on the McBeans menu has been developed incorporating the knowledge from our kitchen's activities. This is where we devise a satisfactory ratio of ingredients for an item which will be introduced to our outlets, and you insist that we immediately expense all the costs associated with that item. Catherine, all test batches are *development*! Every one brings us closer to the final product which will appear on our menu, even if we subsequently decide that the particular item isn't going to be adopted (remember when we were working on new desserts and we invented Pink Punk ice cream with the cookie shaped like a razor blade sticking out of it? The board of directors didn't think that fit our family image so we modified the recipe slightly and produced our highly successful Strawberry Cloud dish). You won't let us start deferring costs until we begin modifying our production line for a new item. Our selling price doesn't just cover the costs incurred when production begins; we have months of prior expenses to recover in that price.

What I'd like to do is to treat all the test kitchen expenses as development. I'd be happy to include in the notes a breakdown between expenditures on the test kitchen and the products in production. Readers know that a careful study of the notes is essential to understanding a company's performance, and they can calculate the effect on the statements of other treatments.

Required

Assume the role of Catherine Anderson and respond to Bob Stewart's suggestions.

Case 60

McGraw Corporation

McGraw Corporation is a medium-sized, privately held Canadian corporation which operates retail stores across Canada selling a wide variety of home exercise equipment. The company was founded in the mid-1970s by a group of entrepeneurs who were convinced that there was an opportunity for a company which catered to the physical fitness boom. After a slow start, McGraw prospered and, in 1994, it owned more than 50 stores.

The company's 1994 fiscal year has just ended and you, as assistant controller, have been involved in preparing draft financial statements. The executive committee, consisting of the company president, four vice presidents, and the controller, spent all Monday morning reviewing the draft financial statements, which you, as assistant controller, had helped prepare.

Following the meeting, Joe Wilson, the controller, called you into his office to brief you on the proceedings. After thanking you for your work on the financial statements, and passing along the general comments of the executive committee, he outlined a number of issues he wished you to investigate.

The committee discussed various changes in accounting policy and practice for the 1994 fiscal year. An inventory accounting error was also discussed. The committee wished to have an explanation of how each item should be reflected in the financial statements and, if possible, of each item's separate dollar impact on net income for 1994. The notes that Mr. Wilson took during the meeting are shown in Exhibit 1.

Also, the committee spent time discussing existing accounting policies and some alternatives which might be adopted in the future. Several committee members were confused about the pros and cons of the alternatives and the effects they would have on the firm's operating results and financial position. Mr. Wilson's notes on this discussion are in Exhibit 2.

Society of Management Accountants, adapted.

EXHIBIT 1 Notes from Financial Statements Review Meeting, Proposed Changes for 1994

1. Change in depreciation method:
   - Was straight-line, $400,000 per year.
   - Proposed change to declining balance, $600,000 for 1994 fiscal year.
   - Based on decision to conform more closely to CCA methods to reduce deferred taxes.
   - Uncertain about whether information is available to restate specific prior years.
2. Leasehold improvements:
   - Leasehold improvements of $450,000 made in fiscal year 1991, useful life estimated at 10 years.
   - "Improvements" now obsolete, major renovations planned for early next month. Useful life should have been four years.
   - President suggests writing undepreciated balance off to retained earnings as cost should have been matched to revenues in prior periods. If not, president favors extraordinary item treatment of write-off.
3. Inventory error:
   - Error in determination of the closing inventory, fiscal year 1992, discovered last week.
   - Inventory as reported approximately $200,000 understated.

Note: Tax rate is 45 percent.

EXHIBIT 2 Notes from Financial Statement Review Meeting, Proposed Policies for Future Implementation

1. Inventory:
   - Proposed change is from FIFO to LIFO inventory valuation.
   - LIFO closing inventory value about $500,000 lower than FIFO for 1994.
   - LIFO opening inventory about $700,000 lower than FIFO for 1994.
   - Other Canadian companies generally use FIFO.
2. Doubtful Accounts:
   - Existing policy is to age receivables and estimate uncollectible portion based on past experience.
   - Proposed change is direct write-off of accounts as soon as they are deemed uncollectible.
   - Tighter credit policy to be instituted for fiscal year 1995.
   - Vice president of administration expects improved collections.
3. Bond Interest:
   - 25-year, $10 million debenture issued in fiscal year 1994, at 1 percent discount amortized on a straight-line basis.
   - Proposal is to use the effective interest method.
4. Warranty Expense:
   - Results from two-year product guarantee on electronic exercise bicycles being offered in fiscal year 1995 for the first time.
   - One alternative is to write off expenses as incurred.
   - Proposed method is to estimate and accrue cost.

To satisfy investors and creditors, management would like to present a steady growth in accounting income. A significant portion of the company's financing is obtained through bank loans, and the bank loan agreements require audited financial statements.

Mr. Wilson has asked you to prepare a report, complete with your recommendations, to be circulated to the members of the executive committee.

Required

Write the report requested by Mr. Wilson.

Case 61

Megadata Ltd.

Megadata Ltd. is a Canadian public corporation with head office in Montreal and branch operations located all over the world. The company is a developer of computer software and provides custom software and predesigned packages to its customers. The related services include scientific and engineering applications, business data processing, education (computer-based training and education is provided through a network of vocational schools established by Megadata), consulting, health care, and small business services. Customers can share the resources of large-scale computer systems or integrate on-site mini- and microcomputing capabilities with proprietary or licenced software and custom-designed data bases. Megadata also offers specialized information services in audience measurement, sports and entertainment ticketing, and a variety of finance and securities industry applications.

The Megadata group includes the operating company and a number of subsidiaries, two of which are Megadata Credit Company Ltd. and Megadata International Banking Corporation (both are wholly owned). Megadata Credit Company Ltd. is engaged in casualty, business credit, and life insurance. The operations of Megadata International Banking Corporation include leasing and consumer and business financing services.

In 1991, Megadata began reporting the activities of Megadata Credit Company Ltd. on a consolidated basis. Previously, the equity method of accounting was used. In a related change, the balance sheet classification of assets and liabilities as current or noncurrent was eliminated because of the significance of nonclassified financial accounts. In its 1991 annual report, management noted that:

> The consolidation method is intended to provide shareholders a more appropriate and complete view of Megadata than did the previous method. The change is due to an evolutionary process of increasing similarities in the businesses of Megadata Ltd. and Megadata Credit Company Ltd., particularly as to small businesses services.

MEGADATA LTD.
Consolidated Balance Sheet
December 31, 1992
(in thousands)

	Restated for Policy Change	*Previous Policy*
Assets		
Cash	$ 8,910	$ 10,390
Information Services/Products:		
Trade and other receivables	52,380	52,380
Inventories	66,760	66,760
Leased and data centre equipment	40,160	40,160
Property, plant, and equipment	30,290	30,290
Financial Services:		
Finance receivables	375,740	339,470
Marketable securities	97,850	93,240
Property, plant, and equipment	3,580	3,580
Other assets	47,470	54,920
Total assets	$723,140	$691,190
Liabilities		
Accounts payable and accrued liabilities	$ 78,160	$ 77,180
Debt obligations	401,800	370,710
Deferred income taxes	12,930	13,050
Noncontrolling interests in consolidated subsidiaries	4,370	4,370
Other liabilities	53,380	53,380
Total liabilities	$550,640	$518,690
Shareholders' Equity		
4.5% cumulative preferred stock, $100 par, authorized 37,114 shares, issued 11,492 shares	$ 1,150	$ 1,150
Common stock, $0.50 par, authorized 10,000,000 shares, issued 3,752,063 shares	1,880	1,880
Additional paid-in capital	48,000	48,000
Retained earnings	123,590	123,590
Other items decreasing shareholders' equity	(2,120)	(2,120)
Total shareholders' equity	$172,500	$172,500
Total liabilities and shareholders' equity	$723,140	$691,190

MEGADATA LTD.
Consolidated Income Statement
Year Ended December 31, 1992
(in thousands except per share earnings)

	Restated for Policy Change	*Previous Policy*
Revenues:		
Information Services/Products:		
Net sales	$169,890	$169,890
Services	123,900	123,900
Rentals	36,320	36,320
Total	$330,110	$330,110
Financial Services:		
Interest and discounts	66,900	62,230
Insurance premiums	26,830	26,830
Investment and other income	10,190	10,030
Total	103,920	99,090
Total revenues	$434,030	$429,200
Expenses:		
Information Services/Products:		
Cost of sales	$118,860	$118,860
Cost of services	72,420	72,420
Cost of rentals	12,740	12,740
Selling, general, administrative	69,300	69,300
Technical expenses	32,590	32,590
Interest expense	10,040	10,040
Total	$315,950	$315,950
Financial Services:		
Interest expense	$ 35,860	$ 32,340
Operating expenses	32,920	32,660
Provision for credit losses	5,430	5,350
Insurance losses and reserves	20,940	20,940
Total	95,150	91,290
Total expenses	$411,100	$407,240
Earnings before income taxes and other items:		
Information Services/Products	$ 14,160	$ 14,160
Financial Services	8,770	7,800
Total	22,930	21,960
Provision for income taxes	6,760	6,310
Earnings before other items	$ 16,170	$ 15,650
Noncontrolling interests and equity in operations of affiliates	(660)	(140)
Net earnings	$ 15,510	$ 15,510
Earnings per share	$ 4.11	$ 4.11

MEGADATA LTD.
Supplemental Information Treating
Megadata Credit Company Ltd.
as a Nonconsolidated Subsidiary
(in thousands except per share earnings)

Condensed balance sheet information (December 31, 1992):	
Current assets	$125,910
Investment in Megadata Credit Company Ltd.	80,850
Leased and data centre equipment	40,010
Property, plant, and equipment	28,750
Other assets	17,670
Total assets	$293,190
Liabilities and shareholders' equity:	
Current liabilities	$ 74,000
Long-term obligations, less current portions	13,180
Amounts due Megadata Credit Company Ltd., less current portions	22,340
Deferred income taxes	1,850
Other noncurrent liabilities	5,000
Noncontrolling interests in consolidated subsidiaries	4,320
Shareholders' equity	172,500
Total liabilities and shareholders' equity	$293,190
Condensed earnings information (year ended December 31, 1992):	
Revenue	$318,260
Expenses	301,770
Earnings before income taxes	$ 16,490
Provision for income taxes	4,650
Noncontrolling interests and equity in operations of affiliates	(890)
Net earnings excluding Megadata Credit	$ 10,950
Net earnings of Megadata Credit (equity method)	4,560
Net earnings	$ 15,510
Earnings per share	$4.11

Operations of Megadata Ltd. and Megadata Credit Company Ltd. are now principally reported as Information Services/Products and Financial Services, respectively. The computer-related small business services (revenues of approximately $10,000,000 in 1991) of Megadata Credit are, however, reported with Information Services/Products.

In 1992, Megadata Ltd.'s management began consolidating the results of Megadata International Banking Corporation. The Accounting Policies note mentioned that the statements included the accounts of Megadata

Credit and that the accounts of most of the international subsidiaries were included as of November 30 to facilitate timely reporting. A separate note, entitled "Changes in Basis of Consolidation and Accounting Principle," stated that:

> Effective January 1, 1992, Megadata Ltd. has changed its method of accounting for its investment in Megadata International Banking Corporation from the equity method to consolidation. Management believes that consolidation is preferable because it provides a more comprehensive view of the company's financial position and results of operations since the lending and funding activities of Megadata International are very similar to other financial services businesses of Megadata Ltd. Prior years' financial statements have been restated; however, the change had no effect on net earnings or shareholders' equity.

Required

Assess (individually) the impact that consolidation of Megadata International Banking Corporation and Megadata Credit Company Ltd. had on the results of Megadata Ltd. Is consolidation of these results more or less informative than the previous presentation?

Case 62

Metro City Art Gallery

The Metro City Art Gallery (MCAG) is the leading art gallery in Canada. MCAG has the largest art collection in Canada and usually mounts four to six major exhibits per year, both national and international in scope. The Metro City area, served by MCAG, has a population base of 4 million people.

During the 1993 fiscal year, it became increasingly obvious that there would be a large (unplanned) deficit for the year. The original budget for 1993 showed MCAG in a break-even position, following a devastating deficit of $1,500,000 in 1992. The original 1993 budget had based improvements in operating results on a major membership drive that was expected to raise over $1 million in incremental revenues. Additional bottom-line improvements were expected from a reduction in staffing levels and from severe restraint on operating expenditures.

Unfortunately, by the third quarter of 1993, revised budgets showed a projected 1993 deficit of $1,400,000 (see Exhibit 1). Staff indicated three reasons for the shortfall. First, the membership drive in the first quarter, which was very successful, did not increase 1993 revenues as expected. Second, MCAG received disappointing grant support from Metro City and the province. Finally, MCAG had cancelled a major international exhibit in the second quarter of 1993, because costs, especially insurance, could not be accommodated within MCAG's tight budget. Attendance fell accordingly.

Tristan Akerly-Smith is a member of the board of directors. The board will shortly be asked to make decisions relating to the operating policies to be followed in 1994. The goal will be to break even or try to recover part of the operating shortfall of 1992 and 1993. Some measures that have been suggested are: further staff cuts, reduced advertising, reduced hours of operation, closure of conservation and research areas, drastic curtail-

---

Adapted, with permission, from the Atlantic School of Chartered Accountancy.

EXHIBIT 1 Metro City Art Gallery Financial Information—Operations

METRO CITY ART GALLERY
Statement of Income and Expenditures
(in thousands)

	1993 (Budget; Revised)*	1992
Revenues:		
Memberships	$ 680	$ 420
Admission fees	800	890
Government grant—provincial	1,425†	1,425
Government grant—city	1,200†	1,100
Contributions	415	475
Endowment fund revenue	942	786
Course fees; auxiliary service revenue	175	149
Total revenues	5,637	5,245
Expenditures:		
Salaries and benefits	4,100	3,800
Custodial and insurance	1,142	1,073
Depreciation	760	695
Other operating costs	1,035	1,177
Total expenditures	7,037	6,745
Excess of expenditures over revenues	$1,400	$1,500

* Three quarters at actual; fourth quarter at budget.
† At actual; original budget showed $1,825 and $1,400, respectively, for provincial and city grants.

Accounting Policies—Operations

1. Admission fees are recognized as monies are collected, as are "contributions," or unrestricted donations to cover operating costs.
2. Income from membership fees is recognized as time passes; for example, a four-year membership, paid in advance as required, would be recognized in income evenly over the four-year period.

Cash collections have been as follows (000s):

	1990	*1991*	*1992*	*1993*
One year	$292	$295	$310	$400
Two year	47	51	58	60
Four-year*	—	—	220	664

* New in 1992.

EXHIBIT 1 *(concluded)*

METRO CITY ART GALLERY
Accounting Policies—Operations

3. MCAG capitalizes all operational fixed assets at acquisition cost, which is fair market value. Depreciation is charged on all fixed assets as follows:

Office equipment	straight-line	10 years
Automobiles	straight-line	4 years
Facilities	straight-line	40 years

   "Facilities" represents the MCAG premises, which was newly built in 1989 at a capital cost of $20 million. It was fully funded by provincial, federal, civic, and private donations, as are all operational assets.
4. Additions to the art collection are made from segregated funds and capitalized in that fund. Detail in this exhibit covers only operating and certain endowment activities.
5. Endowment fund revenue is recorded as received and consists of interest and dividends received, as well as realized capital gains. Operating endowment fund revenue as reported in this statement is available to cover operating expenditures in an unrestricted fashion. Restricted endowment fund activity is recorded in a separate fund.
6. Volunteer services are not recorded.

ment of special exhibits, summer programs, community education programs, and so on.

Mr. Akerly-Smith has asked you, CA, to examine the financial statements and accounting policies and to comment on whether you think these policies are appropriate. His concern is that the financial statements were designed for members, contributors, and government bodies that provide monetary support to MCAG. He has asked you to consider whether:

1. The statements are appropriate for the contributor group.
2. The statements are appropriate for the decisions at hand.

If present policies are not appropriate, a recommended alternative should be developed.

Required:

Write a report to Mr. Akerly-Smith, dealing with the issues raised. *Do not* comment on the proposals for 1994 cost-cutting.

Case 63

Midnight Express Ltd.

Midnight Express Ltd. is a trucking company and an audit client of the CA firm where you are employed. The company is privately owned, and it has an audit primarily to satisfy the chartered bank that provides long-term, fixed-rate financing for its truck fleet and short-term demand loans to finance working capital requirements at various peak seasons.

Doug McKenzie, the controller, is a competent professional who believes in giving the auditors "a hard time." One of his recurring themes is accounting rules that Midnight must follow to get an unqualified audit report—and that McKenzie does not agree with or does not think meaningful.

Two weeks before this year's audit field work was to begin, Mr. McKenzie sent a letter to the partner-in-charge of the audit, outlining his objections to comprehensive tax allocation and deferred taxes (see Exhibit 1). The partner has asked you to prepare some notes outlining McKenzie's objections and opposing arguments, for him to refer to in his upcoming discussion with Mr. McKenzie.

Required

Respond to the request of the partner.

EXHIBIT 1 Letter to Partner

Midnight Express Ltd.

January 14, 1994

Mr. Bob McGraw, Partner,
Audit & Co.,
100 Main Street,
Anytown, British Columbia

Dear Bob,

I wish to take this opportunity to lay out my objections to the accounting rules that require Midnight Express Ltd. to set up deferred taxes each year. If possible, I would like to eliminate this accounting policy for the 1993 year just ended.

First of all, the way our truck fleet has been growing, and is expected to grow over the foreseeable future, timing differences caused by the depreciation versus CCA problem will never reverse. If they never reverse, why should we set them up?

Even if we held our truck fleet at a constant size, the increase in truck prices would also guarantee that timing differences would not go down. This year we're replacing trucks that originally cost $27,000 with those costing $47,000. Some of this price differential is caused by a decision to upgrade the fleet, but the result is the same.

Secondly, our legal liability is only to pay the taxes payable on the tax form. Why set up this ''thing'' called deferred taxes when we don't owe it to anyone? After all, it's taxable income that incurs tax, not accounting income.

Finally, my bank manager, who is the major reason we have an audit and conform to all these rules, seems to be more interested in ''cash from operations'' than anything else. All he seems to be concerned about is that we can make our loan payments, and his calculations always seem to involve ''adding back'' things like deferred taxes. Why don't we produce statements that are tailored to his needs?

I look forward to seeing you and your staff in a couple of weeks when we will have the opportunity to discuss these issues further.

Yours truly,

Doug McKenzie

Case 64

Miller Manufacturing Limited

Miller Manufacturing is a small private company in the plastic molding business. The market is very competitive for these products, but Miller has a good reputation for quality products delivered on time.

Your firm, Audit & Co., has been appointed auditors of Miller for the 1994 fiscal year-end. Miller's bankers, who provide an operating line of credit secured by inventory and receivables, and long-term financing secured by capital assets, have requested an audit. Previously, Miller had your firm review the statements and attach a "Review Engagement Report," Audit & Co. also has prepared tax returns.

You are part of the audit team, and have been assigned to the capital assets section. Analysis of the various accounts has been provided to you (see Exhibits 1 and 2). The senior in charge of the audit has asked you to examine the accounts, comment on the acceptability of Miller's policies, and prepare any journal entries necessary.

Required

Respond to the requests of the audit senior.

EXHIBIT 1 Miller Manufacturing Limited—Capital Asset Accounts

Land

Balance, January 1, 1994	$400,000
Adjustment, November 22, 1994	320,000
Balance, December 31, 1994	$720,000

The "Adjustment" recorded increases land to its fair market value ($720,000) per appraiser's reports. The credit was made to "Unusual item—gain on land value increase," an income statement item.

Buildings

Balance, January 1, 1994	$329,000
Additions during year:	
New roof, June 24, 1994	20,000
Paint and general repairs, July 19, 1994	17,000
Balance, December 31, 1994	$366,000

Automotive Equipment

Balance, January 1, 1994	$41,900
Balance, December 31, 1994	$41,900

Note: During 1994, John Miller, the major shareholder, gave the company a 1990 Chevy Van, which his children had used but no longer wanted. No entry was made to record this asset, as it was acquired at no cost to the company. It was worth $5,000.

Manufacturing Equipment

Balance, January 1, 1994	$129,400
Additions during the year:	
Injection molder, March 31, 1994	12,000
Packaging equipment, December 31, 1994	6,000
Balance, December 31, 1994	$147,400

The injection molder was bought used, at a bankruptcy sale. Miller estimated it was really worth $17,000, but they got a bargain. It cost $2,000 to transport and install the machine. This was expensed.

Packaging equipment had an invoice price of $15,000. Miller got a $9,000 government grant, under an upgrading program, to partially offset the purchase price.

EXHIBIT 2 Miller Manufacturing Limited—Depreciation

Depreciation is recorded at rates sufficient to amortize the cost of capital assets over their useful life.

Buildings—4 percent, straight-line
Automotive—20 percent, straight-line
Equipment—15 percent, straight-line

A full year's depreciation is charged in the year of acquisition unless the item was not used in the year of acquisition, in which case no depreciation is charged.

Depreciation expense, buildings	$13,040

Note: An existing storage building, original cost, $40,000, was not used in 1994, so no depreciation was charged (matching).

Depreciation expense, automotive equipment	$ 8,380
Depreciation expense, manufacturing equipment	$22,110

Case 65

Mills' Audio Limited

Mills' Audio Limited was a small but aggressive company that began by manufacturing hearing aids, but it has since expanded into the production of speakers for car stereos. It was controlled by the company president and founder, Mr. T. Mills, who owned 63 percent of the company's shares. The remaining shares were owned by five individuals who all served on the company's board of directors.

At a recent meeting, the board had discussed possible ways to continue expansion, including going public. The board, therefore, asked Mr. Mills to meet with Jim Acta, the company controller, to discuss the preparation of the 1993 financial statements. Future expansion plans will depend on the profitability of the company in 1993, and the board needs an estimate of the pretax income as quickly as possible. In addition, the directors want to be advised of any accounting issues that may affect the estimated income and, thereby, influence the expansion plans.

Immediately after the meeting with the president, Jim Acta sat down with his assistant, Art Simpson, to discuss the financial statements for the year just ended. Art presented Jim with a first draft of the balance sheet and income statement for the year ended December 31, 1993 (Exhibit 1).

The following conversation ensued:

Jim:

I see you have made all of the usual adjusting entries. What problem areas did you run into this year?

Art:

First, our January 2, 1993, purchase of 30 percent of Lanibald Limited has yielded the results we expected. This year our purchases from Lanibald totaled $421,000 and inventory of their product at year-end totaled $50,000. They deliver twice as fast as last year, but sell to us on the same terms as anyone else. They work on a 25 percent markup over cost.

Institute of Chartered Accountants of Ontario, adapted.

EXHIBIT 1

MILLS' AUDIO LIMITED
Balance Sheet (first draft)
As at December 31, 1993

Assets	
Cash	$ 17,000
Accounts receivable	1,034,000
Inventory	1,320,000
Prepaid expenses	81,000
Total	2,452,000
Land	284,000
Building	493,000
Equipment	2,060,000
Accumulated amortization	(1,039,000)
Total	1,798,000
Investment in Lanibald Limited	300,000
Total assets	$ 4,550,000
Liabilities and Equity	
Bank loan	$ 190,000
Accounts payable	980,000
Accrued expenses and liabilities	240,000
Total	1,410,000
Promissory notes payable	225,000
Bonds payable	1,320,000
Term bank loan	420,000
Total	1,965,000
Capital stock	360,000
Retained earnings	815,000
Total liabilities and equity	$ 4,550,000
Revenue	$11,372,000
Cost of goods sold	9,458,000
Gross profit	1,914,000
Expenses:	
Administrative and selling	$ 910,000
Interest	268,000
Pension	196,000
Other	192,000
Total	$ 1,566,000
Income before income taxes	$ 348,000

EXHIBIT 2

LANIBALD LIMITED
Condensed Balance Sheet
At December 31, 1993

	Book Value	*Fair Value*
Current assets	$ 540,000	$555,000
Land	120,000	184,000
Plant (net)	180,000	220,000
Equipment (net)	345,000	345,000
Goodwill	10,000	?
Total	$1,195,000	
Current liabilities	$ 370,000	$370,000
Long-term debt	365,000	345,000
Common stock	125,000	—
Retained earnings	335,000	—
Total	$1,195,000	

1. All of the differences between fair value and book value of current assets relate to inventory.
2. The plant has a remaining useful life of 20 years.
3. The goodwill arose 10 years ago when Lanibald Limited purchased 100 percent of Mimdar Inc. The goodwill is being amortized over a 30-year period on a straight-line basis.
4. The long-term debt matures on December 31, 1997.

When we purchased the shares, I recorded it as a $300,000 investment. There had been five shareholders, each owning 20 percent of the common shares. We bought an equal amount from each one, so each now owns 14 percent. We paid each shareholder $15,000 cash and gave each a $45,000 note, noninterest bearing, due January 1, 1998, even though we would have borrowed at 12 percent from the bank. The promissory notes payable on our balance sheet are still recorded as $225,000. The details on acquisition book values and fair market values are here [Exhibit 2].

The Lanibald accountant says their consolidated net income for 1993 is $123,000. No dividends were declared and no common shares were issued during 1985. Our share has not been recorded on our draft statements, although it would be nice if we could justify increasing our income by including our share of Lanibald's income.

Jim:

I can see why Lanibald is a problem area. What's next?

EXHIBIT 3 Memorandum

To: Jim Acta
From: Art Simpson
Re: Equipment Lease

The details of the lease are as follows:

Effective date:	July 1, 1993.
Term:	10 years.
Payments:	$70,000 annual payments beginning July 1, 1993.
Disposition at the end of the lease:	Two options available at that date: Option A: pay $20,000 to acquire title to the equipment. Option B: return equipment and pay $20,000; lessor will refund proceeds when he sells equipment.

We could have purchased the equipment in July 1993 for:

Sales price:	$450,000.
Salvage value:	$30,000 at the end of 10 years; 0 at the end of its 12-year estimated useful life.
Bank interest rate:	12%.

Art:

We entered into an equipment lease agreement on July 1, 1993. The $70,000 annual payment was paid on that date. I expensed one half of it and set up the remainder as a prepaid on the draft statements. Here is a summary of the details [Exhibit 3].

Jim:

We will have to examine that in greater detail. What is number three on your list of problem areas?

Art:

The employees are very happy about the new pension plan introduced at the end of 1993. Each year of employment provides 2 percent of the employee's final year salary. It is a noncontributory plan; the average employee age is 36.

The actuary used the accrued benefit valuation method to project the present value of past service pension costs. We paid the trustee $96,000, which will provide for the past service obligation over the 15 years allowed by law. The current service costs were an additional $100,000. I recorded both of these amounts as pension expense. It's too bad the law required a 15-year maximum period for funding. If we were allowed to fund over 20 years, our payments would have dropped to $84,000.

Required

Assume that you are Jim Acta. Prepare a report to the president which addresses the concerns of the board of directors. The report should identify the relevant reporting issues and present recommendations that are appropriate for the company's reporting situation. Clearly indicate the impact that your recommendations will have on the company's financial statements and the notes thereto. You need not prepare revised statements.

New pretax income for this co.

Case 66

Moonbeam Mining Ltd.

Moonbeam Mining Limited (MML) is a federally incorporated company with shares traded on Canadian stock exchanges. The company has a number of public issues of bonds outstanding, and bond covenants contain restrictions regarding the ratio of consolidated debt to shareholders' equity. In addition, top executives of MML receive bonuses based on net income measured in accordance with generally accepted accounting principles (GAAP).

MML operates several silver mines in Canada. In 1993, 3.6 million ounces of silver were produced at the mines. Independent mining engineers have estimated that, as of January 1, 1994, the company's proven and probable silver reserves are about 24.3 million recoverable ounces.

In April 1994, MML issued to the public $25 million of 8.5 percent silver-indexed bonds due April 15, 2009. The bonds were issued at par. Each $1,000 face value bond is payable at maturity in $1,000 cash or 50 ounces of silver at the holder's option. The bonds are secured by an agreement entitling the trustee to receive, upon default, and on behalf of the bondholders, 3.7 percent of the annual mining production of MML, limited to not more than an aggregate of 50 ounces of silver per outstanding bond.

The transaction may be viewed as an issuance of convertible debt. Debt securities are often issued with a conversion feature which permits the holder to convert a bond into a predetermined number of common shares, whereas MML bonds permit the holders to convert a bond into a predetermined number of ounces of silver. This call option on silver allowed MML to issue the bonds initially at a substantially higher price than it could have obtained for a bond with an 8.5 percent interest rate but without the call option on silver. Major considerations in deciding how MML should account for the proceeds from the issuance of the convertible debt are:

1. The valuation of the liability at the date of issuance and subsequently.
2. The measurement of interest expense in each period the debt is outstanding.
3. The treatment of the bond retirement at maturity.

One possibility for accounting for the bonds at issuance, though not one proposed by management, is to view the convertible debt as possessing the characteristics of both a debt and a call option on silver. Consistent with this view, a portion of the proceeds could be allocated to the call option and credited to a separate account. The amount so allocated would be a measure of the excess of the fair value of the bond liability expected at maturity over its par value. The remainder of the proceeds would be allocated to the debt. To reflect the bond liability at its par value, the recording of a bond discount would be required. The amount assigned to the call options could be measured as the excess of the amount received for the bonds over the estimated price that could have been obtained for similar bonds without the call option on silver, since estimation can be made with reasonable accuracy. The amount recorded in the deferred credit account would be included in the liabilities of the company's balance sheet. The following entry reflects this interpretation (all amounts are hypothetical):

Cash	1,000	
Discount on silver-indexed bond	300	
Silver-indexed bond payable		1,000
Deferred credit—call option on silver		300
To record the issuance of one silver-indexed bond.		

Consistent with this method, the bond discount would be amortized to interest expense in each year the debt is outstanding. The deferred credit would be adjusted upward or downward each year to reflect changes in the fair value of the call option on silver because of changes in the market price of silver. Any such adjustment would be charged or credited to interest expense in each year.

The entry at maturity, assuming the market price of silver is $40 per ounce, at that time, is as follows (all amounts are hypothetical):

Silver-indexed bond payable	1,000	
Deferred credit—call option on silver	1,000	
Revenue from the sale of silver		2,000
To record the delivery of 50 ounces of silver to the trustee to satisfy the debt obligation on one silver-indexed bond.		

Alternatively, the management of MML has proposed another method to record the silver-indexed bond in a manner consistent with a "debt only'' view of the transaction. The bonds would be recorded at their face value. Interest expense reported in each period would reflect the coupon rate of interest. If bondholders elect to take silver as payment at maturity, management proposes to record the delivery to the trustee as a sale of silver at $20 per ounce.

This method would result in the following journal entry at maturity (all amounts are hypothetical):

Silver-indexed bond payable	1,000	
Revenue from the sale of silver		1,000

To record the delivery of 50 ounces of silver to the trustee to satisfy the debt obligation on one silver-indexed bond.

Under management's proposed method, MML would realize, at maturity, a loss or profit from the delivery of silver depending on whether or not the cost of producing silver exceeds $20 per ounce at maturity. If the market price of silver at maturity falls below $20 per ounce, bondholders will take cash, rather than silver, to satisfy the debt obligation, so all of the company's silver production would be sold in the normal course of operation.

The silver-indexed bonds of MML reflect an unusual and unique response to inflation; namely, providing bondholders with a hedge against inflation. If inflation continues in the economy, we are likely to see an increased number of debt obligations similar to that of MML which are convertible into various commodities such as silver, gold or oil, all of which give the bondholder the opportunity to share in the appreciation of nonmonetary assets over long periods of time. These types of complicated option contracts are likely to put considerable pressure and strain on transaction or exchange-based accounting, since such transactions or exchanges may effectively be held open for many years.

Required

a. Discuss the advantages and disadvantages of the silver-indexed bonds with respect to the financial management of the issuing company.

b. Provide a critical evaluation of both the accounting treatment proposed by management and the alternative accounting treatment illustrated in the question for the silver-indexed bonds. Conclude by stating which treatment you consider as most appropriate and why.

Case 67

National Design Productions Ltd.

You have just returned from a meeting with a client who is considering an opportunity to invest in nonvoting shares of National Design Productions Ltd. (NDP). Your client was very enthusiastic about the company, pointing out the company's high return on assets, low long-term debt/equity ratio and high operating margin on production activities. Your client is also impressed with NDP's large positive cash flow from operations.

NDP is offering to sell 100 shares of nonvoting common shares to private investors for $10,000 per share. The nonvoting shares would receive the same dividends as the voting shares. Before investing in a few of these shares, however, your client wants to have your advice on the apparent advisability of the investment. The client has given you the audited financial statements of NDP and some additional background information on which to base your opinion.

National Design Productions is a private Ontario corporation that was founded in 1973 by Cy Gilbert. Cy was a fashion consultant who was often called on to help stage fashion shows and other promotional events in the fashion industry. Cy began to videotape the shows and promotions to use as sales tools to show other prospective clients the type of work that he could do and then realized that videotape could in itself be a useful promotional tool. He, therefore, established National Design Productions as a video production company, initially dedicated to fashion productions.

Institute of Chartered Accountants of Ontario, adapted.

NATIONAL DESIGN PRODUCTIONS LTD.
Consolidated Balance Sheet
December 31

	1992	*1991*
Assets		
Current assets:		
Cash and deposits	$ 510,000	$ 683,000
Accounts receivable (Note 2)	2,289,000	1,068,000
Inventories:		
NDP	233,000	187,000
Stores	100,000	628,000
Total current assets	$3,132,000	$2,566,000
Furniture and fixtures—stores	1,401,000	4,916,000
Accumulated amortization	649,000	2,371,000
Total amortization	752,000	2,545,000
Other assets:		
Notes receivable—franchisees (Note 3)	805,000	400,000
Deferred production costs (Note 1)	2,429,000	1,688,000
Total assets	$7,118,000	$7,199,000
Liabilities and Shareholders' Equity		
Current liabilities:		
Bank operating loan (Note 6)	$1,100,000	$ 500,000
Current portion of term loan (Note 6)	—	306,000
Accounts payable: NDP	462,000	277,000
Stores	201,000	635,000
Income taxes and accrued expenses	119,000	87,000
Total current liabilities:	$1,882,000	$1,805,000
Long-term debt:		
Term loan payable (Note 6)	1,519,000	2,994,000
Deferred income taxes (Note 7)	1,392,000	383,000
Shareholders' equity:		
Common shares (Note 8)	500,000	500,000
Retained earnings	1,825,000	1,517,000
Total shareholders' equity	$2,325,000	$2,017,000
Total liabilities and equity	$7,118,000	$7,199,000

NATIONAL DESIGN PRODUCTIONS LTD.
Consolidated Statement of Income and Retained Earnings
Year Ended December 31

	1992	*1991*
Revenue from production activities:		
Contract production revenue	$3,219,000	$1,797,000
Video sales and rental	1,327,000	1,113,000
Less: allowance for returns	(116,000)	(97,000)
Total	4,430,000	2,813,000
Other revenue:		
Franchise fees (Note 5)	$1,124,000	$ 881,000
Total revenue from continuing operations	$5,554,000	$3,694,000
Net revenue from store operations:		
Store revenue (Note 4)	$1,396,000	$4,710,000
Store operating expenses	1,384,000	4,569,000
Total	12,000	141,000
Gains on sale of stores	572,000	73,000
Revenue from operations being discontinued	584,000	214,000
Total revenue	6,138,000	3,908,000
Expenses:		
Contract production costs	$1,514,000	$1,344,000
Amortization of production costs (Note 1)	599,000	432,000
General selling and administration	862,000	738,000
Interest expense	369,000	276,000
Income tax expense (Note 7)	1,286,000	514,000
Total expenses	4,630,000	3,304,000
Net income	1,508,000	604,000
Balance of retained earnings, January 1	1,517,000	1,413,000
Dividends on common shares	(1,200,000)	(500,000)
Retained earnings, December 31	$1,825,000	$1,517,000

Before long, NDP had built a solid reputation for video productions, and the rapidly growing company began producing videos for other commercial and promotional ventures outside of the fashion industry. Within 20 years, the company had grown to encompass video productions of many types and had become a vertically integrated video company with owned and franchised operations across Canada.

NATIONAL DESIGN PRODUCTIONS LTD.
Consolidated Statement of Changes in Financial Position
Year Ended December 31

	1992	*1991*
Operations:		
Net income	$1,508,000	$ 604,000
Amortization of production costs	599,000	432,000
Deferred income taxes	1,009,000	319,000
Excess of dividends over equity earnings in subsidiary	10,000	—
Gains on disposal of stores	(572,000)	(73,000)
Net changes in receivables, inventories, and payables	(1,361,000)	(637,000)
Cash provided by operations	1,193,000	645,000
Financing activities:		
Repayment of term loan	(1,781,000)	(226,000)
Dividends declared and paid	(1,200,000)	(500,000)
Cash provided (used) in financing activities	(2,981,000)	(726,000)
Investing activities:		
Investment in video production	(1,340,000)	(513,000)
Proceeds from sale of stores	2,365,000	360,000
Cash provided (used) in investing activities	1,025,000	(153,000)
Increase (decrease) in cash	$ (763,000)	$(234,000)

Notes to Financial Statements, Year Ended December 31, 1987

1. Accounting Policies

Consolidation: All subsidiaries are consolidated with the accounts of National Design Productions Ltd.

Revenue: (*a*) Revenue from video sales is recognized when the videotapes are shipped to the dealers. Rental revenue is recognized monthly as the rental receipts are reported by the dealers to NDP. (*b*) Revenue on cost-plus contracts is recognized as the contracts proceed, using the percentage of cost completion basis. Retainers are recognized when the contract is signed. (*c*) Franchise fees are recognized when all substantive effort has been performed by NDP and the franchisee has begun operations.

Production costs: The costs of producing videos for sale and rental are capitalized and amortized to income on a straight-line basis over four years at rates of 15 percent, 30 percent, 30 percent, and 25 percent per year consecutively.

Notes to Financial Statements, Year Ended December 31, 1987 (*continued*)

Income taxes: NDP uses the full allocation basis of reporting income taxes, whereby the future or past income tax effect of revenues and expenses is reported in the income statement in the period in which the related items of revenue and expense are themselves recognized in income.

Furniture and fixtures: The store furniture and fixtures are reported at cost less accumulated amortization. Amortization is straight line at a rate of 8 percent per year.

2. Accounts Receivable

	1992	*1991*
Dealers	$ 443,000	$ 325,000
Production contracts	431,000	407,000
Retainers	1,101,000	213,000
Franchise fees	510,000	263,000
Total	$2,485,000	$1,208,000
Allowance for returns	(116,000)	(97,000)
Allowance for doubtful accounts	(80,000)	(43,000)
Net accounts receivable	$2,289,000	$1,068,000

3. Notes Receivable—Franchisees

The notes receivable from franchisees are due over a period of four years and mature as follows:

	1992	*1991*
Due in 1993	$345,000	$260,000
Due in 1994	260,000	140,000
Due in 1995	200,000	—
Total	$805,000	$400,000

4. White Heat Stores

In 1990, NDP acquired a group of 16 retail video stores operating under the name of White Heat Video. NDP has undertaken a program of selling these stores on an individual basis to be operated by the purchasers as White Knight franchises (Note 5). Twelve of the stores have been sold, 3 in 1991 and 9 in 1992. The remaining four stores are expected to be sold in 1993. The assets, liabilities, revenues, and expenses relating to these stores are segregated in these financial statements.

Notes to Financial Statements, Year Ended December 31, 1987 (*concluded*)

5. Franchises

NDP has established the name of White Knight Video Stores as a trademarked name and sells this name as part of a franchise operation. Fourteen such franchises were sold in 1992 (1991: 8). The former White Heat Video stores are operated as franchises by the purchasers under the White Knight name.

6. Bank Loans Payable

National Design Productions Ltd. carries an operating line of credit with the CIBC, which is limited to 60 percent of billed accounts receivable, excluding franchise fees. The operating loan is payable on demand and bears interest at the rate of 2 percent above the prime rate, as established on the 15th of each month.

As part of the acquisition of White Heat Video Stores in 1991 (Note 4), NDP arranged a seven-year term loan with the CIBC. This loan is payable in blended payments of not less than $434,000 per year for seven years. As the result of the disposition of most of the stores, loan repayment is well ahead of schedule and thus there is no current portion due at the end of 1992.

NDP is the unconditional guarantor of the debentures issued by Video Equipment Leasing Ltd.

All of the aforementioned liabilities are secured by a first fixed and floating charge against the assets of National Design Productions Ltd. and its subsidiaries. Accounts receivable are specifically assigned as security for the operating loan.

7. Deferred Income Taxes

Deferred income taxes arise from the fact that income tax expense on certain items of revenue and expense are recognized for income tax purposes in a different year than their recognition in the income statement. The items to which these differences apply are franchise fees and deferred production costs for NDP and CCA amortization for VEL.

8. Share Capital

There are 300 common shares issued and outstanding. There is no public market for the shares, and there were no transactions in these shares in 1992 or 1991.

NDP's core business is still the production of videos, but the scope of the business has increased dramatically. About 60 percent of the production volume is for videos made under contract for commercial users. About two thirds of that volume is done under retainer, wherein the customer signs an annual contract to pay a flat amount per month plus the cost of any videos produced. The flat fee is, therefore, NDP's profit, and NDP gets to keep that amount whether the customer wants a dozen productions or none during the year. Of course, the size of each customer's fee is set in relation to the past and expected volume of production for that customer.

NDP recognizes the full amount of the retainer as revenue when the retainer contract is signed. The customer makes 12 equal monthly payments throughout the contract year. NDP began the retainer programme in 1991 and has been placing increasing emphasis on retainer contracts. Retainer contract signing was particularly heavy in the last quarter of 1992; those contracts run into the third and fourth quarter of 1993.

The remaining one third of the commercial production volume is performed under individual cost-plus-fixed-fee contracts.

The other 40 percent of the video production volume consists of independent productions of adult videos undertaken by NDP. These videos are exhibited commercially in Quebec and British Columbia, with a specially edited version exhibited in Ontario. The videos are also rented and sold at retail by the exhibitors as well as by other video outlets across the country. The exhibitors are unrelated to NDP but pay a percentage of their gross receipts to NDP as a rental fee.

The costs of producing these adult videos are capitalized and amortized. The amortization period is four years on a modified straight- line basis of 15 percent, 30 percent, 30 percent, and 25 percent per year consecutively.

The video stores that rent and sell the adult videos are of three types. The first type is independent dealers who buy the videos (with the right to return up to 30 percent of unsold and unopened videos) and rent or sell them.

The second type is the remnants of a chain of video outlets called White Heat Videos that operates mainly in British Columbia. This chain had been an independent company, but 100 of its stores were purchased by NDP in 1990. NDP has been following a policy of reselling these stores as independent units tied to a franchise agreement. The franchise name (and the new name under which former White Heat stores operate) is White Knight Video.

The third type is stores that are franchised by White Knight. Most of the franchisees are in Quebec and have been opened during the past two years (i.e., since NDP acquired White Heat). Twenty-two franchises have been sold during the past two years, and NDP management expects that franchise sales will decline in future years. The franchise fee is recognized as revenue when the franchisee is substantially open for business. The franchisee pays most of the price of the franchise over a period not to exceed three years after opening.

NDP also has a leasing subsidiary, Video Equipment Leasing Limited (VEL). VEL was founded by NDP to acquire the equipment and other capital assets needed by NDP and to lease it to NDP. VEL also leases to other, smaller production companies, but NDP accounts for about 85 percent of VEL's leasing volume. NDP management felt that it was easier to pass the rental costs of equipment on to the customers than it was to pass on amortization allocations. NDP guarantees the secondary debt of VEL by which the equipment was financed.

Required

Submit a report to your client in which you discuss the advisability of investing in nonvoting shares of NDP. Support your recommendations with specific numerical analyses that are relevant to the prospective investment decision. Ignore income tax considerations.

Case 68

New Horizons Ltd.

New Horizons Ltd. was incorporated in 1993, with common shares owned equally by the three principals: Christine Newell, Nelson Wong, and Reginald Lee. Previously, these three engineers held positions in the research group of a large public plastics company. New Horizons was formed to develop, produce, and sell a process that would render various types of packaging "tamperproof," a booming market.

Newell, Wong, and Lee had been working on this concept for their previous employer. However, when the project was shelved, the three decided to go ahead with it on their own. They agreed to pay their previous employer a royalty of 3 percent of sales in exchange for the use of research done to date, and left in 1993 with their employer's blessing and promises of their old jobs back if "things did not work out."

The year 1993 was spent developing the process to the point where it was technologically and economically viable. By February 1994, New Horizons's operations were well under way. A coordinated marketing effort and careful recruitment of sales representatives, as well as a little help from their previous employer, resulted in good manufacturer acceptance of the line. New Horizons dealt mostly with small manufacturers.

Since every application was unique, the machinery and process was custom tailored to each manufacturer's needs. This turned out to be easier than anticipated, although New Horizons had to provide engineering support for the first month or two of production to iron out any problems that developed.

From the beginning, the firm's accounting and related clerical activities were supervised by Dave Madden, a recent B. Comm. graduate with a background in accounting. Initially, attention was directed toward controlling cash, establishing cost records, and implementing a cost control system. Orders from customers were accepted after reference to a credit-rating service.

It is now the end of 1994, and various accounting policies have to be established before the 1994 statements can be prepared. The principals wish to pick policies they will not have to change later, especially if they are successful in their ultimate goal of taking the company public.

They have asked Dave Madden to evaluate the alternatives for recording bad debt expense: direct write-off, setting up a percentage of sales, or aging the receivables and/or attempting some provision based on percentages or specific identification.

At present, the principals prefer the direct write-off method. It seems to them to be the only one based on objective, real events. They point out that there is no history on which to base a percentage for either percentage of sales or an aging method. Specific identification makes them uncomfortable, as they point out that if a particular firm were not creditworthy, they never should have accepted the sale.

Required

Adopt the role of Dave Madden and write a brief report evaluating the alternative policies for calculating bad debt expense.

Case 69

Nile Manufacturing Ltd.

Jaspar Jones is the president of Nile Manufacturing Ltd. (Nile), a small, privately owned company. The company manufactures numerous products. The family that owns the company prefers to remain out of the day-to-day operations because they have complete trust in Jaspar's judgement. In fact, they are so pleased at having Jaspar on the management team that they have instituted a bonus for him based on net income before taxes and extraordinary items. The family elected you as Nile's auditor at a recent board of directors meeting. Their only instruction to you was that they consider everything material. You have done all the audit work for the December 31, 1994, statements and have requested a meeting with Jaspar to discuss the following items:

1. One of Nile's capital assets is a machine that makes doors. The unique characteristic of these doors is that they are very difficult to open and close due to their weight. The company felt that this would be a safety factor in that it would slow down a burglary. You have noticed that sales of this product have not broken any records. In fact, the only door that Nile has made is still in inventory after two years. The machine was very expensive and cannot be used for any other purpose. You have suggested that the value of both the door and the machine be written off. Jaspar agrees with you—he fully supports a charge against either 1993 net income (since it was known last year that the product would not be successful) or 1994 net income as long as it is disclosed outside operating items. You are willing to consider Jaspar's ideas.

2. On a tip from his broker, Jaspar had Nile purchase 10 common shares of British Enterprises during 1994. (British Enterprises is a major Canadian public company, which trades on stock exchanges all over the world.) Jaspar intends that Nile hold these shares for many years, unless some cash is needed to meet the payroll. The shares cost $38 each and were trading for $35 each on December 31, 1994.

During the year, British Enterprises paid a dividend of $2 per share and reported basic earnings per share of $4. Jaspar recorded the following journal entries:

	Dr	Cr
Cash	20	
Dividend income		20
To record receipt of dividend.		
Investment in British Enterprises	40	
Income from investment		40
To record earnings attributable to common shares for 1989.		

3. Nile has a product that is both extremely successful and very profitable—a battery-operated swizzle stick. The company can hardly produce this item fast enough. At a New Year's Eve party Jaspar ran into one of Nile's customers, who said that he had been meaning to phone the company to order 100,000 of the swizzle sticks. They will be used as gifts to the employees at the customer's annual Valentine's Day party. Jaspar told the customer to phone him personally to arrange a cut price, full refund if not satisfied, deal on the sale. You have noticed a journal entry dated December 31, 1994, recording this sale "in anticipation."

Required

Present your analysis and recommendations for the treatment and disclosure of each of the above items on Nile Manufacturing Ltd.'s December 31, 1994, financial statements.

Case 70

Northern Lights Limited

Northern Lights Ltd. (NLL) is one of the largest federally incorporated companies in Canada. It is involved in transportation, steel, forest products, and other natural resources. It is a major employer in seven provinces.

By the end of 1993, NLL had fallen upon hard times. The steel and forest products industries were in recession, and company earnings were adversely affected. (See Exhibit 1.) NLL's cash flow situation was dismal, as they had invested heavily in fixed assets beginning in 1991. The majority of these expenditures had been financed by debt. In 1992 alone, NLL doubled its level of long-term borrowings and more than tripled its short-term borrowings. The effect of this was to increase the debt/equity ratio from close to 3:1 in 1990 to 5.7 to 1 shortly before the 1993 year-end.

A significant portion of NLL's debt was U.S. denominated, raised privately in the United States in the late 1980s. One of the covenants associated with this debt was that the debt/equity ratio could not exceed 5.5 to 1. Since the interest rate on the debt was favourable to NLL, and less attractive to the lenders in 1993, there was little question but that violation of this covenant, putting NLL into technical default, would trigger a demand for debt repayment. There was some considerable doubt about whether NLL would be successful in negotiating another loan deal to replace this one, as the company's cash flow problems were growing serious and were well known. It became clear that new financing would only be available at high interest rates.

Budgets for 1994 indicated a projected loss of $600 million. This would further erode the equity base and exacerbate the cash flow problem. Concern was widely expressed over the company's short-term viability,

---

This case is loosely based on "The Curious Accounting Treatment of the Swedish Government Loan to Uddeholm," Stephen Zeff and Sven-Eric Johansson, *The Accounting Review,* April 1984, pp. 342–49.

EXHIBIT 1 Operating Statistics (in millions)

	Net Income (Loss)	*Capital Expenditures*
1986	$ 92	$107
1987	44	124
1988	32	126
1989	176	118
1990	486	120
1991	238	288
1992	(155)	531
1993 (unaudited)	(448)	477

and the spectre of widespread layoffs was raised. The government came under pressure to lend some aid.

Under the free trade deal with the United States, the Canadian government was not permitted to give a direct operating subsidy to NLL. Since NLL sold many of its products in the United States, such a subsidy would be viewed as giving NLL, in competition with unsubsidized U.S. firms, an unfair advantage. Instead, the government extended a $600 million loan to NLL. This loan was made to NLL on December 28, 1993, three days before the close of the 1993 fiscal year. No funds were actually transferred between the government and NLL; the transaction was more in the nature of a guaranteed line of credit that would allow NLL to draw upon the government as it needed funds in 1994.

The loan was repayable only when NLL wished to pay dividends to its common shareholders; that is, there were no fixed principal repayments required. Repayment had to be "substantially" complete, or a payment scheme approved between NLL and the government, before any dividends could be declared on common shares. In spite of this indefinite term, the company and the government clearly envisioned reasonably prompt repayment of the loan. Neither side viewed the company's cash flow problems as anything other than temporary, as the resource and transportation industries were strong and expected to expand through the next decade. The financial community agreed with this assessment. Thus, the capital the government extended was clearly viewed as a temporary loan and not permanent equity.

While the $600 million would solve NLL's cash flow problems over the next year or so, it did not address the difficulty over the bond covenant specifying an acceptable debt/equity ratio. Under *CICA Handbook* rules on accounting for government assistance, the loan was to be recorded as just that: a loan. This would worsen the debt/equity ratio, not improve it.

The *CICA Handbook* is considered to be the source of accounting principles which federally incorporated companies must use to prepare

EXHIBIT 2 Extracts from the Canada Business Corporation Act and Regulations, 1975

Canada Business Corporation Act

Financial Disclosure

149. (1) Annual financial statements.—Subject to section 150, the directors of a corporation shall place before the shareholders at every annual meeting
(*a*) comparative financial statements as prescribed relating separately to
(i) the period that began on the date the corporation came into existence and ended not more than six months before the annual meeting or, if the corporation has completed a financial year, the period that began immediately after the end of the last completed financial year and ended not more than six months before the annual meeting, and
(ii) the immediately preceding financial year;
(*b*) the report of the auditor, if any; and
(*c*) any further information respecting the financial position of the corporation and the results of its operations required by the articles, the by-laws or any unanimous shareholder agreement.

* * *

163. (1) Examination.—An auditor of a corporation shall make the examination that is in his opinion necessary to enable him to report in the prescribed manner on the financial statements required by this Act to be placed before the shareholders, except such financial statements or part thereof that relate to the period referred to in subparagraph 149(1)(*a*)(ii).

Canada Business Corporations Act Regulations

Part V—Financial Disclosure

General

44. The financial statements referred to in section 149 of the Act and the auditor's report referred to in section 163 of the Act shall, except as otherwise provided by this Part, be prepared in accordance with the recommendations of the Canadian Institute of Chartered Accountants set out in the *CICA Handbook*.

their annual financial statements. The requirement for financial statements is found in Section 149 of the Canada Business Corporations Act. The *Handbook* is endorsed in the Regulations (see Exhibit 2). However, regulations can be changed by a simple resolution of the federal cabinet and no piece of formal legislation is required.

The board of directors of NLL has approached the government to request an amendment, through an Order-in-Council, to Regulation 44 of the CBCA. They have requested that Regulation 44 endorse the *CICA Handbook,* except for their specific loan, which would be a revenue item. That is, they wished to debit a receivable from the federal government and credit revenue for $600 million in 1993. Repayment would be an expense of the period in which the loan was paid off. NLL has pointed out, quite correctly, that such an amendment is fully within the power of the government.

NLL, a large company and a major employer, has significant political influence. Obviously, they had enough power to obtain the loan. They argue that if the situation is serious enough to warrant a loan, then an accounting rule, which after all costs nothing, and which is necessary to avert their potential crisis, is relatively minor. Also, Canada's interests (hopefully a major concern of the political system) would be well served by such a one-time exception. They also point out that this loan, regardless of how classified, will not violate the free trade agreement.

You are a staff member, working for one of the cabinet ministers who is being intensively lobbied to support this proposal for a change in Regulation 44. He has asked you to prepare a report, outlining the pros and cons of the government taking such an action.

Required

Prepare the report.

Case 71

Northern Telecom Limited

Northern Telecom Limited is a supplier of fully digital telecommunications switching equipment. The company's principal subsidiaries, most of which are 100 percent owned, are located in Canada, the United States, Mexico, England, Australia, the Netherlands, Germany, Italy, Belgium, France, the Republic of Ireland, Hong Kong, Japan, Malaysia, Thailand, and the People's Republic of China. Northern Telecom operates 55 manufacturing plants worldwide; research and development is conducted at 24 of these facilities, and by Bell-Northern Research Ltd., a subsidiary that operates R&D facilities in Canada, the United States, the United Kingdom, and Japan.

At December 31, 1991, Northern Telecom's consolidated net assets, including finance subsidiaries, totalled (millions of $U.S.) $3,918.8 ($3,467.5 at December 31, 1990).

The company's common shares trade on the Toronto, Montreal, Vancouver, New York, London, and Tokyo stock exchanges; the annual report does not specify the exchanges where the preferred shares are listed. The financial statements are prepared in accordance with Canadian generally accepted accounting principles.

Northern Telecom describes its accounting policy for translation of foreign currencies as follows:

> The consolidated financial statements are expressed in U.S. dollars as the greater part of earnings and net assets of Northern Telecom is denominated in U.S. dollars.
>
> Self-sustaining operations, which comprise most of the Corporation's subsidiaries, are those whose economic activities are largely independent of those of the parent company. Assets and liabilities are translated at the exchange rates in effect at the balance sheet date. Revenues and expenses, including gains and losses on foreign exchange transactions, other than long-term intercompany advances, are translated at average rates for the period. The unrealized translation gains and losses on the parent company's net investment in these operations are accumulated in a separate component of shareholders' equity,

EXHIBIT 1

Selected Notes from the Financial Statements for the Year Ended December 31, 1991

Long-Term Debt

	1991	*1990*
Finance subsidiaries:		
Variable-rate bank loans bearing interest at an average rate of 9.3% for 1991, 9.7% for 1990	$ 15.6	$ 90.0
Nonrecourse fixed-rate notes bearing interest from 8.8% to 10.9% due 1992 to 1995	184.3	245.3
Fixed-rate notes bearing interest from 7.9% to 9.1% for 1991, 8.4% to 9.3% for 1990, due 1992 to 1996	56.0	60.0
1.70% variable redemption amount notes, due 1996, swapped to variable interest rate of 5.8% and 8.2% at December 31, 1991 and 1990, respectively	20.0	20.9
	275.9	415.3
Other:		
Variable-rate notes bearing interest at an average rate of 11.5% due December 15, 1995 (pounds sterling)	43.2	—
9.75% notes due December 18, 1992, (pounds sterling)	112.4	113.3
9.60% Notes due in equal annual instalments, December 30, 1993 to 1997	100.0	100.0
9.25% notes due October 19, 1993	100.0	100.0
9.25% notes due June 2, 1994	200.0	200.0
8.25% notes due June 13, 1996, swapped to sterling principal and interest of 10.60%	280.6	--
8.75% notes due June 12, 2001, swapped to sterling principal and interest of 10.75%	280.8	—
7.75% subordinated debentures due February 15, 1998	22.0	—
Fixed-rate bank loans bearing interest at an average rate of 9%	5.9	41.0
Obligations under capital leases	25.2	15.0
7.0% subsidiary convertible bonds (French francs)	—	8.0
	1,170.1	577.3
	1,446.0	992.6
Less amount included in current liabilities	284.6	194.9
	$1,161.4	$797.7
Finance subsidiaries' interest expense	40.2	59.1
Other interest expense	221.0	80.0
Total interest expense	$ 261.2	$139.1

EXHIBIT 1 (*continued*)

Selected Notes from the Financial Statements for the Year Ended December 31, 1991

Nonrecourse fixed-rate notes represent debt issued with holders granted a security interest in the associated lease and notes receivable and equipment on lease. Repayment of this debt is limited to collection of payments with respect to these assets.

Variable-rate notes due December 15, 1995 (pounds sterling), are redeemable at the option of the holder semiannually from June 15, 1992. The notes are redeemable at the option of the Corporation semiannually from June 15, 1995, and when less than 25% of those originally issued are outstanding.

At December 31, 1991, the amounts of long-term debt payable for the years 1992 through 1996 were $284.6, $186.1, $279.9, $41.6, and $321.9, respectively.

Preferred Shares

The Corporation is authorized to issue an unlimited number of Class A Preferred Shares and Class B Preferred Shares, without nominal or par value, issuable in series. Class A Preferred Shares have been issued for consideration denominated in Canadian dollars (C$).

	1991		*1990*	
	Number of Shares	*Dollars*	*Number of Shares*	*Dollars*
Cumulative Redeemable Retractable Class A Preferred Shares Floating Rate Series 3, issued August 29, 1984, for consideration of C$200 million	7,882,630	$169.8	8,000,000	$172.9
Cumulative Redeemable Class A Preferred Shares, Series 4, issued June 25, 1985, for consideration of C$100 million	200	$ 73.3	200	$ 73.3

The series 3 preferred shares are presented in U.S. dollars after translation at the exchange rate in effect at the balance sheet date. The series 4 preferred shares are presented in U.S. dollars after translation at the exchange rate in effect at the date of original issue.

The dividend rate on the series 3 preferred shares is calculated each quarter. The quarterly dividend rate is one quarter of 70 percent of the average of the prime

EXHIBIT 1 (*continued*)

Selected Notes from the Financial Statements for the Year Ended December 31, 1991

rates established by two major Canadian chartered banks for stated periods. The series 3 preferred shares are redeemable at the option of the Corporation at C$25 per share. The holders of series 3 preferred shares may require the Corporation to redeem any or all of their series 3 preferred shares on October 25, 1992, at C$25 per share. On October 25, 1990, 117,370 series 3 preferred shares were retracted for C$25 per share.

The dividend rate on the series 4 preferred shares is determined by auctions held at intervals of approximately one month on the business day immediately preceding the commencement of each dividend period. The Corporation can neither participate, nor oblige any subsidiary to participate, in the auction procedures. The annual dividend rate may not exceed the Bankers' Acceptance Rate in effect on the auction date plus 0.40 percent. The rate in effect on December 31, 1991, was 4.39 percent. The Corporation may call all or a part of the series 4 preferred shares for redemption at a price of C$500,000 per share, on the business day immediately preceding any auction date.

Dividends on each of the outstanding series of preferred shares are declared and payable in Canadian dollars. Amounts equal to accrued and unpaid dividends are payable by the Corporation upon redemption or retraction of Class A Preferred Shares. In the case of series 4 preferred shares, the applicable dividend must be declared prior to redemption.

Currency Translation Adjustment

Following is an analysis of the currency translation adjustment included in shareholders' equity at December 31:

	1991	*1990*
January 1	$25.2	$(102.0)
Translation of self-sustaining operations	63.5	144.4
Losses on hedges	(83.9)	(17.2)
December 31	$ 4.8	$ 25.2

Information on Business Segment by Geographic Areas

Business segment

The Corporation operates in one business segment, telecommunications equipment, which consists of the research and the design, development, manufacture, marketing, sale, installation, financing, and service of central office switching equipment, business communications systems and terminals, transmission equipment, cable and outside plant products, and other products and services.

EXHIBIT 1 *(continued)*

Selected Notes from the Financial Statements for the Year Ended December 31, 1991

Geographic area

The point of origin (the location of the selling organization) of revenues and the location of the assets determine the geographic areas.

The following table sets forth information by geographic area for the year ended December 31:

	1991	*1990*	*1989*
Total revenues:			
United States			
customers	$4,335.7	$3,938.3	$3,615.7
Transfers between geographic areas	309.9	205.3	165.1
Total	$4,645.6	$4,143.6	$3,780.8
Canada			
customers	$2,304.2	$2,422.4	$2,172.6
Transfers between geographic areas	865.5	771.6	605.3
Total	3,169.7	3,194.0	2,777.9
Europe			
customers	1,346.6	219.2	192.5
Transfers between geographic areas	4.3	0.1	—
Total	$1,350.9	$ 219.3	$ 192.5
Other			
customers	$ 196.0	$ 188.8	$ 124.7
Transfers between geographic areas	77.1	68.6	75.0
Total	273.1	257.4	199.7
Elimination of transfers between geographic areas	(1,256.8)	(1,045.6)	(845.4)
Total customer revenues	$8,182.5	$6,768.7	$6,105.5
Operating earnings:			
United States	$1,211.6	$1,081.6	$ 899.7
Canada	705.8	678.4	625.4
Europe	223.6	(19.9)	(15.9)
Other	10.2	6.9	7.1
Operating earnings before research and development and general corporate expenses	2,151.2	1,747.0	1,516.3
Research and development expense	(948.3)	(773.7)	(729.8)
General corporate expenses	(371.9)	(324.2)	(277.6)
Operating earnings	831.0	649.1	508.9
Other income less nonoperating expenses	(120.8)	(30.5)	6.2
Earnings before income taxes	$ 710.2	$ 618.6	$ 515.1

EXHIBIT 1 *(concluded)*

Selected Notes from the Financial Statements for the Year Ended December 31, 1991

Identifiable assets:			
United States	$3,893.2	$3,141.8	$3,084.3
Canada	2,228.2	2,170.2	1,911.1
Europe	4,091.3	517.1	325.9
Other	332.2	243.3	176.0
Adjustments and eliminations	(1,565.9)	(706.6)	(429.3)
Identifiable assets	$8,979.0	$5,365.8	$5,068.0
Investments*	235.6	1,154.0	966.8
Corporate assets	319.6	322.5	274.7
Total assets	$9,534.2	$6,842.3	$6,309.5

Transfers between geographic areas are made at prices based on total cost of the product to the supplying segment.

Customer revenues by destination for the year ended December 31 were:

	1991	*1990*	*1989*
United States	$4,105.6	$3,747.3	$3,510.3
Canada	1,960.9	2,153.5	2,006.8
Europe	1,434.3	335.3	275.6
Other	681.7	532.6	312.8
Total	$8,182.5	$6,768.7	$6,105.5

Of the total customer revenues, including research and development, revenues from Bell Canada and other subsidiaries and associated companies of BCE, including associated companies of Northern Telecom, accounted for $1,478.1, $1,637.1, and $1,513.3 for 1991, 1990, and 1989, respectively.

Operating earnings represent total revenues less operating expenses. In computing operating earnings, none of the following items have been added or deducted: equity in net earnings of associated companies, investment and other income (net), interest charges, foreign currency exchange gains and losses, general corporate expenses, research and development expense, and provision for income taxes.

Identifiable assets are those assets of Northern Telecom that are identified with the operations in the geographic area. Corporate assets are principally cash and short-term investments and corporate plant and equipment.

* In unconsolidated associated companies, primarily U.K.

described in the consolidated balance sheet as currency translation adjustment. Exchange gains or losses on preferred shares (retractable) and certain debt designated as partial hedges of foreign self-sustaining operations are also included in the currency translation adjustment. These gains and losses may become realized on the payment of dividends by, or a change in the equity capital of, a self-sustaining operation, in which event an appropriate portion of currency translation adjustment is transferred and reflected in consolidated net earnings.

Integrated subsidiaries are financially or operationally dependent on the parent company. Translation exchange gains or losses of integrated subsidiaries are reflected in consolidated net earnings.

Required

Using the information presented in Exhibit 1, analyze the effectiveness of the hedge identified above. Critique the company's disclosure of the issue, and speculate on the reasons for this particular financial transaction.

Case 72

Oak Tree Arena Ltd.

Oak Tree Arena Ltd. is a public company that owns an arena in Timmins, where hockey games and rock concerts are held. Prior to the 1989 year-end, the company sold all its interest in the local hockey team. The arena is partially subsidized by the government of the province of Ontario.

Because of the limited applicability of the *CICA Handbook* recommendations to government bodies, the Public Sector Accounting and Auditing Committee was established by the CICA in 1981. The committee's objective is to set accounting and auditing standards for both senior and local government levels.

Required

Part A. Identify two user groups who would be interested in the financial statements of the government of the province of Ontario and two *different* user groups who would be interested in the statements of Oak Tree Arena Ltd. For each of the four groups you have identified, specify the following:

1. The user group.
2. This group's objective in relying on these financial statements.
3. A brief explanation of each objective identified in (2); specifically relate your answer to the financial statements of the government and the arena.

Part B. Identify two accounting difficulties that would be specific to the preparation of senior government financial statements. For each item, briefly explain why you feel this might be a problem.

Institute of Chartered Accountants of Ontario, adapted.

Case 73

Olympia & York

On May 14, 1992, Olympia & York Developments Ltd. (O&Y) filed for bankruptcy protection under Canada's Companies Creditor Act and under Chapter 11 of the U.S. Bankruptcy Code. The filing protects $8.6 billion of Canadian and U.S. assets from seizure. The Canadian filing covered 29 companies. The Chapter 11 filing named five O&Y affiliates; the operating companies were left unprotected.

A British court ruling that the company must pay $290 million on 1 of its 11 Canary Wharf buildings precipitated the filings. During the previous week, O&Y had defaulted on $1.5 billion of debts. One of the debts was a progress payment on O&Y's contribution to the British government's subway line construction to the Canary Wharf project, located in London's Docklands.

O&Y is a privately owned Canadian real estate development company, incorporated provincially in Ontario. Each of the company's buildings is owned by a separate subsidiary. The subsidiaries lend to each other and guarantee each other's debt.

O&Y's total debt is estimated at $13.5 billion (Cdn); $8.6 billion is owed to Canadian lenders. A court ruled that O&Y must identify and segregate its Canadian revenue according to the properties producing the income. Each building is responsible for its own expenses. The company can apply any remaining funds to the restructuring costs, estimated at $36 million. O&Y may not sell assets without adequate notice to creditors and the court.

On May 28, O&Y asked a British court to protect Canary Wharf from $8.8 billion in creditor claims. The British government had refused a bailout request and indicated that no government offices would move into the development unless this proved cost effective.

In July, audited figures at January 31 were released. In fiscal 1992 the company lost $2.1 billion. The loss from operations was $651 million, compared to a profit in fiscal 1991 of $205 million. The shareholders' deficit at January 31, 1992, was $134 million.

Write-downs in fiscal 1992 totalled $1.4 billion. Of the total write-down, $553 million related to real estate assets and $229 million was for investments in Gulf Canada Resources Ltd. and Abitibi-Price Inc. There was a provision against the Trizec Corp. Ltd. investment. There was no write-down of the $3.6 billion investment in Canary Wharf. As a result the auditors, Price Waterhouse, qualified the audit report.

Canadian and U.S. legislation allow O&Y to continue to manage its affairs. Chapter 11 legislation places new lenders first for repayment. The U.K. Administration Act does not allow the petitioner to continue to manage its properties; the court appoints the administrators.

A summary of the survival plan proposed by O&Y is:

Debt maturities to be extended for five years, except for certain loans tied to marketable securities, which would be liquidated within a year; secured creditors would have the opportunity to seize the collateral wherever they chose.

The issue of O&Y common shares to creditors; unsecured creditors would be offered control.

The division of loans into convertible and nonconvertible debt.

One-year and two-year business plans to be approved by a committee of creditors.

The liquidation of all securities on an orderly basis, except for core holdings, such as shares in Gulf Canada Resources Ltd., Abitibi-Price Inc., and Trizec Corp. Ltd.

Required

Do conditions exist for a quasi reorganization of Olympia and York Developments Ltd.? Describe the impact a quasi reorganization would have on the company's financial statements. Discuss the public's right to financial information about O&Y prior to the company's bankruptcy filing.

Case 74

Paul Burnham

Several years ago, Paul Burnham inherited some money. He invested it in GICs until last year, when he purchased 2,000 shares in Jordan Enterprises, a company that trades on the Montreal Stock Exchange. The shares cost $4 each. Jordan Enterprises has never declared a dividend.

This year (1993), Paul bought more securities. He also approached his bank manager about a loan for a company he wishes to incorporate. The bank manager wants to see a list of Paul's assets before making a decision on the loan.

Paul had the following transactions in 1993:

June—purchased 800 shares of Taylor Inc. for $5 each.

September—purchased 500 shares of Taylor Inc. for $4 each.

November—purchased 10 percent Hydro bonds for their face value of $100,000.

December—sold 200 shares of Taylor Inc. for $3 each.

Taylor Inc. and Hydro bonds trade on the Toronto Stock Exchange. Taylor Inc. declared a divident of 10 cents per share in October. Hydro bond interest is payable on April 30 and October 31.

At December 31, 1993, the market values of Jordan Enterprises and Taylor Inc. shares were $1.00 and $2.75, respectively. There were rumours that Jordan Enterprises was close to bankruptcy. By January 31, 1994, Taylor Inc. shares were trading for $3.50.

In December interest rates fell and the Hydro bonds were trading for $101,500 (face value only) at the year-end.

Required

What value would you assign to Paul Burnham's portfolio at December 31, 1993? Explain your selections.

If the banker requested financial statements prepared in accordance with generally accepted accounting principles, what items would appear on Paul's balance sheet and income statement? What note disclosure would you include?

Case 75

PIP Grants

The National Energy Policy, legislation of the Canadian federal government, established Petroleum Incentive Program (PIP) grants for the oil industry in 1982. These were created to encourage oil and gas exploration in Canada at a time when energy self-sufficiency in the face of high world energy prices was a top priority. PIP grants replaced a system of "super depletion" allowances and investment tax credits for oil exploration. This latter system was phased out.

The CICA rule on such government grants, according to Section 3800 of the *CICA Handbook,* "Accounting for Government Grants," is that grants must be amortized to income over the life of the related exploration assets. If the exploration assets were to be amortized straight line over 10 years, so, too, should the government grant be amortized. When these rules were developed, there was no particular objection made by the oil industry or the federal government.

The introduction of PIP grants in early 1982 abruptly changed that. Under the 1982 rules for investment tax credits (the old exploration incentives), any tax credits received in the year would be treated as income, or a reduction of expense, in the year.[1] There were no deferrals, and income was boosted. Under the new system, which changed the form of government assistance from investment tax credits to government grants, the impact of government assistance was to be shown over a period of years.

---

[1] Today, investment tax credits also must be deferred and amortized. Immediate recognition was GAAP in 1982.

The oil companies were very unhappy at this prospect, particularly since their earnings were drastically reduced by other provisions of the National Energy Policy.

The difference to net income would be material. For example, Norcen Energy Resources recorded energy exploration grants in income on the cash flow, or immediate recognition, basis in its 1981 quarterly statements. Its nine-month report, dated September 30, 1981, noted that, if the CICA (deferral) rule had been used, earnings per share would have been reduced to $1.26 from $1.71, a decrease of more than 25 percent.

The oil companies represent a powerful lobby group in Ottawa. Getting nowhere with the CICA, they approached the federal government to change the accounting rule through the provisions of the Canada Business Corporations Act. The regulations to this act specify that the generally accepted accounting principles required in the act are to be those principles prescribed by the *CICA Handbook*. However, the federal cabinet was asked to amend the regulations by an Order in Council, which would require *CICA Handbook* treatment for everything except PIP grants, which would be recorded on a cash flow basis.

The oil companies used the following arguments to defend their request:

1. Cash flow treatment for PIP grants was consistent with the treatment for investment tax credits, which PIP grants replaced.
2. Deferral would cause a lower net income to be reported by oil companies, which would reduce their attractiveness to investors and, thus, increase their cost of capital.
3. With a higher cost of capital, fewer exploration programs would be undertaken. This would be contrary to the expressed policy of the federal government: energy self-sufficiency by the 1990s.

The CICA was opposed to such an exception. The research director, R. D. Thomas, pointed out that the only way a company should earn income is to earn revenue on its capital assets. Grants are not income. The basic accounting principle of matching revenues and expenditures period by period requires that the grants be deferred.

A letter, sent by 14 of the major accounting firms, was sent to cabinet ministers supporting the CICA position.

The Ontario Securities Commission (the OSC), which requires *CICA Handbook* rules for all companies listed on the Toronto Stock Exchange (TSE), indicated that they would not automatically accept a federally legislated exception to those rules. Their position was that they would require a public hearing to determine if such statements were misleading in any way. At the same time, the OSC made it clear that they supported the accounting profession and its independence. They strongly objected to government influence or the setting of policies to suit government positions.

Eventually, the federal government decided to leave the accounting rules as they were and not interfere.

Required

Outline the arguments for and against government intervention in the standard setting process, using the PIP Grant case as an example. What are the benefits of an "accounting theory" in this context?

Case 76

Pension Issues

For organizations with defined benefit pension plans, the actuary's estimate of the organization's obligation for pension benefits must be disclosed. The market value of pension plan assets available to satisfy that obligation is also disclosed in the notes to financial statements. Within accounting circles, there is considerable debate as to whether it is more appropriate to disclose this information in the notes, or recognize the net status of the plan as an asset or obligation on the face of the balance sheet, as is required in the United States. Consider, for example, the following conversation, which took place at a social gathering between the chief financial officer (CFO) of a large corporation and a financial analyst (FA) from a brokerage firm:

FA:

I'm sick and tired of having to adjust liabilities on the balance sheet for footnote liabilities, such as the pension obligation! The obligation is that of the organization, not the pension fund, and it belongs, along with related plan assets, on the organization's balance sheet.

CFO:

I was under the impression that it was the extent of disclosure, not the form, that mattered to you analysts.

FA:

That's not the point. A balance sheet must be complete to be useful. It seems to me that the pension obligation meets any reasonable definition of a liability, and it belongs on the balance sheet along with other liabilities. Besides, some users might be misled because they expect the balance sheet to contain all liabilities.

CFO:

I have some concerns about putting the pension obligation on the balance sheet. For one thing, the pension fund is a separate legal entity. Take my organization for example. We have agreed with our union to work towards a goal of having the plan, which is currently underfunded, fully funded by 2005. Our only obligation is to make contributions to the pension fund as suggested by the actuary in order to achieve our funding objective.

For another thing, I believe that the obligation is too soft a number to warrant balance sheet recognition along with other liabilities. There are many uncertainties related to measurement. For example, consider our plan formula, which provides for an annual postretirement pension benefit of 2 percent of the employee's career average earnings for each year of service, to be paid each year beyond retirement until death. All payments are fully indexed to cost-of-living increases after retirement.

And one more thing. How is our auditor supposed to be able to express an opinion as to whether the obligation on the balance sheet is fairly presented? That means a lot of hours spent with the actuary, hours that our organization will have to pay for! Things are much simpler for the auditor when the obligation appears in a footnote only.

FA:

The need to make estimates about the future is not unique to pensions. I wonder whether the claim about uncertainties related to measurement is just an excuse you executives use to conceal your real concerns.

CFO:

Well, to be honest, our organization does have concerns about the economic consequences resulting from putting the pension obligation and the plan assets on the balance sheet. Our stock price could be adversely affected, not to mention our credit rating, borrowing capacity, and management compensation contracts.

FA:

It seems that the controversy regarding pension accounting continues!

Required

Discuss the issues raised.

Case 77

Petro Ltd.

In 1993, Petro Ltd. incurred its second loss in four years. This one was only $280,000, not bad for a company this size in the erratic oil and gas business.

Petro Ltd. has been drilling a series of unprofitable sites. The company has paid no taxes for the past few years while it used up all its loss carryforwards. At the beginning of 1993, the company had net accumulated timing differences of $255,000 due to capital cost allowance exceeding amortization. The average tax rate during the company's existence had been 46 percent. This fell to 45 percent for 1993. The maximum allowable capital cost deduction in 1993 was $120,000, although Petro's management decided not to take any deduction in 1993. The annual $100,000 amortization expense had been correctly recorded.

In 1994, Petro Ltd. returned to profitability, with net income before tax totalling $216,000; this will be taxed at 45 percent. The maximum capital cost allowance deduction this year is $126,000; amortization expense is again $100,000.

Required

Part A. For the year ended December 31, 1994, present the comparative income statement for Petro Ltd., beginning with "Net income (loss) before taxes." Disclose the breakdown of tax expense between current and deferred directly on the statement. Show details of your calculations and clearly state any assumptions you make.

Part B. Since many financial statement readers use the statements as a predictor of cash flows, the taxes payable method of tax expense recognition seems a more logical basis than the Canadian standard of comprehensive allocation. Discuss this statement.

Institute of Chartered Accountants of Ontario, adapted.

Case 78

Plastics Ontario

Plastics Ontario (PO) has recently been incorporated under federal legislation. All the shares are owned by one man, Jimmy Arbuckle. PO will be active in the molded plastics industry, making everything from custom lettered signs to consumer products (e.g., toys) and industrial products (e.g., car dashboards). They will also supply chemicals to other, smaller plastic molding operations.

Arbuckle has 20 years' experience in both production and sales with a large Canadian plastics firm. He took advantage of several recent bankruptcy sales to acquire the manufacturing and molding equipment necessary to start his own firm. He has obtained a 10-year, fixed-interest loan from the Federal Business Development Bank, a line of credit from a chartered bank for working capital, and he has invested $200,000 of his own money. Both banks require audited annual financial statements.

The major pieces of equipment acquired cost $350,000. Another $30,000 will be spent transferring them to PO's new leased facility. Arbuckle estimates another $40,000 will be spent "debugging" the equipment.

Sales are expected to be made on three bases:

1. Custom signs on a prepaid basis. Signs would normally be completed within five business days but could take up to a month for a large order or if volume was high.

2. Direct sales to distributors and manufacturers on terms of 2/10, n/30. Interest on overdue accounts will be 1.4 percent per month. Customers can return defective goods for full credit, and, in common with the industry, goods carry a six-month warranty.

3. Consumer goods to retail outlets on a consignment basis. Arbuckle does not expect to be able to run his molding equipment at full capacity from "outsider" orders for at least two years. Therefore, he plans to design and market a few consumer products—cassette tape holders, doll houses—to keep his operation busy. Several large retail chains have expressed interest in carrying these items but only on a consignment basis. Arbuckle estimates that it will cost $20,000 to design and develop these items.

Arbuckle hopes to break even in his second year of operation and show a profit in his third year. Losses are anticipated in the first year. He has planned to take an extremely low salary for the first three years until he is satisfied that the company can prove its viability. Arbuckle has established relatively low salary levels for his management team but has promised them all generous bonuses based on net income.

Arbuckle has approached you, CA, to act as a financial adviser. He has requested advice on accounting policies and any other relevant issues.

Required

Adopt the role of adviser to Mr. Arbuckle, and draft a report responding to his request.

Case 79

Provincial Hydro I

Provincial Hydro (PH) is an electric utility that generates, supplies, and delivers electric power throughout a small Canadian province. It is incorporated as a Crown corporation, which operates as a cooperative partnership with the relevant municipalities and the provincial government. It is a financially self-sustaining company without share capital, regulated by the provincial government. Its primary customers are the municipalities (which serve about 600,000 end users), 40 large industrial companies (direct service), and 100,000 rural retail customers. PH operates various generating stations, including both nuclear and fossil fuel fired plants. As a result, it is very capital intensive. This, in turn, makes PH sensitive to the cost of money.

PH plays a major role in attracting industry to the province by maintaining competitive rates for electricity. It is profoundly affected by various pieces of provincial legislation.

The financial statement results are used to set utility rates, although there are specific rules about which expenses are permissible and at what time. Many accounting policies are chosen based on the rules for rate recovery. Profits of the corporation are to be applied toward the reduction of the cost of power for the municipalities with whom it has a cooperative partnership.

Management and the municipalities are very sensitive to political pressures. PH is in the public spotlight, and financial results and policies can generate considerable publicity.

A major component of the cost of electricity is fuel cost, which includes the following components: fuel (quantity and price), interest on funds tied up in inventory, transportation, overheads, and a provision for future irradiated fuel transportation, storage, and disposal. The last component relates only to nuclear plants (PH has three) and is provided for based on estimates of future disposal costs.

For example, if the estimate of future cost for disposal of 10 years' accumulated irradiated fuel (also known as nuclear waste) was $60 million, the following annual entry would be made:

Costs	$ 6,000,000	
Liability for future disposal		$ 6,000,000

To accrue one tenth of the cost of disposal.

The problem of disposal has yet to be satisfactorily resolved, however. It seems clear that the solution will involve large elements of fixed cost for even minimum quantities.

There are some that suggest the following alternative treatment for the $60 million estimate:

Costs	$ 6,000,000	
Deferred costs	54,000,000	
Liability for future disposal		$60,000,000

To accrue one tenth of the cost of disposal.

A third alternative is to treat the cost of future disposal as a contingency: while the probability of payment is known (i.e., definite), the amount is not determinable. Thus, the issue should simply be disclosed in the notes to the financial statements. The proponents of this alternative point out that no technology currently exists to "safely" dispose of the irradiated fuels. Estimates, such as the $60 million, are based on a number of assumptions, some of which have already proven false.

At present, PH follows the first alternative and has done so for four years. None of the cost is included in utility rate formulas.

PH is in the process of reexamining a number of their accounting policies. Accordingly, they have hired you as an external adviser in this area. They have requested that you write a report on this issue, incorporating your recommendations.

Required

Assume the role of external adviser and prepare the report.

Case 80

Provincial Hydro II

Provincial Hydro (PH) is an electric utility that generates, supplies, and delivers electric power throughout a small Canadian province. It is incorporated as a Crown corporation, which operates as a cooperative partnership with the relevant municipalities and the provincial government. It is a financially self-sustaining company without share capital, regulated by the provincial government. Its primary customers are the municipal utilities (which serve about 600,000 end users), 40 large industrial companies (direct service), and 100,000 rural retail customers. PH operates various generating stations, including both nuclear and fossil fuel fired plants. As a result, it is very capital intensive. This in turn makes PH sensitive to the cost of money.

PH plays a major role in attracting industry to the province by maintaining competitive rates for electricity. It is profoundly affected by various pieces of provincial legislation.

The financial statement results are used to set utility rates, although there are specific rules about which expenses are permissible and at what time. Many accounting policies are chosen based on the rules for rate recovery. Profits of the corporation are to be applied toward the reduction of the cost of power for the municipalities with whom it has a cooperative partnership.

Management and the municipalities are very sensitive to political pressures. PH is in the public spotlight, and financial results and policies can generate considerable publicity.

A major component of the cost of electricity is fuel cost, which includes the following components: fuel (quantity and price), interest on funds tied up in inventory, transportation, and overheads.

PH has two mothballed generating stations, which are not producing energy at present but may be used during peak demand periods when needed. The plants, all oil-fired, were mothballed as more efficient generation methods were developed.

PH has chosen to reflect the situation by accelerating the rate of depreciation to "reflect the reduced economic value" of the assets. PH has produced demand forecasts (which are regularly updated) that predict when and how much energy will have to come from the mothballed plants. Based on these probability factors, PH established an amortization rate, higher than the original rate, which takes the change of circumstances into account. Depreciation is only charged when the plant is used. Care is taken to avoid premature write-off while the plant may still be useful.

PH uses the CANDU reactor in its nuclear stations. This reactor has relatively low fuel cost but must use "heavy water," H_2O_2 (versus "light water," H_2O, which other reactors use). Heavy water is not consumed in the fissioning process but acts as a moderator of the process. With periodic in-station upgrading to remove impurities, heavy water has an indefinite life.

Heavy water costs, plus interest on inventoried heavy water designated for future use, are capitalized. These capital costs are being written off over 60 years, which is the date PH estimates heavy water will be replaced by new technology. However, the last committed CANDU nuclear unit is due to be retired in 40 years. Management has indicated that nuclear units are regularly upgraded by replacing pressure tubes, which extends their useful life. In addition, the useful life of heavy water does not depend on the life of the station since it can be transferred to another station.

Inventories of fossil fuels are expensed based on an average cost system where the average is calculated monthly on a rolling basis. Average cost was chosen as it seemed the most fair to current and future customers and had a smoothing effect on price fluctuations. Recently, however, with significant declines in fossil fuel prices, there was considerable public comment when electricity prices did not fall accordingly. Management is beginning to consider the alternatives and their advantages and disadvantages.

Management has reminded you that one-time write-downs are not permissible costs in utility rate-setting formulas, nor is it possible to make retroactive changes to the rate structure.

PH has asked you, an external adviser, to consider accounting issues raised. They have requested a report incorporating your recommendations.

Required

Prepare the report.

Case 81

Quebec Sturgeon River Mines

Quebec Sturgeon River Mines (QSRM) is a Canadian public company that directly and through subsidiaries mines several properties in Quebec and the Timmins area of Ontario. Mining operations have been continuous from 1934 when the company was formed.

Recently, a potential investor in the company brought the financial statements to you, a professional accountant (see Exhibit 1), and has asked you to thoroughly evaluate the inventory valuation policy of QSRM, the impact this policy has had on the 1986 financial statements, and industry practice in the mining industry in general.

You have also collected the industry data in Exhibit 2 and the price data shown in Exhibit 3.

Required

Respond to the request.

EXHIBIT 1 QSRM Financial Statement Extracts

QUEBEC STURGEON RIVER MINES LTD.
Extracts from
Annual Report, December 31, 1986

From Significant Accounting Policies
(c) Revenue recognition and bullion on hand

In accordance with industry practice, the company records as revenue the estimated realizable value of bullion awaiting sale at the London second fixing, the U.S. dollar value of which is translated at the noon rate on the last day of the fiscal year.

Financial Statements
Consolidated Balance Sheets
As at December 31, 1986 and 1985

	1986	*1985*
Assets		
Current assets:		
Cash and short-term deposits	$11,246,150	$11,889,751
Bullion on hand	1,219,583	1,787,403
Accounts receivable	1,078,674	237,952
Exploration funds receivable	698,821	403,417
Mining supplies—at cost	239,423	323,001
Prepaid expenses and deposits	47,222	30,819
Marketable securities—at cost (market value $264,455)	218,896	—
	14,748,769	14,672,343
Mining properties	3,844,625	1,844,070
Fixed assets	7,046,060	7,993,996
Investment in joint venture	2,195,984	3,166,823
Deferred expenditures:		
Preproduction and development	7,088,079	7,575,141
Exploration	14,304,758	10,091,628
Incorporation and financing	1,772,145	1,869,309
	23,164,982	19,536,078
Other assets	250,169	85,769
Total assets	$51,250,589	$47,299,079

EXHIBIT 1 (*concluded*)

QUEBEC STURGEON RIVER MINES LTD.
Consolidated Statement of Earnings (Extracts)
For the Years Ended December 31, 1986, 1985, and 1984

	1986	*1985*	*1984*
Revenue:			
Bullion production	$10,581,393	9,568,937	$ 9,241,840
Expenses:			
Mining	4,429,313	4,709,858	4,979,526
Milling	1,704,639	1,715,412	1,765,140
Mine—general	1,690,441	1,404,726	1,573,104
Surface diamond drilling	140,801	58,009	228,406
Depreciation and amortization	1,802,386	1,840,589	1,822,536
	9,767,580	9,728,594	10,368,712
Mine operating income (loss)	813,813	(159,657)	(1,126,872)
Other income (expense)			
Interest earned	878,562	1,048,815	1,361,156
Investment income	116,641	—	—
Administration expense	(1,179,413)	(1,036,509)	(968,483)
Interest expense	(70,478)	(1,699,683)	(102,426)
Joint venture operators' fees	—	56,426	208,974
Total	(254,688)	(1,630,951)	499,221
Earnings (loss)	$ 559,125	$(1,790,608)	$ (627,651)

EXHIBIT 2 QSRM Industry Data

Extracts from
Financial Reporting by Canadian Mining Companies
Deloitte Haskins & Sells, 1982

Inventories

All of the survey companies disclosed the basis of valuation of inventories as recommended in Paragraph 3030.10 of the *CICA Handbook*. Table 3.7 (*a*) summarizes the bases of valuation. From this table it may be concluded that most inventories are valued at the lower of cost and/or net realizable value.

* * *

A practice frequently followed within the industry is to value concentrates and/or bullion produced at estimated net realizable value. Of the 11 companies that produced concentrates and/or bullion, 8 of them valued these inventories at estimated net realizable value. Two of the three remaining companies used the lower of cost and net realizable value method, and the 11th company chose to value its concentrates and/or bullion at the lower of average cost of production and net realizable value.

Table 3.7(*a*)

	*Basis of Inventory Valuation**				
	Integrated	*Metals*	*Uranium & Coal*	*Gold*	*Total*
Lower of cost and/or net realizable value	5	4	1	1	11
Estimated net realizable value	1	3	1	3	8
Lower of average cost and replacement cost	1	1	1	—	3
Average cost less allowances for obsolescence	1	—	—	1	2
Current selling price	1	1	—	—	2
Cost	2	—	—	—	2
Estimated realizable metal prices	—	—	1	—	1
Lower of cost and replacement cost	1	—	—	—	1
Lower of cost or market	—	—	1	—	1

* Some of the bases apply to only part of the inventory, so a company may use more than one basis.

EXHIBIT 3 QSRM Price Data

	Selected Prices		
	1986	*1985*	*1984*
Gold prices in U.S. funds:			
High	$423.50	$329.80	$386.50
Low	339.10	299.30	320.10
Close	391.00	321.90	320.10
U.S. dollar:			
Canadian equivalent of $1 U.S.			
December 31	$1.3895	$1.3654	$1.2949

Sources: Gold prices are stated in *Statistics,* Standard & Poor's, 1991.
Exchange rates from *International Money Markets,* Royal Bank of Canada, 1991.

Case 82

S Limited

S Ltd. is one of the wholly owned subsidiaries of R Ltd. All these companies are incorporated under the Canada Business Corporations Act. The shares and debt of R Ltd., which manufactures various types of electronic equipment, are publicly held in Canada. S Ltd. was incorporated one year ago to help diversify the operations of R Ltd. S Ltd. arranges construction, then owns and leases commercial properties.

The first year-end of S Ltd. is rapidly approaching, and accounting principles and policies must be chosen for the company. During the last three months of this first year, S Ltd. completed construction on its first two buildings; the first building is to be leased for 20 years to C Ltd., another subsidiary of R Ltd., slightly below market rates; and the second has 12 floors, 6 of which are under lease to the federal government on a 10-year basis with lessee options extending for a further 20 years. Only two other floors in the second building are presently under contract, with occupancy to commence in six months.

Management of S Ltd. has proposed the following:

1. All buildings are to be depreciated on a 40-year life using the sinking fund method with an interest factor of 6 percent per annum. Depreciation is to commence when 60 percent of the building is occupied.

2. The present value of future lease payments less expected maintenance and similar costs will be computed annually, using a 6 percent after income tax rate. If this sum is less than S Ltd.'s carrying value of each building, the carrying value will be written down to the present value. If a building is not fully leased, the present value would be compared on a proportionate basis. (For example, if the building is 60 percent occupied,

---

Adapted, with permission from the *Uniform Final Examination Handbook,* (1979). © The Canadian Institute of Chartered Accountants, Toronto. Changes to the original questions and/or suggested approaches to answering are the sole responsibility of the authors and have not been reviewed or endorsed by the CICA.

the present value of lease payments would be compared to 60 percent of the carrying value to ascertain whether a write-down is necessary.)

3. Revenue recognition will be on a cash basis, being recorded on receipt of rental cheques from lessees.

4. Any public relations expenditures are to be capitalized as building costs.

5. Property taxes on land held for future building are to be capitalized as part of the cost of land.

6. Any building acquired by trading with other owners is to be recorded at fair market value of the higher valued building at the date of exchange. (S Ltd. is presently considering trading building 2 for another building close to 1. The only cash to be exchanged is minimal, representing the difference between the mortgages outstanding on the two buildings.)

CA has obtained the audit of S Ltd. and for years has held the audit of R Ltd. R Ltd. depreciates its buildings and machinery on a straight-line basis over periods of up to 40 years.

The treasurer of R Ltd. and the controller of S Ltd. have arranged a meeting with CA to discuss these accounting policies, and they have informed CA that they consider the amounts involved material. They desire an unqualified audit report and want to discuss whether the above proposals are acceptable. Whether the proposals are acceptable or not, the client wishes to know CA's opinion, with reasons about the most appropriate alternative in each case.

Required

Assume the role of CA and prepare a position paper on the matters to be discussed at the upcoming meeting.

Case 83

SBL Corporation

SBL Corporation is a Canadian public corporation, incorporated under the CBCA and listed on the Toronto Stock Exchange. A significant block (35 percent) of its shares are owned by the children of the two company founders; they are not involved in the day-to-day management of the company. Remaining shares are widely held and actively traded. Operating results over the last two years have been disappointing and share price has declined accordingly. Management has a bonus plan based partially on comparisons of actual-to-budget, and partially on share price performance.

SBL Corporation is a major producer of small appliances—toaster ovens, irons, coffee makers, and the like—which it makes under its own brand name and also under contract for house brands. Products are sold in Canada and the United States. Five years ago, SBL acquired 80 percent of the outstanding common shares of Tiny Toys Limited, an industry leader in children's toys and baby products. The acquisition was structured as a leveraged buyout. Unfortunately, the operating performance of Tiny Toys has been less than impressive, and is the major reason SBL's consolidated results have stagnated. However, Tiny Toys is still well regarded and has significant market share.

At its last board of directors' meeting, the SBL board approved a spin-off of Tiny Toys Limited. The shares of Tiny Toys will be distributed directly (or "spun off") on a pro-rata basis to the shareholders of SBL. Instead of controlling Tiny Toys indirectly, through SBL, they will control it directly. Shareholders may then decide for themselves whether to sell or retain the Tiny Toys shares. Since Tiny Toys is also a public company, the investment is liquid.

Adapted, with permission, from the Atlantic School of Chartered Accountancy.

Two alternatives have been suggested to account for the spin-off:

1. The spin-off is recorded at book value, as a property dividend.

Dividends	$100,000	
Investment in Tiny Toys (book value)		$100,000
(amounts in thousands)		

   This method recognizes that there has been no change in control, and no transaction with third parties. Other companies have used this method to account for a spin-off.

2. The spin-off is recorded at market value, as a property dividend.

Dividends (market value)	$175,000	
Investment in Tiny Toys		$100,000
Gain on distribution of long-term investments		75,000

   This method uses the market price of the shares to value the transaction, in accordance with the *CICA Handbook* section on Non-Monetary Transactions.

Required

1. The board has asked you, the controller, to evaluate these two alternative accounting treatments and make a recommendation as to the preferred treatment. Your analysis should be thorough and include an examination of the effect on users, income, and equity.
2. In the year of the spin-off, how would the operating results of Tiny Toys be reflected in the financial statements?

Case 84

Scientific Delivery Corp.

Scientific Delivery Corp. (SDC) is a Canadian company founded in 1985; it went public in 1989 and acquired existing businesses in the United States and Great Britain. The founder and original president, Jonathan Claxon, retired in 1991 after developing a strong management team and training his successor.

SDC's product is laser beam technology. A laser is a beam of light whose energy can be directed onto small surfaces; laser technology is used for product labeling, coding of electronic components, welding, drilling, cutting, spectroscopy (identification of the atoms or molecules in an unknown substance), and delicate surgery (e.g., removal of cataracts and replacement of the lens). Different laser radiation wavelengths are required for different purposes; therefore, there is a range of laser products (gas, solid state, dye, excimer). The difference among them is the material which produces the laser light. SDC's products are primarily in the scientific and components coding lines.

In 1992, the company's management realized that expansion of sales in the component coding area would continue only if more electronic components could be made laser markable; as a result, SDC began a program to develop new coating materials for the components. In 1992, several events affected SDC's results. One was the introduction by the company of a dye laser. SDC's sales of excimer lasers had been decreasing because the two types are usually purchased together, and it was hoped that the addition of the dye laser to the product line would help the company overcome a competitive disadvantage. Also in 1992, the effects of worldwide cutbacks in government funding for research were felt. In addition, all North American scientific instrument manufacturers had problems in pricing their export sales due to wide fluctuations of most European currencies.

The 1993 results showed continued effects of the 1992 setbacks; however, near the end of 1993, SDC received an order for $1.2 million in solid-state lasers for use in surgery. The company was also in the process of developing applications of gas laser technology for use in military defence.

In 1991, management changed the policy for capitalization and amortization of research and development costs. Below are extracts from SDC's most recent financial statements:

Research and Development Costs

Development costs relating to specific products that in the company's view have a clearly defined future market are deferred and amortized on a straight-line basis over three years, commencing in the year following the year in which the new-product development was completed.

Provision for Income Tax

The company uses the tax allocation method of accounting for taxes.

Details from the past five financial statements, as originally issued, are as follows (in thousands):

	1993	*1992*	*1991*	*1990*	*1989*
Sales	3,000	4,300	3,500	3,200	3,500
Net income (loss) before tax	(475)	450	400	350	650
Expenditure on research and development*	1,625	1,425	900	1,200	1,125
Current year's R & D expensed*	0	0	0	1,200	1,125
Previously deferred development costs expensed	1,175	1,075	925	0	0
Deferred development balance at year-end	2,875	2,425	2,075	0	0
Total assets	5,700	6,000	4,800	3,800	3,000
Tax rate	0.48	0.48	0.48	0.48	0.48

* 1985–88: $450 per year.

Required

Comment on SDC's accounting policies for research and development and income taxes. Include in your discussion your recommendations for the measurement and disclosure of the taxable loss carryforward in 1993.

Case 85

Shaw Cablesystems Ltd.

Shaw Cablesystems Ltd. is a publicly owned company listed on the Toronto and Alberta stock exchanges. Revenues are derived principally from cable television services in Canada and, to a lesser extent, from radio broadcasting. Once in the newspaper publishing business, Shaw has either sold or is in the process of selling these divisions; they are shown as discontinued operations in 1991.

Shaw reports total assets of $347 million in 1991, and it generated profits of $15 million from revenues of $141 million (see Exhibit 1). Intangible assets represent $170 million of the asset base.

EXHIBIT 1 Shaw Cablesystems. Financial Statement Extracts

SHAW CABLESYSTEMS LTD.
Consolidated Balance Sheet
As at August 31

	1991	*1990*
Assets		
Current:		
Cash and term deposits	$ —	$ 36,587,000
Accounts receivable	6,616,000	4,747,000
Prepaid expenses	1,382,000	1,427,000
	7,998,000	42,761,000
Discontinued operations	3,320,000	9,056,000
Other investments and deposits on acquisitions	787,000	4,866,000
Property, plant, and equipment	163,072,000	138,818,000
Deferred charges	1,686,000	585,000
Subscriber base, broadcast licenses, and goodwill	170,067,000	81,212,000
Total assets	$346,930,000	$277,298,000

EXHIBIT 1 *(continued)*

SHAW CABLESYSTEMS LTD.
Consolidated Balance Sheet
As at August 31

Liabilities and Shareholders' Equity

	1991	*1990*
Current:		
Bank indebtedness	$ 3,074,000	$ —
Accounts payable and accrued liabilities	13,100,000	14,529,000
Income taxes payable	2,174,000	2,593,000
Unearned subscriber revenue	9,535,000	6,950,000
Current portion of long-term debt	15,977,000	13,616,000
	43,860,000	37,688,000
Long-term debt	154,499,000	115,116,000
Deferred income taxes	17,501,000	15,608,000
Shareholders' equity:		
Share capital	27,861,000	13,859,000
Contributed surplus	53,375,000	54,901,000
Retained earnings	49,834,000	40,126,000
Total equity	131,070,000	108,886,000
Total liabilities and shareholders' equity	$346,930,000	$277,298,000

Consolidated Statement of Income
Year Ended August 31

	1991	*1990*
Income:		
Cable television	$130,407,000	$102,734,000
Radio broadcasting	9,903,000	8,582,000
Other	606,000	589,000
	140,916,000	111,905,000
Expenses:		
Cable television:		
Operations and administration	36,325,000	31,978,000
Network fees	21,292,000	18,196,000
Agreement and franchise charges	6,264,000	4,896,000
Copyright fees	4,815,000	2,633,000
Radio broadcasting	8,295,000	7,721,000
Other	347,000	114,000
	77,338,000	65,538,000
Operating income	63,578,000	46,367,000
Investment income	1,545,000	4,153,000
	65,123,000	50,520,000

EXHIBIT 1 (*continued*)

SHAW CABLESYSTEMS LTD.
Consolidated Statement of Income
As at August 31

	1991	*1990*
Depreciation and amortization	$ 19,386,000	$ 15,539,000
Interest:		
Long-term debt	17,208,000	14,491,000
Current debt	73,000	23,000
	36,667,000	30,053,000
Income before the following	28,456,000	20,467,000
Gain on sale of investment	—	18,682,000
Gain on pension plan conversion	1,498,000	—
Income before income taxes	29,954,000	39,149,000
Income taxes:		
Current	12,005,000	11,295,000
Deferred	2,090,000	2,850,000
	14,095,000	14,145,000
Income before the following	15,859,000	25,004,000
Equity in earnings of investee companies	—	598,000
Discontinued operations	(773,000)	(749,000)
Net income	$ 15,086,000	$ 24,853,000
Earnings per share:		
Before discontinued operations	$ 0.69	$ 1.14
Discontinued operations	(0.04)	(0.04)
Earnings per share	$ 0.65	$ 1.10

Selected Notes

1. Accounting Policies:
   Subscriber base, broadcast licenses, and goodwill.
   The excess of cost of shares over the fair value of net tangible assets acquired is allocated between subscriber base or broadcast licenses and goodwill, if any. Amounts allocated to subscriber base or broadcast licenses are not amortized unless, in the case of cable subscribers, the number of subscribers falls below the level at date of acquisition, or the Company believes there has been a decrease in value. . . .

* * *

Leave license as identify asset.

EXHIBIT 1 *(continued)*

SHAW CABLESYSTEMS LTD.
Selected Notes
As at August 31

3. Business Acquisitions:
A summary of net assets acquired through business acquisitions, accounted for under the purchase method is as follows:

	1991	*1990*
Identifiable net assets acquired at assigned fair values:		
Working capital	$ —	$ 34,000
Fixed assets	16,781,000	1,932,000
Subscriber base	88,860,000	3,298,000
Broadcast licenses	—	8,684,000
Total assets	105,641,000	13,948,000
Working capital deficiency	3,016,000	—
Long-term debt	23,572,000	2,401,000
Deferred income taxes	(158,000)	5,000
Total liabilities	$ 26,430,000	$ 2,406,000
Purchase price	$ 79,211,000	$11,542,000

The company purchased the following cable television companies during the year:

(*a*) Vercom Cable Services Ltd., Vernon, B.C., effective September 1, 1990, for $10,756,000, including 58,877 Senior Preferred Shares, Series II, valued at $5,888,000.
(*b*) Cranbrook Cable Television Limited and Creston Cabled-Video Ltd., Cranbook/Creston, B.C., effective September 1, 1990, for $9,442,000, including 21,550 Senior Preferred Shares, Series II, valued at $2,155,000.
(*c*) Merritt Cablevision Ltd., Merritt, B.C., effective November 1, 1990, for $2,298,000 in cash.
(*d*) Saskatoon Telecable Ltd., Saskatoon/Prince Albert, Saskatchewan, effective February 1, 1991, for $50,516,000. Consideration for the purchase included the issuance of 5,000 Redeemable Convertible Preferred Shares, Series I, valued at $5 million and vendor financing in the amount of $35 million. The balance of the purchase price was satisfied with cash.
(*e*) Panorama Cable Systems Ltd., Invermere, B.C., effective April 1, 1991,for $2,375,000, including 4,500 Senior Preferred Shares, Series III, valued at $450,000.
(*f*) Crowsnest Cablevision Ltd., in southwest Alberta, effective July 1, 1991, or $3,386,000, including 8,875 Senior Preferred Shares, Series IV, valued at $888,000.
(*g*) Uniacke Cablevision Limited, Mt. Uniacke, N.S., effective August 31, 1991, for $438,000 in cash.

* * *

EXHIBIT 1 (*concluded*)

SHAW CABLESYSTEMS LTD.
Selected Notes
As at August 31

6. Subscriber Base, Broadcast Licenses, and Goodwill:

	1991	*1990*
Subscriber base	$149,866,000	$61,011,000
Broadcast licenses	19,280,000	19,280,000
Goodwill (acquired prior to 1974)	921,000	921,000
Total	$170,067,000	$81,212,000

Shaw's cable operations have grown primarily through acquisitions—for instance, seven cable television companies were acquired in 1991, for aggregate consideration of approximately $79 million. Proceeds are generally allocated to the "subscriber base" of the acquiree, or "broadcast licenses." No portion of a purchase price has been allocated to "goodwill" per se since before 1974. Goodwill acquired before 1974 did not have to be amortized; the subscriber base and broadcast licenses (awarded by the CRTC and periodically reviewed) have never been amortized.

A professional accountant, you have just started work in the controller's department. The controller has given you your first assignment:

> "We'd like a pair of fresh eyes to take a look at our financial position. How would an analyst assess our financial strengths and weaknesses? Why don't you pick five of the most important ratios for Shaw, and explain how we stack up.
>
> "We also have to take a look at our policies for accounting for intangibles, in light of the CICA's requirements for accounting for Capital Assets, Section 3060 of the *CICA Handbook*. This section is effective for Shaw's 1992 fiscal year. We don't honestly feel that the subscriber base or broadcast licenses have a finite expected life—well, maybe sixty years is reasonable. What can we do to minimize the impact on earnings?"

Required

Prepare the requested report.

Case 86

Silverado Investments Limited

Silverado Investments Limited (SIL) began operations in 1985 when Eldon Silver left his job as head project engineer for Alis-Dan Construction and started his own real estate development company. The company was an immediate success, resulting from a combination of Silver's entrepreneurial skills and the significant demand for residential rental units.

The normal development process for a residential apartment project starts with a promoter (SIL or an outsider) syndicating the project and setting up a limited partnership. SIL then finds a site, arranges for interim and mortgage financing, and constructs the building (usually employing subcontractors). Mortgage advances approximating 85 percent of the total cost are made to SIL as the building progresses. Upon project completion, SIL receives the final payment of approximately 15 percent and would then turn the project over to an independent property manager.

In the 1990s, successful real estate development has become much more difficult. The phase-out of various tax incentives, the volatility of interest rates, the recession, and flat demand for rental housing in various Canadian urban centers, have all led to a decline in the attractiveness of rental projects to investors. To sell an investment syndication now, the developer must play a much more active role.

Accounting policies for various unique aspects of certain of these real estate projects have yet to be established. (See Exhibit 2.) Silver is

---

Adapted, with permission from Manfred Schneider.

concerned that these policies should be the correct ones and that they can be consistently applied to future projects. His concern is magnified by the fact that bank and securities commissions (under whose jurisdictions these limited partnership offerings are promoted), now want audited statements for the corporation as a whole.

Silver has contacted you, a professional accountant, to provide a complete analysis of the issues and to give recommendations for policies. The company's 1994 draft financial statements (Exhibit 1) and description of current projects (Exhibits 2 and 3) have been provided.

EXHIBIT 1 Silverado Investments Limited, Financial Statements

SILVERADO INVESTMENTS LIMITED
Balance Sheet (unaudited)
at September 30
(in thousands)

	1994 (*draft*)	*1993*
Assets		
Properties:		
Income-producing	$ 1,400	$ 1,500
Held for future development	1,500	800
	2,900	2,300
Projects under construction with sales agreements net of mortgage advances	4,100	6,500
Cash	1,650	—
Due from joint venture	863	754
Mortgage advances receivable	2,900	4,875
Investment in joint venture, at cost	1,000	1,000
Other assets	800	780
	11,313	13,909
Total assets	$14,213	$16,209
Liabilities		
Accounts payable related to projects under construction	$ 7,280	$10,610
Accounts payable—other	2,175	1,610
Total liabilities	$ 9,455	$12,220

EXHIBIT 1 (*concluded*)

SILVERADO INVESTMENTS LIMITED
Balance Sheet (unaudited)
at September 30
(in thousands)

	1994	*1993*
Shareholders' Equity		
Share capital	$ 1	$ 1
Retained earnings	4,757	3,988
Total equity	4,758	3,989
Total liabilities and shareholders' equity	$14,213	$16,209

Statements of Income and Retained Earnings
For the Year Ended September 30

	1994	*1993*
Revenue:		
Residential project sales	$15,000	$19,000
Rental and other	154	145
	15,154	19,145
Expenses:		
Cost of projects sold	12,756	16,250
Rental	142	130
General and other	1,125	830
	14,023	17,210
Net income for the year	1,131	1,935
Retained earnings at beginning of year	3,988	2,053
Dividends	362	—
Retained earnings at end of year	$ 4,757	$ 3,988

EXHIBIT 2 Current Projects—Silverado Investments Limited

1. *Income-Producing Properties*—consists of a 40-unit apartment building owned and operated by SIL since 1989. The building is in a rapidly developing urban harbourfront area. SIL has applied to the municipality to obtain approval for condominium status. If the approval is granted, it is expected that the units could be sold for $100,000 each. Approximately $1.1 million would be needed for improvements at that time. The company has stopped depreciating the building because the site is already undervalued on the books.
2. *Held for Future Development Properties*—consists of a 15-acre site on the outskirts of Montreal. SIL has subdivided the land in Phase I and since August 1994 they have been selling the individual lots. Additional information with respect to this project follows:

   a. Phase I—Consists of 25 single-family lots on four acres and a one-acre lot suitable for 25 multiple-unit dwellings (i.e., duplexes, townhouses, and so on).
   Phase II—Plans have not been finalized on this 10-acre parcel. The mix of units is expected to be similar to Phase I.
   b. Development costs of $300,000 have been incurred to construct roads and water mains. These costs are expected to benefit each phase equally.
   c. The sales prices are estimated to be $25,000 each for the single-family lots and $15,000 per unit for the multiple-dwelling lots in Phase I. In Phase II, prices will be $30,000 and $20,000, respectively.
   d. Five single-family lots have been sold since September 30, 1994, and 15 more are expected to be sold soon. It is expected that 10 multiple-dwelling lots will also be sold by the end of December.
   e. Revenue from lots sold has been recorded, but no cost has yet been expensed.

3. *Projects under Construction*—consists of a major development project (255 units) for which an agreement has been signed with a group of limited partners. When the project is completed, in July of 1995, the building will be sold to the partners, who will pay SIL as follows:

Cash, provided by first mortgage from Confidential Insurance	$11,000,000
Cash, payments by the investors to SIL	1,000,000
6% notes receivable to SIL from the investors, payable in four equal installments on the anniversary of the turnover date	2,000,000
Five-year 18% second mortgage provided by SIL	1,500,000
Total	$15,500,000

The estimated total costs of the project are $12,300,000. SIL plans to record the profit ($3,200,000) in July 1995, when the building is completed. The assets received in consideration (listed above) would be recorded at that time.

EXHIBIT 3 Information on Development Project under Construction— Silverado Investment Limited

SIL is currently constructing a 255-unit luxury apartment complex, which will be completed by July 1995. (See item 3, Exhibit 2.) This project differs from former development projects in both the manner of financing and in the number of indemnities and covenants that SIL must provide. The turnover date, referred to below, is the date the Limited Partnership assumes ownership of the project. It occurs when the project is finished and 90 percent leased.

Extracts from Offering Memorandum

SIL Second Mortgage. The SIL mortgage will be in the principal amount of $1.5 million and will bear interest at the rate of 18 percent after the turnover date.

The SIL mortgage will be for a five-year term beginning on the turnover date. The mortgage will include the following terms:

1. The mortgage will be without recourse to the limited partners.
2. Payment of principal and accrued interest at maturity only to the extent that proceeds are available from the refinancing of the first mortgage; and the mortgage to be renewed for any unpaid balance for a further term, without interest.
3. The Limited Partnership will have the right to set off amounts owing by it under the SIL mortgage against amounts by which SIL is in default under the Purchase and Development Agreement.

Initial Leasing Period Indemnity

The Purchase and Development Agreement provides that SIL will operate the project on behalf of the Limited Partnership and will indemnify the Limited Partnership for all losses incurred in operating the project during the initial leasing period which ends on the turnover date.

Cash Flow Guarantee

SIL has covenanted to provide interest-free loans to the Limited Partnership for the following purposes:

i. To fund, as required, for a period of 10 years from the turnover date, the amount, if any, by which the total operating expenses of the project (including payments on account of principal and interest due on the mortgages, but excluding noncash items such as depreciation and reserves for replacement of equipment and chattels) exceed the aggregate gross income receipts from the project.

ii. To fund during the period commencing on the turnover date and ending on December 31, 1997, the amount (the "Guaranteed Amount"), if any, by which the actual net cash flow is less than the amounts set forth opposite "Net Distributable Cash Flow" contained in the "Forecasts."

*Note: The "Forecasts," which are not contained in these exhibits, are cash flow predictions outlining the expected positive cash flow available for distribution to the partners.

EXHIBIT 3 (*concluded*)

Management of the Project

SIL will be appointed manager of the project for a term of 10 years and will be paid 5 percent of the monthly gross income receipts.

The management agreement will provide that SIL will be responsible for the ongoing leasing of apartment units comprising the project, maintenance and repairs, collection of rents, payment of all expenses properly incurred in connection with such duties out of revenues received from the project, including all amounts payable under the mortgages, the maintenance of fire and liability insurance on the project, the preparation of a budget for each fiscal year for the project, and the annual remittance of cash surpluses to the Limited Partnership.

Required

Respond to Silver's request.

Case 87

Smith Wesley Ltd.

Smith Wesley Ltd. is a manufacturer and supplier of paper products. It specializes in a broad range of office needs, including photocopier paper and stationery, as well as corrugated (paperboard) boxes for packaging, newsprint, and so forth. The company is fully integrated, owning timberland, milling and manufacturing facilities, and sale and distribution centers.

Smith Wesley is 29 percent owned by a large American multinational company. The remaining common shares are widely held and traded on the Toronto Stock Exchange. Recently, the company's management has suspected that shares are being quietly accumulated by a group of investors interested in a takeover bid.

Smith Wesley's operating results have not met its own or analysts' expectations over the last three years. This was due to two factors: a softening of product prices in reaction to increased competition, and increased production costs. Smith Wesley recently completed an aggressive capital expansion program, resulting in state-of-the-art, highly efficient production facilities. Unfortunately, the facilities are only highly efficient if run at peak capacity, which sales volume has not been able to support. Product costs, therefore, have exceeded expectations.

Smith Wesley is concerned that its seemingly poor operating results will encourage existing shareholders to divest, and make the company an easy target for a takeover attempt. Accordingly, it is examining its reporting practices to see if its financial position is being well represented.

Currently, inventories are valued on the last-in, first-out (LIFO) method, to facilitate performance evaluation by the major American shareholder. The first-in, first-out (FIFO) system has been used for tax purposes. The following values (in thousands) have been calculated:

Inventory	*LIFO*	*FIFO*
December 31, 1994	$115,398	$162,998
December 31, 1993	$111,261	$150,861
December 31, 1992	$106,419	$140,421

EXHIBIT 1 Smith Wesley Ltd Financial Statement Extracts

SMITH WESLEY LTD.
Statement of Income and Retained Earnings
For the Year Ended December 31
(in thousands)

	1994	*1993*
Sales	$1,673,250	$1,840,360
Costs and expenses:		
Cost of sales	1,316,260	1,330,040
Selling and general	293,740	306,670
Financing costs	175,090	157,760
	1,785,090	1,794,470
Income (loss) before tax	(111,840)	45,890
Provision for tax (recovery)	(48,090)	19,730
Net income (loss)	$ (63,750)	$ 26,160
Retained earnings, beginning of year	247,830	221,670
Retained earnings, end of year	$ 184,080	$ 247,830

Management is considering changing their inventory costing system from LIFO to FIFO to make their statements more comparable with other Canadian companies.

Required

1. Recast the 1994 and 1993 income statement (only) using FIFO as an inventory costing policy. The tax rate is 43 percent.
2. Comment on the desirability of the proposed change. Your analysis should include the predicted reaction of the stock market to the change.

Case 88

So-fine Foods Ltd.

So-fine Foods Ltd. (SFL) is a large Canadian supermarket chain, with common shares, preferred shares, and corporate debentures sold publicly.

SFL prides itself on the quality of its annual report, which has several times won awards for its informativeness. Accordingly, the controllers' department at SFL takes a serious interest in accounting trends and standard changes.

EXHIBIT 1 So-fine Foods Ltd Deferred Tax Data

a. Calculation of provision for tax:

	Accounting Income	*Taxable Income*	*Effect on Deferred Taxes*
Income before tax	$5,390,000	$5,390,000	
Plus:			
Depreciation		605,000	$ 605,000
Reserve for obsolete inventories		100,000	100,000
Club dues	10,000	10,000	
Foreign advertising	20,000	20,000	
Less:			
Dividends from taxable Canadian corporations	(120,000)	(120,000)	
Capital cost allowance		(1,750,000)	(1,750,000)
	$5,300,000	$4,255,000	$(1,045,000)
Tax rate, 42%	$2,226,000	$1,787,100	$ 438,900

EXHIBIT 1 *(concluded)*

		Taxable Income	*Effect on Deferred Taxes*
b. Balance in deferred taxes, end of current year, including adjustment for current year			$1,258,200 cr.
Consisting of:			
1. Provision for obsolete inventory ($100,000 × $0.42) Provision in current year income Deductible for tax when incurred, expected next year			$ 42,000 dr.
2. Net Book Value versus UCC:			
Net book value, end of year		$6,785,000	
Undepreciated capital cost, end of year		3,485,000	
Difference		3,300,000	
Rate of accumulation		$0.394	1,300,200 cr.
Balance in deferred taxes			$1,258,200 cr.

c. Additional information:

1. Tax rates are expected to stay stable for the next two years, then increase by 1 percent per year for the next five years. These rates have not been enacted.
2. The Net Book Value/UCC timing difference is expected to reverse as follows (1 is next year, 5 is fifth subsequent year, etc):

Year	*Amount*
1	$ 430,000
2	475,000
3	500,000
4	540,000
5	560,000
6	795,000
Total	$3,300,000

Current year's timing differences reverse in Year 3 ($400,000), Year 4 ($540,000), and Year 5 ($205,000).

Note: New originating timing differences are not considered in the above schedule, which shows how the $3,300,000 of existing timing differences would reverse if no capital assets are acquired. If new capital assets are acquired on schedule, no reversals are expected after Year 2.

An analysis of the deferred tax account and calculation of the latest year's "Provision for Tax" is contained in Exhibit 1. You, a junior accountant in the controller's department, have been asked to prepare a brief summary of the financial statement impact of three independent scenarios:

1. A change to the accrual method from the deferral method. SFL defines the accrual method as measuring the future liability for taxes at the current enacted tax rate.
2. A change to partial tax allocation from full tax allocation. SFL defines partial tax allocation as considering only those timing differences expected to reverse in the next three years (apply this using the accrual method).
3. A change to discounting deferred taxes from a nondiscounting system. A discount rate of 10 percent should be used (apply this using the accrual method).

Required

Prepare the requested analysis.

Case 89

Sousa Ltd.

Sousa Ltd. is a small privately owned company engaged in the plastic molding industry. Audited financial statements are prepared annually, and the year-end is December 31.

Recently, it leased three pieces of manufacturing equipment from the leasing subsidiary of a major chartered bank. It could have borrowed money from the same bank, using the equipment as collateral, at prime plus 3 percent, or about 10 percent interest. Management decided to use leases as the financing method. The lease contracts are shown in Exhibits 1–3.

The leased manufacturing equipment has an approximate useful life of seven years. Other such equipment is depreciated using the straight-line method.

You, a member of Sousa's accounting department, have been asked by the controller to do an analysis that will show the impact each *separate* lease will have on net income, the balance sheet, and the notes to the financial statements.

Required

Prepare the requested analysis for each lease individually.

EXHIBIT 1 Sousa Ltd Lease #4921

Alberta Lease Co.

Equipment Lease

LESSEE NO	LEASE NO
1426	4921

ALWAYS REFER TO THESE NUMBERS

LESSEE		SUPPLIER OF EQUIPMENT	
LESSEE NAME Sousa Ltd.		NAME X Machinery Co.	
ADDRESS 100 Any Street		ADDRESS 400 Main Street	
CITY Metropolis	PROV Alta.	CITY Metropolis	PROV Alta.
POSTAL CODE A1A 2B3	TELEPHONE NO 991-9999	POSTAL CODE A2A 7B9	TELEPHONE NO 997-1111
CONTACT Mr. Smith		SUPPLIER REPRESENTATIVE Mr. Jones	

EQUIPMENT LOCATION IF OTHER THAN ABOVE — ADDRESS — CITY — COUNTY — PROV

n/a

LANDLORD — ADDRESS

n/a

NO OF UNITS	MODEL NO	YEAR	DESCRIPTION	LIST PRICE	SERIAL NO
1	40902	1994	Molding Equipment	$72,000	

TERMS OF PAYMENT (total subject to any provincial sales tax % changes)

TERM IN YEARS	NO OF RENTAL PAYMENTS	PAYMENTS WILL BE MADE	FIRST RENTAL DUE DATE (M D Y)	AMOUNT OF EACH RENTAL PAYMENT EXCLUDING SALES TAX	INSURANCE COSTS	TOTAL AMOUNT EACH PAYMENT	SECURITY DEPOSIT	PURCHASE OPTION PRICE AND DATE
3	3	☑ YEARLY ☐	07 01 94	$ 19621	$ 1,175	$ 20,796	$	$ n/a AT END OF OF THE LEASE TERM

TERMS AND CONDITIONS OF LEASE

For and in consideration of the covenants and agreements by the Lessee to pay the total rental payment herein provided for and to perform the terms, covenants and conditions on the Lessee's part herein contained, the Lessor hereby leases, and lets unto the Lessee, and the Lessee hereby leases and takes from the Lessor, each unit of equipment described above and hereinafter referred to as "said equipment", for the term set forth above (commencing on the date of the first delivery of any of the said equipment to the Lessee) and upon and subject to the covenants, conditions and provisions hereinafter set forth. Notwithstanding the foregoing, in the event that such first delivery takes place before the First Rental Due Date the term of this Lease shall be extended by the number of days from and including the date of the first delivery of any part of the said equipment and the First Rental Due Date.

1. RENTAL. For the use of said equipment, the Lessee shall pay to the Lessor at the Lessor's office, at 100 Main Street, Metropolis, Alta a total rental payment equal to the amount of each rental payment specified above multiplied by the number of rental payments specified above. The first rental payment and Security Deposit shall become due on the First Rental Due Date indicated above. Subsequent rental payments shall become due in every consecutive month or period, as the case may be, thereafter on the same date of each such month or period as the First Rental Due Date indicated above, or in the event that there is no such corresponding date, the last date of the said month. Rental payment hereunder is payable without abatement.
2. EQUIPMENT DESCRIPTION. The Lessee authorizes the Lessor to complete the description of said equipment above with the insertion of serial numbers and other details specifically identifying said equipment.
3. REPRESENTATIONS AND WARRANTIES. Each unit of said equipment leased hereunder is of a size, design and capacity personally chosen and selected by the Lessee and the Lessee is satisfied that the same is suitable for its purposes and the Lessor has made no representation or warranty with respect to the suitability or durability of any such unit for the purposes or uses of the Lessee, or any other representation or warranty express or implied with respect thereto.

   The Lessee acknowledges that said equipment hereby leased was personally chosen and selected by the Lessee for business purposes, and purchased at the Lessee's request from a supplier designated by the Lessee. Consequently, the Lessee takes full responsibility for the choosing and the selection, and will look only to the supplier for warranty against latent defects or other matters, the Lessor hereby conveying expressly and without reserve to the Lessee all warranties, if any, resulting from the sale of said equipment entered into with the supplier. The Lessee renounces the right to any claim or defence against the Lessor relating to said equipment. In the event of an action brought by the Lessor for default under the provisions of this Lease, the Lessee waives all defences predicated on the failure of said equipment to perform the function for which it was designed and further acknowledges and agrees that such failure shall not be deemed to be in breach of this Lease.
4. GOVERNING LAW. This lease shall be interpreted and enforced in accordance with the laws of the Province wherein said equipment is to be located according to the terms hereof. Lessor and Lessee hereby acknowledge that they have required this Lease and all related documents to be drawn up in the English language. Le Locateur et le Locataire reconnaissent avoir exigé que le présent crédit-bail et les documents qui s'y rattachent soient rédigés en anglais.

The Undersigned Agree to All Terms and Conditions Set Forth Above and in Consideration Thereof Hereby Execute This Lease.

Date June 15 19 94

Lessor

By Alberta Lease Co.
Authorized Signature

Name of Lessee SOUSA LTD.
(Legal Name of Firm)

By ____________
Authorized Signature and Title

By ____________
Authorized Signature and Title

LESSEE COPY

EXHIBIT 2 Sousa Ltd Lease #4922

Operating lease.

Alberta Lease Co.

Equipment Lease

LESSEE NO	LEASE NO
1426	4922

ALWAYS REFER TO THESE NUMBERS

LESSEE	SUPPLIER OF EQUIPMENT
LESSEE NAME Sousa Ltd.	NAME X Machinery Co.
ADDRESS 100 Any Street	ADDRESS 400 Main Street
CITY Metropolis PROV. Alta.	CITY Metropolis PROV. Alta.
POSTAL CODE A1A 2B3 TELEPHONE NO. 991-9999	POSTAL CODE A2A 7B9 TELEPHONE NO. 997-1111
CONTACT Mr. Smith	SUPPLIER REPRESENTATIVE Mr. Jones

EQUIPMENT LOCATION IF OTHER THAN ABOVE ADDRESS CITY COUNTY PROV.
n/a

LANDLORD: ADDRESS:
n/a

NO. OF UNITS	MODEL NO.	YEAR	DESCRIPTION:	LIST PRICE	SERIAL NO.
1	40170	1994	Molding equipment	$115,000	

TERMS OF PAYMENT (total subject to any provincial sales tax % changes)

TERM IN YEARS	NO. OF RENTAL PAYMENTS	PAYMENTS WILL BE MADE	FIRST RENTAL DUE DATE M D Y	AMOUNT OF EACH RENTAL PAYMENT EXCLUDING SALES TAX	INSURANCE COSTS	TOTAL AMOUNT EACH PAYMENT	SECURITY DEPOSIT	PURCHASE OPTION PRICE AND DATE
5	5	☑ YEARLY ☐	07 01 94	$ 28,484	$ 1,300	$ 29,784	$	$ n/a AT END OF OF THE LEASE TERM

TERMS AND CONDITIONS OF LEASE

For and in consideration of the covenants and agreements by the Lessee to pay the total rental payment herein provided for and to perform the terms, covenants and conditions on the Lessee's part herein contained, the Lessor hereby leases, and lets unto the Lessee, and the Lessee hereby leases and takes from the Lessor, each unit of equipment described above and hereinafter referred to as "said equipment", for the term set forth above (commencing on the date of the first delivery of any of the said equipment to the Lessee) and upon and subject to the covenants, conditions and provisions hereinafter set forth. Notwithstanding the foregoing, in the event that such first delivery takes place before the First Rental Due Date the term of this Lease shall be extended by the number of days from and including the date of the first delivery of any part of the said equipment and the First Rental Due Date.

1. RENTAL. For the use of said equipment, the Lessee shall pay to the Lessor at the Lessor's office, at 100 Main Street, Metropolis, Alta a total rental payment equal to the amount of each rental payment specified above multiplied by the number of rental payments specified above. The first rental payment and Security Deposit shall become due on the First Rental Due Date indicated above. Subsequent rental payments shall become due in every consecutive month or period, as the case may be, thereafter on the same date of each such month or period as the First Rental Due Date indicated above, or in the event that there is no such corresponding date, the last date of the said month. Rental payment hereunder is payable without abatement.
2. EQUIPMENT DESCRIPTION. The Lessee authorizes the Lessor to complete the description of said equipment above with the insertion of serial numbers and other details specifically identifying said equipment.
3. REPRESENTATIONS AND WARRANTIES. Each unit of said equipment leased hereunder is of a size, design and capacity personally chosen and selected by the Lessee and the Lessee is satisfied that the same is suitable for its purposes and the Lessor has made no representation or warranty with respect to the suitability or durability of any such unit for the purposes or uses of the Lessee, or any other representation or warranty express or implied with respect thereto.

   The Lessee acknowledges that said equipment hereby leased was personally chosen and selected by the Lessee for business purposes, and purchased at the Lessee's request from a supplier designated by the Lessee. Consequently, the Lessee takes full responsibility for the choosing and the selection, and will look only to the supplier for warranty against latent defects or other matters, the Lessor hereby conveying expressly and without reserve to the Lessee all warranties, if any, resulting from the sale of said equipment entered into with the supplier. The Lessee renounces the right to any claim or defence against the Lessor relating to said equipment. In the event of an action brought by the Lessor for default under the provisions of this Lease, the Lessee waives all defences predicated on the failure of said equipment to perform the function for which it was designed and further acknowledges and agrees that such failure shall not be deemed to be in breach of this Lease.
4. GOVERNING LAW. This lease shall be interpreted and enforced in accordance with the laws of the Province wherein said equipment is to be located according to the terms hereof. Lessor and Lessee hereby acknowledge that they have required this Lease and all related documents to be drawn up in the English language. Le Locateur et le Locataire reconnaissent avoir exigé que le présent crédit-bail et les documents qui s'y rattachent soient rédigés en anglais.

The Undersigned Agree to All Terms and Conditions Set Forth Above and in Consideration Thereof Hereby Execute This Lease.

Date June 15 19 94

Lessor

By Alberta Lease Co.
Authorized Signature

Name of Lessee SOUSA LTD.
(Legal Name of Firm)

By ______________________
Authorized Signature and Title

By ______________________
Authorized Signature and Title

LESSEE COPY

EXHIBIT 3 Sousa Ltd Lease #4923

Equipment Lease

Alberta Lease Co.

LESSEE NO	LEASE NO
1426	4923

ALWAYS REFER TO THESE NUMBERS

LESSEE	SUPPLIER OF EQUIPMENT
NAME Sousa Ltd.	NAME X Machinery Co.
ADDRESS 100 Any Street	ADDRESS 400 Main Street
CITY Metropolis PROV. Alta.	CITY Metropolis PROV. Alta.
POSTAL CODE A1A 2B3 TELEPHONE NO. 991-9999	POSTAL CODE A2A 7B9 TELEPHONE NO. 997-1111
CONTACT Mr. Smith	SUPPLIER REPRESENTATIVE Mr. Jones

EQUIPMENT LOCATION IF OTHER THAN ABOVE	ADDRESS	CITY	COUNTY	PROV.
n/a				

LANDLORD	ADDRESS
n/a	

NO. OF UNITS	MODEL NO	YEAR	DESCRIPTION	LIST PRICE	SERIAL NO
1	1724	1994	molding equipment	$179,000	

Because 1/2 of its useful life still remain after the lease & the value is more than 100, thus it is a BPO

TERMS OF PAYMENT (total subject to any provincial sales tax % changes)

TERM IN YEARS	NO. OF RENTAL PAYMENTS	PAYMENTS WILL BE MADE	FIRST RENTAL DUE DATE M D Y	AMOUNT OF EACH RENTAL PAYMENT EXCLUDING SALES TAX	INSURANCE COSTS	TOTAL AMOUNT EACH PAYMENT	SECURITY DEPOSIT	PURCHASE OPTION PRICE AND DATE
4	4	☑ YEARLY ☐	07 01 94	$ 52,600	$ 2,500	$ 55,100	$	$ 100 AT END OF OF THE LEASE TERM

TERMS AND CONDITIONS OF LEASE

For and in consideration of the covenants and agreements by the Lessee to pay the total rental payment herein provided for and to perform the terms, covenants and conditions on the Lessee's part herein contained, the Lessor hereby leases, and lets unto the Lessee, and the Lessee hereby leases and takes from the Lessor, each unit of equipment described above and hereinafter referred to as "said equipment", for the term set forth above (commencing on the date of the first delivery of any of the said equipment to the Lessee) and upon and subject to the covenants, conditions and provisions hereinafter set forth. Notwithstanding the foregoing, in the event that such first delivery takes place before the First Rental Due Date the term of this Lease shall be extended by the number of days from and including the date of the first delivery of any part of the said equipment and the First Rental Due Date.

1. RENTAL. For the use of said equipment, the Lessee shall pay to the Lessor at the Lessor's office, at 100 Main Street, Metropolis, Alta a total rental payment equal to the amount of each rental payment specified above multiplied by the number of rental payments specified above. The first rental payment and Security Deposit shall become due on the First Rental Due Date indicated above. Subsequent rental payments shall become due in every consecutive month or period, as the case may be, thereafter on the same date of each such month or period as the First Rental Due Date indicated above, or in the event that there is no such corresponding date, the last date of the said month. Rental payment hereunder is payable without abatement.
2. EQUIPMENT DESCRIPTION. The Lessee authorizes the Lessor to complete the description of said equipment above with the insertion of serial numbers and other details specifically identifying said equipment.
3. REPRESENTATIONS AND WARRANTIES. Each unit of said equipment leased hereunder is of a size, design and capacity personally chosen and selected by the Lessee and the Lessee is satisfied that the same is suitable for its purposes and the Lessor has made no representation or warranty with respect to the suitability or durability of any such unit for the purposes or uses of the Lessee, or any other representation or warranty express or implied with respect thereto.

The Lessee acknowledges that said equipment hereby leased was personally chosen and selected by the Lessee for business purposes, and purchased at the Lessee's request from a supplier designated by the Lessee. Consequently, the Lessee takes full responsibility for the choosing and the selection, and will look only to the supplier for warranty against latent defects or other matters, the Lessor hereby conveying expressly and without reserve to the Lessee all warranties, if any, resulting from the sale of said equipment entered into with the supplier. The Lessee renounces the right to any claim or defence against the Lessor relating to said equipment. In the event of an action brought by the Lessor for default under the provisions of this Lease, the Lessee waives all defences predicated on the failure of said equipment to perform the function for which it was designed and further acknowledges and agrees that such failure shall not be deemed to be in breach of this Lease.

4. GOVERNING LAW. This lease shall be interpreted and enforced in accordance with the laws of the Province wherein said equipment is to be located according to the terms hereof. Lessor and Lessee hereby acknowledge that they have required this Lease and all related documents to be drawn up in the English language. Le Locateur et le Locataire reconnaissent avoir exigé que le présent crédit-bail et les documents qui s'y rattachent soient rédigés en anglais.

The Undersigned Agree to All Terms and Conditions Set Forth Above and in Consideration Thereof Hereby Execute This Lease.

Date June 15 19 94

Lessor

By Alberta Lease Co.

Authorized Signature

Name of Lessee SOUSA LTD.

(Legal Name of Firm)

By ______

Authorized Signature and Title

By ______

Authorized Signature and Title

LESSEE COPY

Case 90

Southstar Mining Limited

"Well, folks, it's been a rough year, but we've survived." Ben South, president and CEO of Southstar Mining Limited, grimly surveyed the audit committee of the board of directors. Southstar Mining is a small public mining operation with eight mines operating in western Canada. In 1994, low ore prices hit the company hard and record losses had been recorded, eating into the company's hard-won equity base. Dividends were suspended, and new credit facilities were negotiated to finance Southstar during the cyclical swing. By February of 1995, as this meeting was underway, the tide had begun to turn for Southstar: operating costs had been deeply cut, ore prices had stabilized, and the company was projecting a marginal profit for 1995.

Ben South addressed the committee. "As you can see from our balance sheet, our 1994 equity position has eroded to only $115.6 million, down from $189.4 in 1993. (See Exhibit 1.) Hopefully, future profits and a continued "no-dividend" policy will rectify this in years to come. Our debt/equity ratio has climbed to 3.1 to 1 [$358.8/$115.6]. Paying down the debt is a high priority."

John Franklyn, a member of the audit committee, spoke up. "Excuse me, Bill, but isn't that a problem? Doesn't the new long-term debt, negotiated in 1994, specify that our maximum debt/equity cannot exceed 2.5 to 1?"

"Yes, John, it does, and I'm glad that came up. The debt covenants do specify that, using our GAAP statements, 2.5 to 1 is the maximum. Fortunately, though, we've agreed with the lenders that deferred taxes, which will never really have to be paid anyway, are excluded from that ratio. That takes the debt/equity ratio to 2.46 to 1 [($358.8 – $74.6)/$115.6]".

Another committee member joined in. "If it isn't a liability, why do we have it there on the balance sheet?"

Jeremy Seaforth, the chair of the committee, voiced his concerns. "Listen, my real concern is our pension liability. I see here (Exhibit 2) that we're underfunded by $24.6 million [$58.9 – $34.3]. That's an

EXHIBIT 1 Southstar Mining Ltd Consolidated Balance Sheet

Southstar Mining Limited
Consolidated Balance Sheet
As at December 31, 1994
(in millions)

	1994
Assets	
Current:	
Cash and short-term investments	$ 2.6
Accounts receivable	15.8
Inventories	46.6
Prepaid expenses	0.9
Total current assets	65.9
Property, plant, equipment, and related development costs, net of accumulated amortization	330.4
Investment in related company, at cost	76.7
Other assets	1.4
Total assets	$474.4
Liabilities and Shareholders' Equity	
Liabilities:	
Current:	
Accounts payable and accrued liabilities	$ 72.5
Income tax payable	10.3
Total current liabilities	82.8
Long-term debt	137.0
Due to related company	48.0
Deferred income tax	74.6
Other liabilities	16.4
Total liabilities	$358.8
Shareholders' equity:	
Share capital	63.0
Contributed capital	15.2
Retained earnings	37.4
Total shareholders' equity	115.6
Total liabilities and shareholders' equity	$474.4

obligation we'll have to pay over the next 15 years, according to our labour agreements. If the lenders include *that* number, we'll be in violation of our debt covenant for sure! And it's a hard liability—I know they include it on the balance sheet in the United States!"

EXHIBIT 2 Southstar Mining Ltd Additional Information

From the notes to the financial statements

Pension Plans

The company has pension plans for hourly and salaried employees. The dates of the last actuarial reports were January 1, 1992, for the salaried plan, and January 1, 1994, for the hourly plan. At December 31, 1994, the estimated actuarial present value of accrued pension benefits was $58.9 million; the estimated market value of the pension fund assets was $34.3 million. An amount of $7.5 million has been expensed for the year, representing the cost of pension benefits earned in the current year and the amortization, over the expected average remaining service life of current plan members, of the excess of accrued pension benefits over pension fund assets.

"Now, its really not as bad as all that!" said Ben. "After all, we follow GAAP—and if they say to put it in the balance sheet, like deferred taxes, we do. If they say to put it in the notes, like pensions, we do that, too! We're not trying to play games! And anyway, that pension deficit could disappear the next time we have a valuation done . . . as long as we make our regular annual payment, no one is going to ask us to pay out $24.6 million, all at once!

"Look—I'm a miner, not an accountant! Let's have our controller here analyze these issues for us so we can talk about them at our next meeting. OK, Lillian?"

Lillian See, the controller, nodded and made a note in her filofax.

"Great!" said Ben. "Now, back to the statements."

Required

Adopt the role of Lillian See and thoroughly outline the points of view on both sides of the issues raised.

Case 91

Sunbeam Iron Mines Ltd.

The partner in charge of the Sunbeam Iron Mines Ltd. audit has just briefed you on an accounting problem that has developed in the company. You have worked on this audit client for the last two years and are reasonably familiar with the operation. The mining industry is highly cyclical, and the company's fortunes have waxed and waned with fluctuating ore prices. They have been reasonably profitable recently but are keen to minimize fluctuations in income.

At this point in time, the 1994 fiscal year has ended, and the audit work is almost complete. The statements have yet to be finalized, as a major issue has yet to be ironed out, a problem relating to Sunbeam's deferred development expenses (DDEs).

DDEs are a basic principle in accounting for mine operations. When initial development costs are incurred, they are not immediately expensed, but rather deferred as an asset on the balance sheet, to be amortized as the mine property generates revenue in future years. The amortization rate is based on expected future revenues from total proven ore reserves. This is industry practice.

The 1994 draft financial statements currently show $75 million of DDEs on the balance sheet. In previous years, the DDEs had been amortized at the rate of $500,000 to $800,000 per year, and ore reserves appeared vast.

The partner has just seen revised geological reports, prepared by Sunbeam Iron Mines' geologists, that showed a significant drop in proven reserves, down to 20 million tons. Based on this estimate, the partner did an analysis that showed that $55 million of the DDEs should be written off. Net of deferred tax, the write-off would be $35,475,000.

As the partner raised this issue with the company, Sunbeam produced another report, also prepared by their geologists. While it had the same conclusions about proven reserves, it estimated the presence of 74 million tons of inferred ore reserves recoverable by underground mining techniques. The partner felt that this report had been hastily assembled to counteract the effect of the first report on financial markets.

The company told the partner that they prefer to simply disclose the decline in their proven reserves in a note to the financial statements and increase the rate of future amortization. They do not feel a write-down is required as this is a change in estimate, to be accounted for prospectively. This became a major difference of opinion between the partner and the company's management. They also informed the partner that, should a write-down have to be made, it should be presented as a prior period adjustment, not as an unusual or extraordinary item on the face of the income statement.

A meeting of the audit committee has been scheduled for next week, and the partner has asked you to prepare a report for him to use in this meeting. He has specifically asked you to evaluate both sides of the argument, as he wants to ensure that he has given the company's side the consideration it deserves. The report should include your recommendations.

Before starting your report, you did some research into the area of "inferred reserves." The concept of inferred reserves rests on implication. If ore has been found, or regularly found, in one geological formation, then the presence of that same formation in another area has the possibility of ore reserves as well. These are called *inferred reserves*. You also learned that the underground mining techniques necessary to mine Sunbeam's inferred reserves have yet to be fully established. The company currently has commissioned a $2 million study to investigate the feasibility of such techniques.

Required

Respond to the request of the partner and prepare the report.

Case 92

Sunrise Enterprises Limited

Sunrise Enterprises Ltd. is a small manufacturer of pipe fittings with a December 31 year-end. The company is privately owned by Greg Lai, the president and general manager. An annual audit is performed, primarily to satisfy the chartered bank that provides financing for capital assets and working capital.

EXHIBIT 1 Sunrise Enterprises—Capital Asset Data

• Manufacturing Equipment, balance per G/L, December 31, at cost.	$2,700,000
• Accumulated Depreciation, Manufacturing Equipment, balance per G/L, December 31. (Depreciation has not yet been booked for the current year.)	$1,210,000
• Machinery lasts 12–15 years, on average, and is being depreciated straight-line over this period.	
• Current year depreciation, straight-line method.	$ 240,000
• Machinery was used for a total of 1,700 hours in the current year. Total available machine-hours (excluding overtime) in this period were 1,950. The plant was idle due to lack of orders for several weeks during the year. Estimated machine-hours over the remaining life of all manufacturing equipment, approximately 14,700 (Lai's estimate).	
• Usage of machine-hours is not available for any prior year as data was not kept by the company.	

Mr. Lai has raised the following concerns with reference to the depreciation charges on assets:

1. He wishes to change the depreciation method for his manufacturing equipment from declining-balance to "units-of-production," or usage, because he's convinced that units-of-production is a more logical choice and relates to how his equipment wears out. Details are in Exhibit 1.
2. He does not wish to depreciate his factory building at all, as he is confident that the building has actually appreciated in value, not depreciated, over the last year. Sunrise Enterprises is located in a major urban center where appreciation of residential real estate is well documented. Lai has watched several commercial properties around him sell for "fabulous" prices in the past 18 months.

Lai has also asked for an explanation of depreciation in general, as he feels it is a "waste of time." He points out that all the bankers seem to be interested in is cash flow, and whether Sunrise has enough cash to make loan and interest payments. Lai cannot decide what is the "right" way to depreciate, as everyone he talks to seems to do it differently.

Required

Draft a response to Mr. Lai.

Case 93

The Carmanah Giant

The Carmanah Giant is a Sitka spruce that may be the largest tree in the world. The tree is located in a small valley on Vancouver Island. The tree, which was discovered in 1988, is 95 metres tall and 9.5 metres in circumference. Also in the valley are 279 Sitka spruce trees more than 70 metres tall; other types of wood include cedar, hemlock, and Douglas fir. Many of the trees in this valley are 500 years old.

The Carmanah Giant was in the news from 1988 to 1990 because environmentalists were concerned about the extent of logging in the province and were using the tree to focus the public's attention. MacMillan Bloedel Limited held the logging rights for the area. The company intended to log the valley over the next 70 years. The company assured the protesters that they would not cut the Giant. The protesters replied that leaving the spruce unprotected by other trees exposed it to the risks of wind and flooding.

In 1990, the British Columbia government legislated that half the valley would be logged. The other half (which included the Carmanah Giant) was declared a national park, thereby prohibiting logging.

The Forest Industry

The forest industry is a provincial responsibility. In British Columbia, 56 percent of the land is natural area protected by legislation. Twenty-eight percent of the province is manageable forest; the Crown owns most of this land. The ministry of forests issues licences to companies to cut the timber.

There are two types of licences. A tree farm licence gives a company exclusive cutting rights to a specific geographic area for a 25-year term. A forest licence gives a company a government-determined allowable annual cut for a 15-year term (renewable every 5 years for 15 years) in different parts of a timber supply area. The company may exceed the allowance by as much as 50 percent in a year as long as the average annual cut over five years is within 10 percent of the limit. Several licence holders may operate in one area. In return for a licence, companies pay a stumpage fee for the timber they cut. The companies must assume all costs of replanting the area with nursery-grown seedlings.

Each crop of trees takes 40 to 120 years to grow; some may grow for hundreds of years. British Columbia has been harvested for over a century, but replanting only began about 50 years ago. Most of the replacement trees were planted within the past 15 years. The yield from a second-growth forest is about 75 percent of the original forest, although advances in sawmill technology have increased the product per tree. Old-growth trees produce tight-grained wood that is usually knot-free. Second-growth trees have thick rings, because they grow quickly in the early years. Lumber from second-growth trees tends to warp, and it contains knots that weaken it and make it less valuable.

British Columbia's forest policies traditionally have been shaped by royal commissions; the 1945 commission recommended a policy of sustained yield—the replacement of at least the amount of timber cut. The 1976 royal commission commented on the growing concentration among a few large corporations of timber holdings and manufacturing capacity.

The rate of logging has quadrupled in the past 40 years. The annual sustainable level is estimated at 59 million cubic metres.

B.C. tourism generates more than $3 billion a year. Canoeists, hikers, and climbers come to the province because of its natural beauty (less than 1 percent of the province is urban). The tourist industry is expressing concern about unsightly clearcutting. This is the usual technique of logging, in which all the trees in an area up to 80 hectares are cut in one operation.

The Federal Government's Involvement with the Industry

In the early 1980s, Ottawa entered into a Forestry Resource Development Agreement (FRDA) with each province. The agreements deal with the country's reforestation and silviculture and with the planting and care of new trees. They include a provision for provincial and federal cost-sharing. British Columbia's $300 million FRDA expired in 1990. The province requested a new FRDA worth $700 million. It received $200 million, to be financed half from Ottawa and half from the province. FRDAs used to be the responsibility of Agriculture Canada, but the federal government is giving the regions the responsibility for negotiating the new agreements.

MacMillan Bloedel Limited

MacMillan Bloedel Limited is one of North America's largest forest products companies, with integrated operations in Canada and the United States, as well as investments in the United Kingdom and Continental Europe. The company was incorporated in 1911. The head office is in Vancouver.

MacMillan Bloedel's results are affected by newsprint prices, housing starts, and foreign currency values. Additional information about the company is in the attached exhibits.

EXHIBIT 1

MacMillan Bloedel Limited
1991 Sales of Selected Products by Market

	Lumber (MMfbm)	*Newsprint* (k-tonnes)	*Pulp* (k-tonnes)
U.S.A.	787	494	57
Canada	396	90	12
Japan and Orient	293	120	82
Europe and other	147	129	261

Source: MacMillan Bloedel Limited Information Circular and Annual Statutory Report 1991.

EXHIBIT 2

MacMillan Bloedel Limited
Extracts from the Annual Statutory Report
December 31, 1991

Reforestation

To assure a continuing supply of raw materials for the future, the Company maintains an active reforestation program in British Columbia. Company managed lands in British Columbia in the process of being restocked currently represent about three years of logging which is reflective of the restocking process and consistent with the Company's experience over the last two decades. . . .

EXHIBIT 2 *(continued)*

MacMillan Bloedel Limited
Extracts from the Annual Statutory Report
December 31, 1991

Forest Lands

The total area of commercial forest lands under MB's control is:

	Commercial Hectares (Note 1)	
British Columbia (Note 2):		
Area operated on a sustained yield basis:		
Tree farm licences:		
Crown lands (Note 3)	659,000	
Timber licences (Note 4)	125,000	
Owned lands	221,000	1,005,000
Other tenures:		
Timber licences (Note 5)	39,000	
Owned lands	3,000	42,000
		1,047,000
Saskatchewan		309,000
Alabama and Mississippi:		
Owned lands	80,000	
Long-term cutting rights	102,000	182,000
		1,538,000

Notes:

1. Land is considered commercial if it is feasible to grow timber on it which can be economically harvested using present technology. Lands controlled by MB in Alabama, Mississippi, and Saskatchewan are considered commercial. In British Columbia, 60,000 hectares controlled by MB are presently considered inaccessible and, hence, not commercial.
2. On January 2, 1992, the British Columbia government announced a sustainable cut reduction of 418,000 cubic metres in one tree-farm licence. This reduction represents a 5.7 percent decrease in MB's allowable cut from accessible timberlands operated on a sustained-yield basis. With the current unfavourable market conditions, this reduction should not adversely affect production facilities in British Columbia.
3. These are contained within MB's two tree-farm licences. These tree-farm licences were renewed for 25-year terms in the early 1980s.
4. The company owns exclusive rights to harvest timber on the land held under timber licences. A royalty is payable upon harvesting the timber. After the timber is harvested on these lands, the company has the responsibility to reforest them. They then revert to the Crown but will be retained within the tree-farm licences as "Crown lands." Approximately 32,000 hectares of these lands have been logged but not reverted.
5. Included are approximately 14,000 hectares of lands, which already have been logged and will revert to the Crown when restocked at the company's expense.

EXHIBIT 2 (*concluded*)

MacMillan Bloedel Limited
Extracts from the Annual Statutory Report
December 31, 1991

Stumpage and Royalty

A stumpage charge that will generate a revenue target for the British Columbia government is assessed by the government on all Crown timber harvested. On those lands held under timber licences, a fixed royalty is payable when the timber is harvested. No royalty or stumpage charges are payable on timber harvested on company-owned lands.

Countervailing Duty on Canadian Softwood Lumber

In October 1991, the United States Department of Commerce (DOC) announced an investigation into the potential subsidy afforded to Canadian softwood lumber by provincial stumpage systems. About half of the company's harvest in British Columbia is from owned timber. For the Crown timber that the company harvests, it pays economic rent. Consequently, the company applied on November 22, 1991, for an outright exemption from a company specific rate or for any countervailing duty that might result from this investigation. This was denied on January 17, 1992.

These issues are ongoing and, in the opinion of the company, there are cogent arguments for defeating a countervail duty on softwood lumber sold in the United States.

Forestry and the Environment

On January 21, 1992, the provincial government announced an 18-month moratorium covering several harvesting areas on Crown lands under MB's control for review by a special government commission. The commission is charged with the responsibility of developing a land use strategy, including a dispute settlement mechanism to resolve conflicts over the use of forest land for timber harvesting.

Specific areas subject to major action are:

	Commercial Hectares (Note 1)	*Action by*
Clayoquot Sound	106,000	Special interest groups and aboriginal people
Tsitika Valley	3,000	Special interest groups
Temporary moratorium on other areas	57,000	Special interest groups
Total	166,000	

1. In addition, in 1990 approximately 3,600 commercial hectares of forest land in the Carmanah Valley were set aside as a park to preserve old-growth Sitka Spruce believed to be the tallest in North America. Compensation will be payable to MB for timber licences expropriated for the park establishment. The amount and timing are yet to be determined. Compensation will also be payable to MB for timber licences expropriated for a federal park reserve on South Moresby Island in the Queen Charlotte Island chain. These licences contain a significant volume of high-grade Sitka Spruce. (Includes second-growth and old-growth forest lands.)

EXHIBIT 3

MacMILLAN BLOEDEL LIMITED
Extracts from the Financial Statements
December 31, 1991
From the Consolidated Statements of Earnings (Loss) (dollars in millions)

	1991	*1990*	*1989*
Depreciation, depletion, and amortization	156.6	156.5	130.4
Net earnings (loss)	(93.4)	50.8	246.7

From the Consolidated Statements of Changes in Financial Position (dollars in millions):

	1991	*1990*	*1989*
Capital expenditures	241.1	366.5	518.4

From the Consolidated Statements of Financial Position (dollars in millions)

Inventories (Note 2)	483.6	531.3
Property, plant, and equipment:		
Buildings, equipment, and construction in progress, net	1,727	1,841
Timber and land less accumulated depletion	203.2	211.3
Logging roads	12.9	13.4

From the Notes to Consolidated Financial Statements (dollars in millions)

1. *Accounting Policies*
   c. *Valuation of inventories:*
   Inventories of operating and maintenance supplies and raw materials are valued at the lower of average cost and replacement cost or net realizable value. Inventories of manufactured products are valued at the lower of average cost and net realizable value.
   d. *Property, plant, and equipment:*
   Property, plant, and equipment are recorded at cost.

   MacMillan Bloedel employs the units-of-production basis for depreciation of manufacturing assets. Nonmanufacturing assets are depreciated on a straight-line basis.

   The rates of depreciation being applied are intended to fully depreciate manufacturing assets (at normal production levels) and nonmanufacturing assets over the following periods:

Buildings	20 and 40 years
Pulp and paper mill machinery and equipment	20 years

EXHIBIT 3 (*concluded*)

MacMILLAN BLOEDEL LIMITED
Extracts from the Financial Statements
December 31, 1991
From the Notes to Consolidated Financial Statements
(dollars in millions)

Logging machinery and equipment	5 to 7 years
Other manufacturing machinery and equipment	7 to 13 years
Vessels	10 to 13 years

Depletion of timber and amortization of main logging roads are determined on a basis related to log production.

2. *Inventories*

	1991	*1990*
Operating and maintenance supplies	78.8	80.2
Logs, pulp chips, and pulpwood	124.9	154.0
Lumber, panelboards, and other building materials	198.6	210.0
Pulp and paper products	50.7	56.3
Containerboard and packaging products	30.6	30.8
Total inventories	483.6	531.3

Required

Describe specific financial accounting policies, valuations, and disclosures of MacMillan Bloedel that might be affected by changes occurring in the forest industry.

Case 94

The Thomson Corporation

The following extract is from The Thomson Corporation's Management's Discussion and Analysis for the year ended December 31, 1991:

> The Capital Assets accounting standard mandated by the CICA defines capital assets to include intangible assets, such as publishing rights and circulation, and requires these to be amortized over periods not exceeding 40 years. Amortization is purely an accounting concept, which has no effect on TTC's cash flow nor on its underlying value, and we remain fundamentally opposed to the application of this standard in respect of publishing rights and circulation.
>
> The value of a publishing business and its ability to earn profits and to generate cash is dependent upon the quality of its intangible assets. The economic value of publishing rights and circulation does not, in principle, diminish with the passage of time. Such assets are more closely akin to land than to buildings and machinery. A reduction in value only occurs if the publication or service loses its position in the marketplace. Accordingly, TTC believes that such assets should not be subject to periodic amortization but should be written down only where a permanent diminution in value has occurred.
>
> TTC expenses considerable amounts each year on editorial, marketing, selling, and fulfillment costs to protect and enhance the value of its publishing rights and circulation. Additional annual amortization, thus, represents a double charge and distorts TTC's earnings.
>
> While TTC believes that publishing rights and circulation should not be amortized and also that there are grounds under the CICA standard for it to capitalize many costs that are currently expensed, TTC also considers that the accounting, administrative, regulatory, and other problems associated with not amortizing such intangibles or with capitalizing certain costs presently being expensed would be out of all proportion to the benefits obtained.

Required

Discuss the arguments raised above.

Case 95

Total Beauty Ltd.

Total Beauty Ltd. was founded in Windsor, Ontario, almost 50 years ago. The company sells skin care, fragrance, makeup, and glamour products to women through "Network Presentations," private parties held for half a dozen people by a hostess who may also be a Total Beauty counsellor. There are currently 10,000 Total Beauty counsellors located across Canada.

To service these sales, the company owns a plant, Helden Laboratories, which handled $741,000 sales volume in 1984; this increased to $1.6 million during 1985 and required expansion of the plant's capacity. By the end of 1985, the board of directors was planning an expansion into the American market through the acquisition of a small cosmetics company; this would require additional funding. If the move into the United States proved successful, the board intended to enter the European market at a later date.

Total Beauty's earnings history has been erratic. In the 1950s and 1960s, the company was a household name throughout the country. In the late 1960s, the company was purchased by a public corporation; the fit was not a comfortable one, and Total Beauty's image was harmed. By the mid-1970s, the company was unknown. It was at this time that Thomas Elder, a wealthy entrepreneur, purchased a controlling interest in Total Beauty. By 1980, Elder's management had restored the company's national reputation, and Elder and a close group of friends owned all the shares. Just after the 1984 year-end, the current structure of Total Beauty Ltd. was created through a reverse takeover, and the company was listed on the Toronto Stock Exchange.

It is now September 1985, and Thomas Elder has just reviewed the draft financial statements for the year ended August 31. He is not pleased with several of the requirements of Total Beauty's auditors, which he feels present the company in a bad light. He would like to hear some justification of, for example, the requirement that all the reorganization costs be expensed immediately. The reorganization costs represent salaries paid to employees who spent most of the year working on the changes to the company's methods of sales and distribution. Expensing them totally in 1985 seems to be unduly harsh, particularly for a company where items such as working capital are so strong and which has such a promising future.

TOTAL BEAUTY LTD.
Consolidated Income Statement (draft)
For the Year Ended August 31, 1985
(in thousands)

	1985	*1984*
Sales	$ 5,481.0	$4,824.7
Costs and expenses, including depreciation and amortization of $125.6 (1984: $74.7)	5,439.4	4,530.9
Interest expense on long-term debt and capital leases	187.7	125.7
Other interest	77.5	10.2
Operating income (loss) before nonrecurring reorganization costs	$ (223.6)	$ 157.9
Nonrecurring reorganization costs	885.3	
Income (loss) before income taxes	$(1,108.9)	$ 157.9
Provision for (recovery of) income taxes	$ (117.0)	$ 86.0
Net income (loss)	$ (991.9)	$ 71.9

TOTAL BEAUTY LTD.
Consolidated Balance Sheet (draft)
August 31, 1985
(in thousands)

	1985	*1984*
Assets		
Current assets:		
Accounts receivable	$ 184.0	$ 558.1
Due from shareholder	30.0	250.0
Inventories	2,036.8	1,424.6
Income taxes recoverable (Note J)	113.0	
Deferred income taxes (Note J)		8.0
Total current assets	$2,363.8	$2,240.7

TOTAL BEAUTY LTD. (*concluded*)
Consolidated Balance Sheet (draft)
August 31, 1985
(in thousands)

	1985	*1984*
Assets		
Fixed assets:		
Land	$ 533.8	$ 533.8
Building	1,415.9	1,386.5
Furniture and equipment	46.0	21.2
Computer software	53.8	
	$2,049.5	$1,941.5
Less accumulated depreciation	149.8	69.6
	$1,899.7	$1,871.8
Equipment under capital leases	258.1	
Less accumulated amortization	34.7	
	$ 223.4	
Deferred income taxes (Note J)	34.0	26.0
Other assets:		
Goodwill (Note C)	224.8	
Patents and trademarks	39.9	45.0
Total assets	$4,785.6	$4,183.5
Liabilities and Shareholders' Equity		
Current liabilities:		
Bank indebtedness	$ 998.4	$ 540.6
Accounts payable and accruals	932.4	1,186.9
Due to shareholder	15.0	
Current portion of capital lease	38.8	
Income taxes payable	–	120.0
Total current liabilities	$1,984.6	$1,847.5
Long-term debt (Note E)	1,621.7	1,064.1
Capital lease obligation (Note G)	210.3	
Deferred revenue	44.5	
Shareholders' equity:		
Common shares (Note F)	644.6	0.1
Appraisal increment	1,113.8	1,157.0
Retained earnings (deficit)	(833.9)	114.8
Total liabilities and shareholders' equity	$4,785.6	$4,183.5

TOTAL BEAUTY LTD.
Consolidated Statement of Changes in Financial Position (draft)
For the Year Ended August 31, 1985
(in thousands)

	1985	*1984*
Source of funds:		
Increase in long-term debt	$ 700.0	$1,064.1
Issuance of capital stock	644.5	0.1
Increase in capital lease obligation	210.3	
Proceeds on disposal of equipment	81.9	
Total	$1,636.7	$1,064.2
Application of funds:		
Net income (loss)	(991.9)	71.9
Charges to operations not affecting working capital:		
Depreciation and amortization	125.6	74.7
Deferred income taxes	(8.0)	(26.0)
Deferred revenue recognized	(12.2)	
Total to (from) operations	$ 886.5	$ (120.6)
Additions to fixed assets under capital leases	378.0	741.6
Acquisition of business (Note C)	209.5	
Working capital deficiency of acquired business	21.0	
Acquisition of patents and trademarks		50.0
Repayment of long-term debt	142.3	
Increase in deferred revenue	13.4	
	$1,650.7	$ 671.0
Increase (decrease) in working capital	$ (14.0)	$ 393.2

TOTAL BEAUTY LTD.
Extracts from the Notes of the
Consolidated Financial Statements (draft)
August 31, 1985

Note B: Summary of Significant Accounting Policies

Patents and Trademarks

Patents and trademarks are stated at cost less accumulated amortization. Amortization is computed on the straight-line method at 10 percent per annum.

Appraisal Increment

Appraisal increments are transferred to retained earnings on the straight-line method at a rate which approximates but does not exceed the realization on the related assets through depreciation or sale.

TOTAL BEAUTY LTD. *(continued)*
Extracts from the Notes of the
Consolidated Financial Statements (draft)
August 31, 1985

Note C: Business Combination

Pursuant to an agreement dated September 1, 1984, Total Beauty Ltd. issued 3 million common shares in exchange for the outstanding shares of Total Beauty Canada (''Canada''), a private Canadian company. As a result of this transaction, control of the combined companies passed to the former shareholders of ''Canada'' as a group. Legally, Total Beauty Ltd. would be regarded as the parent or continuing company. However, since the former shareholders of ''Canada'' control Total Beauty Ltd. after the acquisition, ''Canada'' is identified as the acquirer and Total Beauty Ltd. is treated as the acquired company. The value of the shares issued has been determined to be $209,500, which represents the portion of the equity of Total Beauty Canada that was given up by the individuals who held the shares of Total Beauty Ltd. immediately prior to the combination.

Being the acquiring company, the net assets of ''Canada'' are included in the balance sheet at book value, and the net assets of Total Beauty Ltd. have been recorded at fair market at the date of acquisition.

The acquisition is summarized as follows:

Assets and liabilities of Total Beauty Ltd. as at September 1, 1984:	
Current assets	$ 0.9
Current liabilities	21.9
Working capital deficiency and net book value acquired	21.0
Assigned purchase value	209.5
Goodwill	$230.5

* * *

Note E: Long-term Debt

Mortgage payable, bearing interest at the mortgagee's prime lending rate, secured by the building and certain of the company's insurance policies, due on June 1, 1985, and extended on a monthly basis since that date	$ 921.7
Debenture maturing November 30, 1989, bearing interest at 10% per annum	300.0
Debenture maturing May 3, 1990, bearing interest at 10% per annum	400.0
Total	$1,621.7

Subsequent to the year-end, the mortgage payable has been renewed until August 31, 1986, with interest at 11.25 percent per annum. Although the mortgage is due within one year of the balance sheet date, it has been classified as a long-term liability as management intends to renew the mortgage or refinance the amount with other long-term borrowings.

TOTAL BEAUTY LTD. *(continued)*
Extracts from the Notes of the
Consolidated Financial Statements (draft)
August 31, 1985

Note F: Capital Stock

	Number Authorized	*Number Issued*
Opening balance	$10,000,000	$ 591,666
Issued to effect the business combination		3,000,000
Issued through private placements		435,000
Issued to employees		5,340
Total	$10,000,000	$4,032,006

The value assigned to the issued shares is calculated as follows:

Balance of Total Beauty Canada capital stock account immediately prior to the business combination	$ 0.1
Assigned purchase value of Total Beauty Ltd.	209.5
Shares issued through private placements	435.0
Shares issued to employees	0
Total	$644.6

Note G: Commitments

The company leases office space, warehouse vehicles, and equipment under the terms of various operating and capital leases. Annual rentals under lease agreements presently outstanding are as follows:

	Capital Leases	*Operating Leases*	*Total*
1986	$ 75.3	$113.8	$189.1
1987	75.3	86.3	161.6
1988	75.3	86.3	161.6
1989	75.3	71.9	147.2
1990	41.9	0	41.9
Total	$343.1	$358.3	$701.4
Amount representing interest	94.0		
Present value of minimum lease payments	249.1		
Less current portion	38.8		
Total	$210.3		

* * *

TOTAL BEAUTY LTD. *(concluded)*
Extracts from the Notes of the
Consolidated Financial Statements (draft)
August 31, 1985

Note I: Related Party Transactions

A shareholder and director of the company owns the $400,000 debenture maturing May 3, 1990, referred to in Note E.

The same shareholder and director receives a fee for providing personal guarantees against the mortgage payable and the bank loan of the company. Such fees amounted to $41,000 during the year.

Note J: Income Taxes

Deferred income taxes arise principally from timing differences in reporting depreciation expense for tax and financial reporting purposes and from accounting for certain lease agreements as capital leases for financial reporting purposes.

The company has tax loss carry-forwards in the amount of $800,000, which expire in 1992.

Required

Revise Total Beauty Ltd.'s Statement of Changes in Financial Position to comply with Section 1540 of the *Handbook*. Do not make any changes to estimates, policies, or classifications before you recast the statement. Analyze the financial health of the company and present your recommendation for the treatment of the reorganization costs.

Case 96

TransCanada PipeLines Limited

TransCanada PipeLines Limited (TCPL) is a Canadian company that was incorporated in 1951; the head office moved to Calgary in 1990. At the end of 1991, TCPL's total assets and long-term debt were $6.6 billion and $3.4 billion, respectively. Income before income taxes and discontinued operations totalled $348.7 million in 1991 ($280.8 million in 1990); the respective net income figures were $251.2 million and $214.9 million.[1] The company's shares trade on all five Canadian stock exchanges and on the New York Stock Exchange.

TCPL purchases, transports, and sells natural gas to regional gas distribution companies throughout North America. The company augments its 11,000-kilometer distribution network by ownership in other connecting pipeline systems.

The National Energy Board (NEB) is the Canadian oil and gas industry regulator. The NEB sets TCPL's tolls and gives permission for changes in pipeline kilometers and compression horsepower. In establishing tolls the NEB considers estimates of a segment's rate base, operating, and financing costs. The rate base is the net book value of the gas plant in service plus an allowance for working capital. For 1991, the NEB has approved a return on equity of 13.5 percent on a deemed common equity ratio of 30 percent of capitalization.

TCPL prepares its statements in accordance with Canadian GAAP. The company includes a note reconciling the differences between Canadian and U.S. practices. One area of difference in TCPL's statements is

[1] For the regulated operations of the Gas Transmission Segment, the company follows the taxes payable method of accounting for income taxes. This method is prescribed by the NEB for tollmaking purposes. Income tax expense in 1991 totalled $97.5 million ($65.9 million in 1990).

accounting for pension plans. Extracts from TransCanada PipeLines Limited's 1991 notes follow.

Note 14—Pension Plans: The Company has a noncontributory pension plan . . . [that] covers all employees who have completed one year of service and provides a defined benefit pension based on length of service and the employee's final average earnings.

The cost of pension benefits earned by employees is determined using the projected unit credit method pro rated over the service life of the employee group. This cost is charged to operations as services are rendered and reflects management's best estimate of expected plan investment performance, salary escalation, terminations, and retirement ages of plan members. Adjustments arising from plan amendments, changes in assumptions, and experience gains and losses are amortized on a straight-line basis over the expected average remaining service life of the employee group.

The components of the Company's pension expense are detailed as follows:

	Year Ended December 31 ($ millions)		
	1991	*1990*	*1989*
Pension costs for benefits earned during the current period	$ 9.7	$ 9.8	$ 9.9
Amortization of transition amount and other	2.2	2.9	3.0
Net pension expense	$11.9	$12.7	$12.9

The Company contributes annually to the pension plan the amount that is determined by the actuary. Contributions are intended to provide for benefits attributed to service to date.

The projected funded status of the Company's pension plan is as follows:

	Year Ended December 31 ($ millions)	
	1991	*1990*
Accumulated benefits based on service to date and current compensation:		
Vested	$129.5	$119.1
Nonvested	14.8	14.7
Accumulated benefit obligation	144.3	133.8
Additional amounts related to projected salary increases	49.1	50.0
Actuarial present value of current accumulated pension benefits	193.4	183.8
Pension plan assets at fair value	171.1	155.2
Deficit	22.3	28.6

Pension plan assets are at average market value using five-year moving average and include marketable equity securities and corporate and government debt securities and mortgages.

The discount rate used in determining the actuarial present value of the projected pension benefit obligations was 8.5 per cent. The rate of return on pension plan assets was estimated to be 8.5 per cent per annum.

Note 20—Significant Differences between Canadian and United States GAAP:

(*c*) Additional disclosure required under U.S. GAAP:

(iii) The components of the Company's pension expense in accordance with U.S. GAAP are detailed as follows:

	Year Ended December 31, ($ millions)		
	1991	*1990*	*1989*
Current service cost	$ 7.5	$ 7.1	$ 6.4
Interest on accrued benefits	15.5	15.3	14.4
Expected return on pension assets	(13.3)	(12.6)	(10.9)
Amortization of prior service cost	2.8	2.1	2.4
Amortization of transition amount	(0.3)	(0.3)	(0.3)
Net pension expense	$12.2	$11.6	$12.0

There is no significant impact on income for any difference between Canadian and U.S. GAAP pension expense, as a major portion of the difference would be deferred and recognized in income in the future when recovered in the tollmaking process.

The funded status of the Company's pension plan for U.S. GAAP purposes is as follows:

	Year Ended December 31 ($ millions)	
	1991	*1990*
Projected benefit obligation	$193.4	$183.8
Pension assets—market value	177.7	152.1
Deficit	(15.7)	(31.7)
Unrecognized net loss*	3.9	0.3
Unrecognized prior service cost	19.1	20.9
Unrecognized net transitional assets	(5.6)	(5.9)
Pension liability	$ 1.7	$(16.4)

* This and the following three tabular lines may be ignored for purposes of this case.

The amount of deficit reported above is less than the amount calculated under Canadian GAAP as a result of differences in the valuation of pension assets. Under U.S. GAAP, pension assets are at market value, whereas under Cana-

EXHIBIT 1 Summary of U.S. Pension Accounting Standards

Assumptions used include the discount rate at which the *projected* benefit could be effectively settled. The impacts of changes in assumptions and experience gains/losses are added together. If the total exceeds 10 percent of the greater of the market value of the assets/projected benefit at the beginning of the year, the excess over the 10 percent is amortized over the "average remaining service life of active employees." Past service costs and the opening net asset/obligation position upon plan adoption are amortized over the "average remaining service life of active employees." Since 1989, an additional liability has been recognized. This is the difference between the *accumulated* benefit (excludes provision for future salaries) and the fair value of plan assets; an intangible asset offsets the liability. The plan assets should be valued at market; average market value over not more than five years may be used in calculating the expected return on assets and experience gains/losses.

dian GAAP such assets are at an average market value using five-year moving average.

Required

Compare Canadian and U.S. pension accounting standards. Analyze TransCanada Pipeline Limited's pension plan disclosure under Canadian and U.S. generally accepted accounting principles. Assess the value to the reader of the additional disclosure required under U.S. GAAP.

Case 97

True North Limited

True North Limited (TNL) was incorporated under the Canada Business Corporations Act three months ago, in June 1993. TNL represents an amalgamation of the talents of six engineers and the money of three moderately wealthy financiers. Prior to June 1993, the six engineers had been employees of other companies. In their spare time, they had formed a partnership that developed and obtained patents on laboratory equipment, which the partners commenced manufacturing in 1989. In addition, they have been experimenting from 1989 to now, September 1993, with other commercial designs for small laboratory equipment. The equipment might be sold to a variety of mining, smelting, oil and gas, pulp and paper, and similar industries, as well as to governments for their research and development activities.

The financiers heard about the partnership in 1992, investigated the commercial designs, and recommended that TNL be incorporated. The financiers had followed a successful strategy in the past of investing in new ventures and selling them when their investment "matured," using the proceeds to invest in other prospects. Early discussions with the engineers had revealed that the engineers would be content with an initial minority (one third) participation in ownership of the new venture. The engineers' long-run strategy was to buy out the financiers' shares of TNL and then take TNL public, retaining effective control. The investment in TNL represented most of the engineers' savings, and their stated long-run objectives were employment security with TNL and growth in their equity investment.

You, CA, are employed with Audit & Company, who have been appointed auditor of TNL. TNL has yet to hire a controller, and, as a special assignment, you will be working full-time for TNL over the next six months, reporting directly to the executive vice president, Mr. Kerr. As a start, he has asked you to analyze financial accounting issues and make recommendations on the preferable methods for TNL to follow. Mr. Kerr has told you the following:

"Remember that I don't want you wearing your auditor's hat while you are here—I want recommendations which suit the company's needs. To get you started, an engineer friend of mine tells me that, in his company, he keeps his bookkeeping and tax costs to a minimum by using direct costing, at standard, for internal statements and for the statements which go to the banker and the tax department. This is an idea for TNL to consider.

"As a young company, our immediate needs are cash management, and tax minimization."

You realize that the threat of a qualified audit report will not necessarily sway Kerr, depending, of course, on the type of qualification and the purpose of the external statements. You also realize that you must consider the needs of two separate groups, the engineers and financiers.

Required

Write a report to Mr. Kerr, responding to his request. Additional information is contained in Exhibits 1 and 2.

EXHIBIT 1 True North Limited Memo to CA

From: Mr. Kerr
To: CA
Re: Accounting Policies

My initial thoughts on our accounting policies are as follows:

1. Revenue Recognition—equipment sold will generate revenue under three different arrangements:
   a. Full payment 90 days after shipment of the product.
   b. Rental over 60 months, with the monthly rental rate being 2 percent of the selling price of the product.
   c. The new basis suggested by the directors, of encouraging financed sales whereby we accept a 10 percent down payment and charge 15 percent per annum on the outstanding balance, which can be paid over 36 months.

I would suggest that, because the products are new, we should record revenue only on receipt of cash for (*a*) above; and, for (*b*) and (*c*), we would record revenue only after we have recovered all of our manufacturing and

EXHIBIT 1 (*continued*)

selling costs. This should enable us to defer income tax payments. Some of our shareholders (directors of TNL) think that this portrays a gloomy picture and will confuse and discourage creditors and other eventual shareholders.

Although we have not yet received any orders for the design and manufacture of special customized small equipment, we are hopeful that this will be a very profitable part of the business. Many contracts will likely be on a "cost plus" basis, especially those conducted for governments. However, because we will want to establish a good name, and may not want to invoice for our inefficiencies, I suggest that we also recognize revenue only when we receive cash from the buyer. This basis will enable us to defer income tax payments.

2. Warranty Costs—All units which are sold, as opposed to being rented or financed, carry a 36-month warranty. Although it is difficult to estimate the warranty cost, because we have not been in business for a sufficiently long time, a rough guess of 5 percent of selling price should be chosen until hindsight proves otherwise. Probably, this sum is 2 percent or so more than we need, but using the higher rate is to our advantage in helping to defer income tax payments.
3. Depreciation—We should probably accept the rates allowed for income tax purposes (20 percent) and depreciate on this basis. A declining or diminishing balance basis seems appropriate, because maintenance costs are likely to increase; also with this method we will have less cash investment in the older machines. Alternatively, we could apply straight-line depreciation, and then accrue expected repair and maintenance costs and get a similar effect on net income.
4. Capitalizing Costs of Equity—Most of the equity infusion received in early July 1993 is to be used for designing and manufacturing special small equipment. Since we are not likely to generate revenue on these products for some months, it seems sensible to recognize a benefit for funds being used during the development stage. This idea is very similar to interest being capitalized during construction. The directors are expecting an after-tax return on equity investment of around 12 percent. Hence, in the year ending June 30, 1994, we would add to deferred product costs 12 percent of about $1,000,000, or $120,000.
5. Intangibles—Our patents probably should be amortized over 10 years; no one seems to know what economic life they might have. We've also capitalized some goodwill representing the creative talents of our 6 engineers. There is no need to amortize this as these individuals will, if anything, increase their skills over the years.
6. Product Investigation Costs—These costs are likely to benefit the company for many years. But, to be on the conservative side, we should amortize them over 10 years on a straight-line basis. Out-of-pocket costs, excluding depreciation, amortization and allocations such as salaries of the executive team, are likely to be:

Year Ending June 30	*Approximate Amount*
1994	$200,000
1995	300,000
1996 and thereafter	400,000

EXHIBIT 1 *(concluded)*

7. Deferred Advertising—At the last executive committee meeting, we agreed to pay $150,000 in October 1993, and a further $100,000 in March 1994, to Gloss Advertising Associates. This sum is required for an extensive public relations and institutional advertising campaign designed to make the company's name well known over the next several years. Product quality will be stressed. Although the benefits of this advertising are expected to extend over a decade, we can be conservative and amortize it over three years.
8. Executive Incentive Plan—Although this plan has not yet been approved by the directors, we must formulate some wording for our annual external statements to indicate that payment is not in cash but in voting shares of the company. The present proposal is that "free" shares would be issued for 10 percent of annual net income (computed in accordance in GAAP) and that these shares would be allocated among the eight executives on a formula basis. This will probably be approved at the next meeting, and should offer tax savings for our executives.

I would appreciate your thoughts on the above.

EXHIBIT 2 True North Limited Additional Information

1. TNL has signed an agreement with True North Sales Limited (TNSL) that makes TNSL their exclusive sales agent. All sales will be made through TNSL, although TNSL will not buy or hold inventory. TNSL will act only to generate orders. They will be paid a 10 percent commission, based on cash received. TNSL is wholly owned by the financier group who own shares in TNL.
2. A pension plan was drawn up for the eight-member executive team of TNL—six engineers and two other executives hired by the financiers. The plan became effective July 1, 1993, and granted the six engineers pension benefits based on age and experience, even though there was no past service with TNL itself. This past service entitlement was a contributing factor in convincing the engineers to join TNL on a full-time basis, as most have only 20 years to work until retirement.

   The past service cost was calculated to be $450,000 as of July 1, 1993, to be funded over 20 years, with the first payment made on that date. Current service cost of $40,000 was also funded on July 1, 1993.
3. In a memo to the president dated June 12, 1993, the financiers as a group indicated that part of their investment would likely take the form of a convertible income bond. The bond would bear interest up to 12 percent per annum to the extent that TNL has sufficient "net income determined in accordance with generally accepted accounting principles." The bond could be converted at any time before June 30, 2014, at the option of the financiers, into common shares based on their appraised market value at June 30, 1994.

EXHIBIT 2 *(concluded)*

4. You discovered a letter addressed to one of the financiers from an underwriter and, with permission, photocopied it. In part, the letter stated: "Our company would be willing to take TNL public by selling its voting shares when its financial statements show a trend of profitability and a solid net income figure. Without these characteristics, potential investors tend to be frightened away by undue risk or lack of stability. TNL's shares might still be sold when risk and uncertainty exist if we can explain the nature of this risk and uncertainty. We, of course, always prefer to see some clearly worded notes to financial statements and other supplementary information to minimize surprises to investors."

Case 98

VMG Products Limited

In April of 1994, the board of directors of VMG Products Limited met to discuss management's recommendations to increase prices for all the firm's major product lines.

VMG is a private company, formed in 1990, with a shareholder group of about 50 individuals and private holding companies. VMG manufactures and distributes patented solar water-heating equipment for residential and commercial use. Due to the high price of fossil fuel and consumers' preference for "environment friendly" products, markets for the product are healthy and growing. Profit performance had been strong from 1990–92, but levelled off in 1993 due to higher costs of components. Prices of these components were expected to increase another 13 to 18 percent in 1994 before stabilizing in 1995. In order to cover the price increases, and make up lost ground from 1993, VMG's management is recommending that the board approve increases of 25 to 35 percent on all product lines.

The following discussion took place at the meeting:

Management

Price increases are clearly supported by the data presented. Our calculations include higher component costs and increased depreciation of equipment based on current replacement costs of plant facilities.

Director 1

But isn't our plant facility fairly new?

Management

Yes. We acquired much of it 3 years ago and expect it will last for another 20 years. Right after our acquisition, costs began to spiral and, thus, it would cost us 40 percent more to replace it today. That's what our figures are based on!

Adapted, with permission from the Atlantic School of Chartered Accountancy.

EXHIBIT 1 VMG Products Limited Additional Information

VMG PRODUCTS LIMITED
Income Statement and Projections
(in thousands)

	1993 actual (historical cost)	*1994 Projection (replacement cost)*
Net sales	$9,146	$12,028*
Cost of goods sold, excluding depreciation	6,651	8,473
Depreciation expense, straight line	210	317
Selling, general, and administrative expenses	1,817	2,080
Interest expense, net	118	100
	8,796	10,970
Pretax income	$ 350	$ 1,058
Other information:		
Increase in current cost of inventories, property, plant, and equipment during 1994	$ 694	
Effect of the general price level	157	
Excess of the increase in specific prices over the general price level	$ 537	

* Reflects price increase—would be $9,550 at current prices.

Director 2

But who says we'd replace it with the same thing in 20 years' time?

Management

(testily) We'd certainly have to replace it with something, and that something wouldn't be cheap.

Director 2

Well, what about our component costs? I thought we'd stockpiled eight months' worth of our major component in order to beat this last round of price increases.

Management

Yes, that's true, and we've expensed that component at its replacement cost in our projections, not the price we paid for it. But we've got to generate funds to replace inventory and not focus on cost recovery, or we'll end up in a cash squeeze.

Director 4

So we'd be making our customers pay more for cheap units made on cheap facilities? Why?

Management

To preserve our future!

Director 3

I don't really understand these numbers! How were they derived? And what would the price increases do to our reported, audited net income?

Required

Discuss the issues as raised by the board of directors.

Case 99

WW Inc. I

Bill Walker is a dentist in Kingston, Ontario. The practice has been very successful, and Bill has decided to invest some excess cash in real estate, in hopes of long-run capital appreciation. During 1993, Bill decided to incorporate a company, WW Inc., which would own a commercial property. Bill estimates that the new corporation will show a loss during the first few years. Bill started the company with a cash injection of $210,000. The following events occurred during 1994:

1. In early January, WW Inc. purchased land and a building on a main street in Kingston. WW Inc. paid $800,000 for the property: $150,000 cash and $650,000 through a 12 percent 25-year mortgage from the First Royal Bank. The building was two storeys. The first floor could be retail space. The second storey had two apartments. Both floors needed extensive work before occupancy. Similar properties on the street were selling for $1,500,000; the land value was approximately $700,000. The building had a useful life of approximately 40 years.

2. By the end of February, Bill and some friends had completed most of the renovations. Materials totalled $208,000; electricians' invoices were $10,120; unpaid labour by Bill's friends was estimated at $57,500; and property taxes to June 30 added another $1,800. To cover these costs, the bank extended WW Inc. a demand loan in early January at a floating rate of interest. The interest rate of 13.5 percent had not changed since January.

3. In March, the owner of a men's clothing business answered an advertisement for a tenant for the first floor. The owner of the clothing business signed a lease, moved in on April 1, and made an immediate payment of $4,800.

Society of Management Accountants, adapted.

4. In April, a tenant signed a one-year lease and moved into an upstairs apartment. The monthly rental was $1,000. The tenant gave WW Inc. a cheque for $2,000, which included the last month.

By June 30, the rent on the apartment was two months in arrears, because the tenant had lost her job. WW Inc. instituted legal proceedings, but the tenant refused to move out. She was optimistic that she would be able to make up the overdue payments. At June 30, the other apartment remained vacant.

5. At June 30, interest payments had been made on both the demand loan and the mortgage, but no principal had been repaid.

Required

Prepare the land and building disclosure on WW Inc.'s balance sheet at June 30, 1994. Clearly state any assumptions you make and show details of all calculations. Ignore taxes.

Case 100

WW Inc. II

Bill Walker is a dentist in Kingston, Ontario. The practice has been very successful, and Bill has decided to invest some excess cash in real estate, in hopes of long-run capital appreciation. During 1993, Bill decided to incorporate a company, WW Inc., which would own a commercial property. Bill estimates that the new corporation will show a loss during the first few years. Bill started the company with a cash injection of $210,000.

The following events occurred during 1994:

1. In early January 1994, WW Inc. purchased land and a building on a main street in Kingston. The building was two storeys. The first floor could be retail space. The second storey had two apartments.

2. By the end of February, Bill and some friends had completed most of the renovations. To cover these costs, the bank extended WW Inc. a demand loan in early January at a floating rate of interest. The interest rate of 13.5 percent had not changed since January.

3. In March, the owner of a men's clothing business answered an advertisement for a tenant for the first floor. The space needed modifications before the tenant could operate his business from this location, and Bill agreed to provide these. Shelving, display cases, rugs, and draperies were installed at a cost of $33,000, financed by an increase in the demand loan on April 1 at 13.5 percent. Due to forecast heavy use, the furnishings had a useful life of only 10 years. The owner of the clothing business signed a lease, moved in on April 1, and made an immediate payment of $4,800.

The lease had a five-year term, with a five-year renewal at the option of WW Inc. The monthly rental was $4,800, plus 5 percent of gross sales revenue; the percentage of sales portion of the rent was due by the middle of the following month. Similar rentals on the street were approximately

---

Society of Management Accountants, adapted.

$4,200 plus a percentage of revenue, but often other landlords were unwilling to modify the premises at their own cost to suit the tenant.

4. In April, a tenant signed a one-year lease and moved into an upstairs apartment. The monthly rental was $1,000. The tenant gave WW Inc. a cheque for $2,000, which included the last month.

By June 30, the rent on the apartment was two months in arrears, because the tenant had lost her job. WW Inc. instituted legal proceedings, but the tenant refused to move out. She was optimistic that she would be able to make up the overdue payments.

5. At June 30, the other apartment remained vacant. WW Inc.'s payments from the clothing store totalled $15,576. Sales in June were twice the average level of April and May.

6. At June 30, interest payments had been made on both the demand loan and the mortgage, but no principal had been repaid.

Required

For WW Inc.'s leases, prepare the components of the balance sheet at June 30, 1994, and an income statement and statement of changes in financial position for WW Inc. for the six months then ended. Clearly state any assumptions you make and show details of all calculations. Ignore taxes.

Case 101

George Weston Limited

Effective January 1, 1990, Section 1590 of the *CICA Handbook* required consolidation of subsidiaries controlled by the parent corporation. Prior to this, Section 3050 of the *CICA Handbook,* "Long-Term Investments," required consolidation of subsidiaries in which the parent company owned more than 50 percent of the voting shares. There were a few rare circumstances established in Section 3050 that would dictate an exception to consolidation.

In 1973, George Weston did not consolidate its 67 percent ownership interest in Loblaw Companies Limited. For the fiscal year ending March 31, 1973, Loblaw Companies Limited reported a loss of $14.8 million, or $1.40 per share of Loblaw stock. George Weston Limited accepted a qualification from its auditors as a result of this policy.

Extracts from Weston's 1973 financial statements are shown in Exhibit 1.

In an address to the Toronto Society of Financial Analysts, G. E. Creber, president and managing director of George Weston Limited, argued that Weston's relatively small $31 million equity holding in Loblaw did not justify a consolidation that would double Weston's assets by adding those of Loblaw. Creber also argued that the fair disclosure provisions should override the recommendations contained in the *CICA Handbook*.

In the introduction to its accounting recommendations, the *CICA Handbook* states:

> . . . no rule of general application can be phrased to suit all circumstances or combination of circumstances that may arise, nor is there any substitute for the exercise of professional judgment in the determination of what constitutes fair presentation or good practice in a particular case. (p. 9, *CICA Handbook.*)

Adapted, with permission from John R. E. Parker.

EXHIBIT 1 Extracts from Financial Statements—George Weston Limited (December 31, 1973)

1. Summary of significant accounting policies:
   a. Basis of consolidation:

   The accompanying financial statements consolidate all subsidiary companies except Loblaw Companies Limited and its subsidiary companies ("Loblaw") which is carried at cost.

   George Weston Limited ("Weston") has voting control of Loblaw through ownership of 67.7 percent of that company's outstanding class B voting shares. The Weston holding of the combined Class A nonvoting shares and the class B voting shares represents 60.3 percent of the total participating shares outstanding. Because of the large minority interests in Loblaw, as well as the substantial minority interest in the Loblaw subsidiary companies themselves, management has felt that consolidation of the Loblaw accounts with those of Weston's would not be the most informative presentation.

   Effective January 1, 1973, the Canadian Institute of Chartered Accountants has recommended that, with rare exceptions, all subsidiaries should be fully consolidated. The effect of this recommendation is that the practice followed in the accompanying financial statements of carrying the investment in Loblaw at cost can no longer be said to be in accordance with generally accepted accounting principles.

   In view of this it is the company's intention to include the accounts of Loblaw in the Weston consolidated financial statements for the year commencing January 1, 1974, the earliest practicable period for which such a step could be taken. To provide a proper starting point for the consolidation, the fiscal year-end of Loblaw has been changed to coincide with that of Weston, effective December 31, 1973. The company proposes to first publish operating results on a fully consolidated basis commencing with the quarter ending March 31, 1974.

   The following information has been extracted from the audited consolidated financial statements of Loblaw for the 52 weeks ended March 31,

EXHIBIT 1 *(concluded)*

1973 (with comparative figures for the previous year as restated by Loblaw):

	1973	1972
	($000s)	
Working capital	$ 71,527	$ 99,588
Total assets	531,282	547,109
Minority interests in subsidiaries	90,266	111,267
Shareholders' equity	95,585	117,099
Sales	2,560,283	2,592,748
Income (loss) before special items	(6,539)	4,095
Net income	(14,764)	7,261
Weston's share of the above consolidated earnings (loss) of Loblaw (after eliminating an intercompany gain of $340,000 in 1973) is as follows:		
Net income (loss)—Total	(9,097)	3,177
—Per share of Weston common stock	(83)¢	29¢
Weston has reflected in its net income the dividends received from Loblaw as follows:		
Dividends received during the year ended December 31—Total	2,510	2,274
—Per share of Weston common stock	23¢	21¢

Weston's share of the undistributed earnings of Loblaw from date of acquisition to March 31, 1973 (after retained earnings adjustments) amounts to $19,705,000.

Required

Discuss Weston's objections to consolidation thoroughly, examining both sides of the issue.

Your discussion should include a discussion and calculation of how Weston's financial statements would change (i.e., net assets, EPS, presentation, and so on) if Weston had consolidated Loblaw in 1973.